Learning to Climb Indoors

Learning to Climb Indoors

Eric J. Hörst

FALCONGUIDES ®

GUILFORD, CONNECTICUT
HELENA, MONTANA

AN IMPRINT OF THE GLOBE PEQUOT PRESS

FALCONGUIDES®

Falcon and FalconGuide are registered trademarks of Morris Book Publishing, LLC.

How to Climb is a trademark of Morris Book Publishing, LLC.

Text design and page design by Casey Shain
All interior photos courtesy of the author, unless otherwise credited
Illustrations by Mike Tea

Library of Congress Cataloging-in-Publication Data
Hörst, Eric J.
     Learning to climb indoors / Eric J. Hörst.
       p. cm. —(How to climb series)
     Includes index.
     ISBN-13: 978-0-7627-3985-1
     ISBN-10: 0-7627-3985-1
     1. Rock climbing—Training. 2. Indoor rock climbing. I. Title. II. Series.
     GV200.2.H683 2006
     796.52'23—dc22

                                                                              2006009213

Manufactured in the United States of America
10 9 8 7 6 5 4 3

To my sons, Cameron and Jonathan,
who are now learning to climb.

C O N T E N T S

Acknowledgments *xi*

Introduction *1*

Chapter 1. Welcome to the Vertical Extreme! *7*

Chapter 2. Equipment and Safety Gear *19*

Chapter 3. Learning the Safety Systems *27*

Chapter 4. The Keys to Rapid Learning of Skills *37*

Chapter 5. Basic Skills and Drills *45*

Chapter 6. Advanced Techniques and Drills *67*

Chapter 7. Lead Climbing and Success Strategies *85*

Chapter 8. Mental Training and Fear Management *101*

Chapter 9. Getting into Climbing Shape *115*

Chapter 10. The Secrets to Climbing Your Best *141*

Afterword *155*

Glossary *159*

Suggested Reading *165*

Resources *167*

Index *169*

About the Author *177*

ACKNOWLEDGMENTS

Writing this book took me on an immensely enjoyable trip down memory lane as I reflected on my formative years as a climber. It was nearly thirty years ago that I was a youngster learning to climb, and my brother, Kyle, is the person responsible for starting me on this incredible journey. Thanks, Kyle! Of course, the learning process never ends, so to this day I continue to glean new distinctions and lessons from my experiences as a climber and from all those whom I meet. Consequently, I must begin by thanking my partners past and present for the many wonderful days climbing together. Furthermore, I appreciate the countless friends I've made, climbers I've coached, and everyone else with whom I've talked training throughout my years and travels.

The idea for this book was born a few years ago, and I thank Jeff Serena and everyone at Falcon and The Globe Pequot Press for seeing this project through. There are many others who contributed along the way, and this book, like all others, was really a team effort. First up I must credit the photographers whose pictures helped save me many thousands of words! Thanks to Randy Levensaler, Keith McCallister, Shawn Brünner, Eric McCallister, artist Mike Tea, and Nicros Wall Division for helping bring the pages of this book to life. I'm also grateful for the patience and superb style of my climbing models Lauri Stricker, Mark Himelfarb, Ezra Levin, Sara Born, Elizabeth Westmark, Nic Oklobzija, Tinen Carlson, and LA, as well as several others from VE–St. Paul who appear in the book. Equally important are the gym owners who so graciously allowed me to shoot instructional photos at their facilities. Thanks to Deb at Rock'n & Jam'n, Jason at Vertical Endeavors, Hayes at Cliffhangers, and the crew at Boulder Rock Club. And after eight months of almost nonstop writing, I was fortunate to have the fresh eyes and constructive feedback of my friends Eric McCallister and Jason Noble.

As a veteran climber who still hits the road on climbing trips and for training-for-climbing seminars, I extend sincere thanks to the companies who continue to support my climbing and numerous projects. I must first acknowledge Nate and Pam Postma, Greg, Kimberly, and everyone else at Nicros, Inc. You guys are such a big part of my various training projects, and I tremendously enjoy working with you all! Likewise, I thank Colin, Jonathan, and Stephanie at La Sportiva for keeping me climbing in the best shoes on the planet; ditto to Paul and Carolyn at Sterling Ropes for supplying my lifelines; and to Christian Griffith for the great Verve threads. Also, many thanks to Maile Buker and Russ Clune of Black Diamond Equipment for providing top-shelf harnesses and hardware.

Finally, I extend heartfelt thanks to my wife, Lisa Ann, for her unconditional love and support; to my sons, Cameron and Jonathan, for all the joyous times we share; and to my parents. I am truly blessed to have all of you in my life.

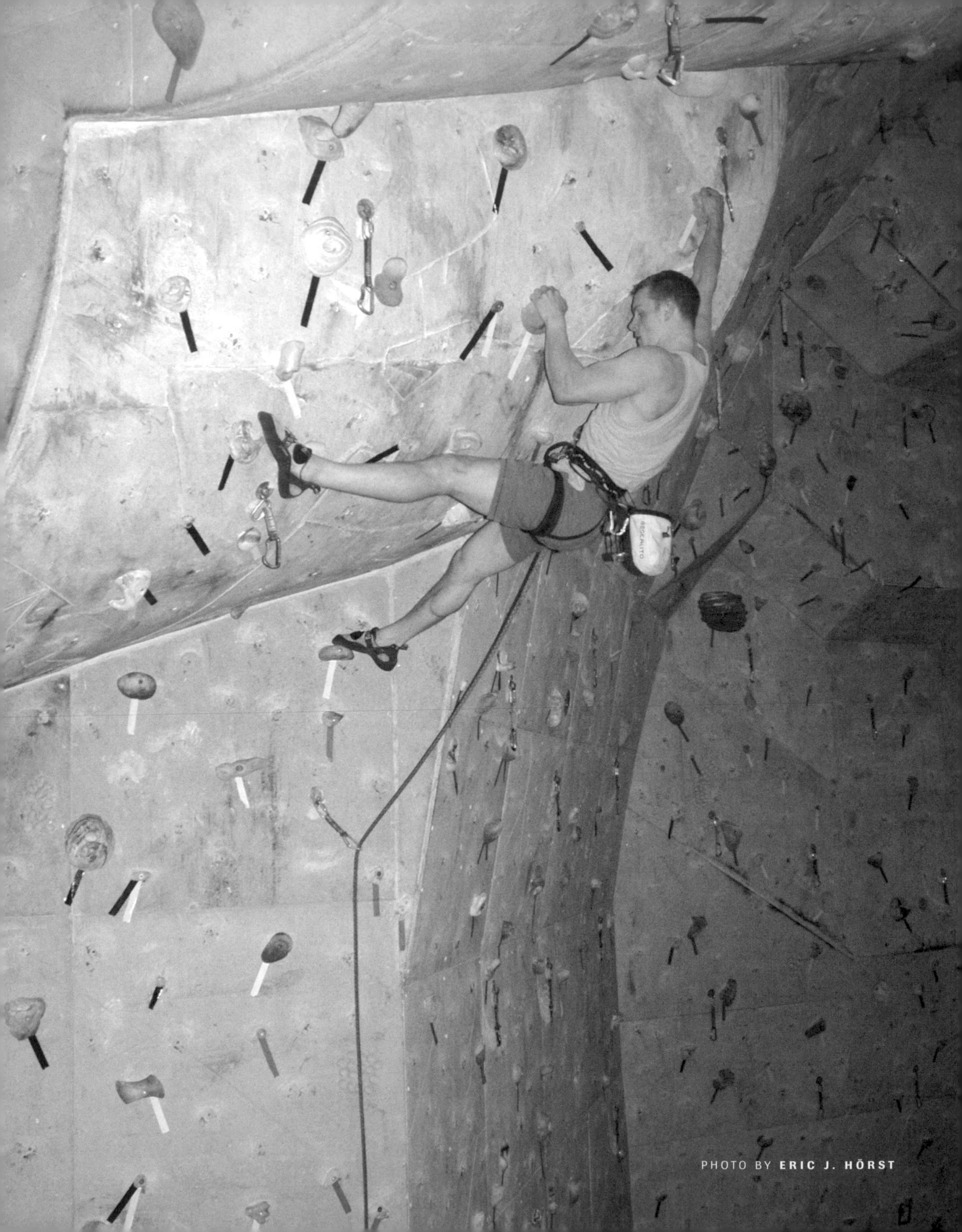

PHOTO BY **ERIC J. HÖRST**

INTRODUCTION

One of the beauties of indoor climbing is the simplicity of engaging the rock wall with just your fingertips, toes, and mind, while all the complexities of life are left behind on the ground.

—Eric Hörst

Welcome to the exhilarating world of indoor climbing! Regardless of your age, background, or level of fitness, indoor climbing will present you with many unique challenges—and rewards—that are far different from other sports. As you will soon discover, the wonder of indoor climbing is the unique way in which it engages both the mind and body. Each climb reveals a novel challenge that offers the opportunity for self-development. Solving a puzzling sequence of hand- and footholds is akin to a vertical chess match requiring a dynamic mix of problem solving, positive thinking, and fear management. Physically, climbing will challenge your flexibility, stamina, body control, and almost every muscle from your legs to your abdominals to your soon-to-be-pumped arms. In aggregate, climbing provides what may be the most complete mind-body workout available. And it's an absolute blast!

Learning to Climb Indoors presents comprehensive instruction on all the vital topics you need to know for your first few days and years in the sport. Chapter 1 begins with an overview of the commercial climbing gym experience. You will gain a sense of the rules of the game and requisite safe-climbing instruction that most gyms mandate. Chapters 2 and 3 will introduce you to the basic gear and safety techniques that make indoor climbing safer than playing soccer or mowing the grass. Yes, climbing is a remarkably safe activity given proper equipment, expert instruction, and diligent use of the safety techniques you will learn in this book.

Chapter 4 is unique among how-to-climb books as it reveals several not-so-well-known strategies for rapid learning of climbing skills. While the majority of new climbers stumble slowly through the maze of trial-and-error learning, you can take a more direct path to improvement by applying the eight powerful learning strategies outlined in this chapter.

The core technical instruction of *Learning to Climb Indoors* is found in chapters 5 through 7. A wise beginning climber will strive to learn—and make habit—the optimal use of hand- and footholds, body positioning, and techniques of movement. These chapters will describe all the fundamental techniques and tactics required for beginner-, intermediate-, and advanced-level climbs. You will learn a variety of technique-building drills as well as several proven strategies for solving difficult routes and programming your brain for success.

Supporting this instruction, you will find dozens of photos depicting the fundamental techniques, body positions, and movements. Many of these photos contain an overlay of symbols and labels (annotations) that reveal optimal application of force to hand- and footholds, as well as proper positioning of the body's center of gravity. It's my hope that these value-added photos will underscore the importance of body awareness and help enhance the learning of proper technique.

Next up, in chapter 8, is an in-depth look at mental training and fear management. It's a fact that climbing requires uncommon discipline and mental fortitude compared with other sports. Thus, elevating your mental game is an essential part of improving your overall ability. To this end, you will learn ten proven techniques for controlling tension, challenging fear, and conquering the fright of flight.

The final two chapters of *Learning to Climb Indoors* complete the circle of becoming a solid all-around climber. Chapter 9 provides a plan for physical conditioning, so that you can develop the strength and endurance needed for climbs of increasing difficulty. Chapter 10 then reveals a few of the secrets for climbing your best, including the keys to staying motivated and upwardly mobile for many years to come. Lastly, I'll provide a primer on what it takes to expand your climbing to the great outdoors, including a review of the unique techniques, risks, and rewards of rock climbing.

Throughout the text, climbing terminology and lingo are bolded on first use. Complete definitions are available in the glossary located in the back of the book.

Please note that each chapter begins with a quote from a famous or legendary climber. It's my hope that you find these quotes inspiring and intriguing, and that you may someday delve deeper into the background and history of rock climbing. You will also discover an afterword that presents some of the climbing wisdom culled from the pages of this book. I trust you'll discover—as I have—that climbing provides many wonderful lessons for effective living on this third rock from the sun.

As you begin your adventures as a climber, I want to wish you a rich and rewarding journey that lasts a lifetime. Be safe and have fun!

Technique Photos: A User's Guide

Climbing is a vertical dance requiring precise hand and foot "steps," body positions, and movement. Unfortunately, this dance is sometimes difficult to illustrate on the static pages of a book. In *Learning to Climb Indoors* I've adopted, from college biomechanics texts, a method of labeling instructional photos with words and symbols that depict the application of force on hand- and footholds. I hope these enhanced photos will underscore the importance of body awareness and help you learn proper technique. Here are the three classes of symbols to look for:

1. Center of Gravity and Line of Gravity

The earth's gravitational pull is most concentrated at your center of gravity—the theoretical point at which gravity's pull acts on you. Standing with your arms by your sides, the center of gravity for males is about an inch above the navel, while for females it averages an inch or two below the navel. (The changing arm and leg positions of a climber in motion, however, can cause the center of gravity to shift side to side and up and down.) Center of gravity is designated here by a bullet or circle, and the earth's gravitational pull, or line of gravity, is indicated by a dashed line and arrow pointing downward.

2. Force Vectors

When you climb, you ascend by contracting your muscles to generate force—a push or pull—that is applied to the rock via the hand and foot points of contact. The direction and amount of force applied at a point of contact is called a force vector. Force vectors are represented in this book diagrammatically by arrows. Each arrow's head depicts the direction you should apply force, while the size of the arrow is scaled to the amount of force—a larger arrow means more force, a smaller one less. You'll find small, medium, and large arrows here.

3. Finesse and Dynamic Moves

Of course the purpose of climbing is to go *up*. Still, sometimes the most efficient way to do that is by twisting—or flagging, deadpointing, lunging, or other angular and dynamic movements. Such finesse movements are illustrated with a dotted line and an arrow.

Photo Symbols

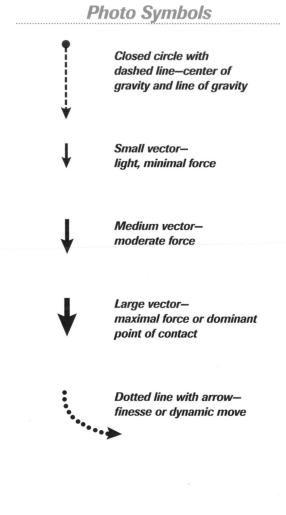

Closed circle with dashed line—center of gravity and line of gravity

Small vector— light, minimal force

Medium vector— moderate force

Large vector— maximal force or dominant point of contact

Dotted line with arrow— finesse or dynamic move

Photo Key

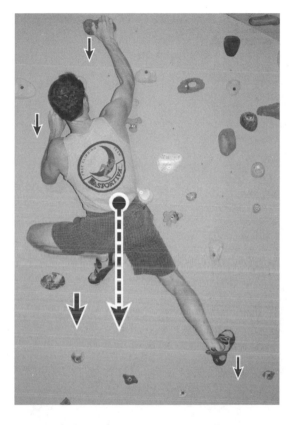 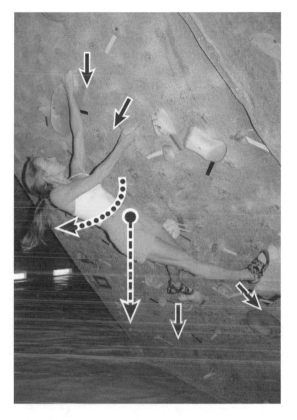

The symbols applied to this photo indicate that the climber uses both of his hands—as well as his right foot—to apply minimal force (note the small arrows, or vectors) to the hold. Meanwhile his left foot carries the bulk of his weight, applying maximal force (indicated by the large arrow, or vector). This positioning is achieved by shifting the center of gravity near—or better yet, over—the left foot.

This climber is using her hands and feet to apply nearly equal force (note the medium vectors). She twists her body (a movement represented by a dotted line) to position her left hip and center of gravity close to the overhanging wall. This shifts the line of gravity closer to her feet, putting more of her body weight onto her feet.

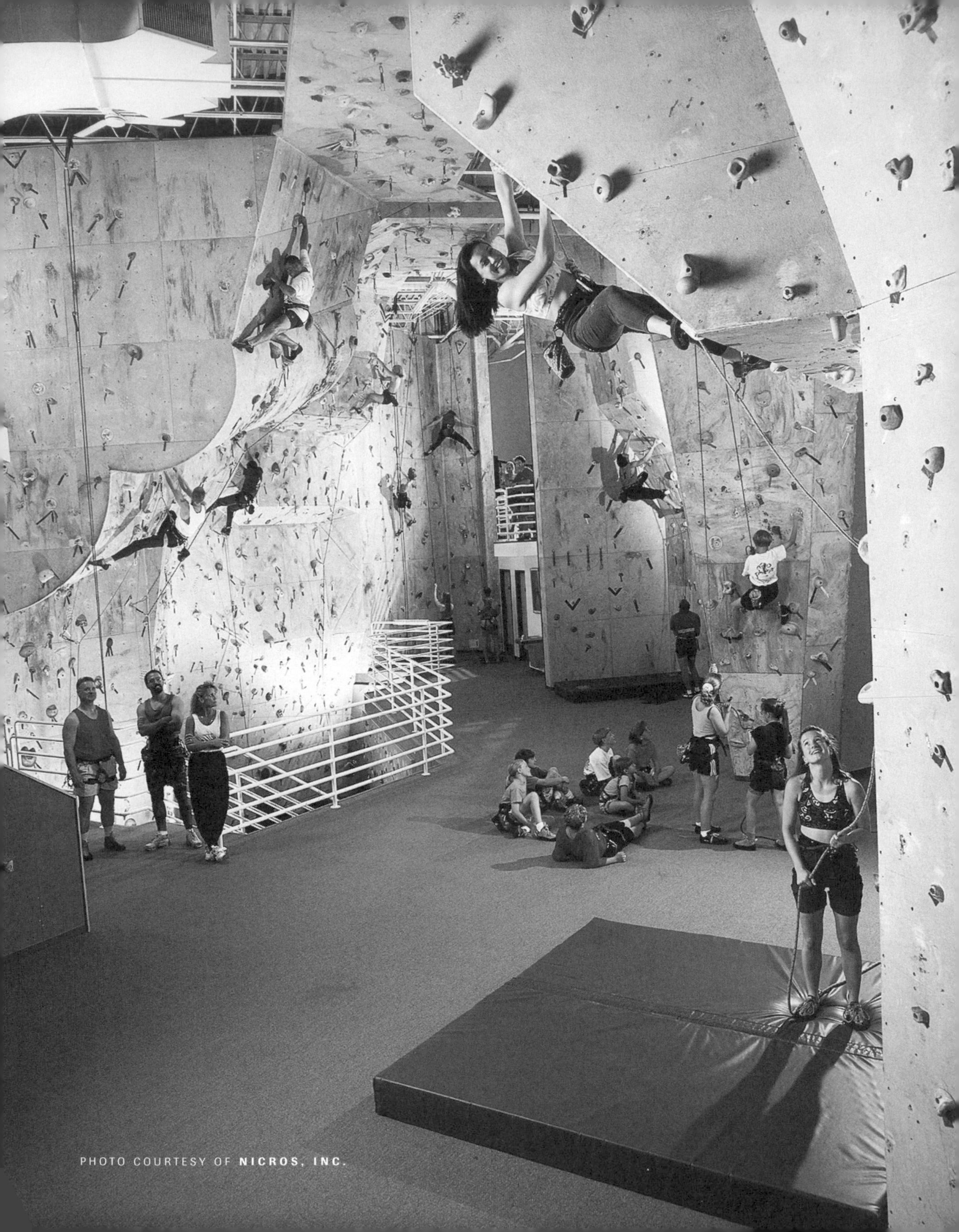

PHOTO COURTESY OF **NICROS, INC.**

Welcome to the Vertical Extreme!

Climbing is a way of life, almost a martial art, and something one practices throughout life—a path of bettering mind and spirit.

—Pat Ament, legendary climber, artist, and author

Are you ready to rock your world? Do you dare leave the plane of flatlander sports and engage the challenges (and rewards) of the vertical extreme? Are you prepared for the intense exhilaration and head-to-toe workout that climbing so uniquely provides? Do you aspire to stretch your personal limits and, in doing so, redefine what you view as possible in your life? If so, read on!

Rock climbing is one of the fastest-growing recreational activities, and it's through the doors of climbing gyms that most people get started. Unlike past generations who learned to climb in the more serious environment of outdoor crags, today's aspiring climbers can gain their skills in a safe, controlled indoor setting that affords rapid learning of skills. It is for this new breed of climber that I have crafted the contents of *Learning to Climb Indoors*.

To begin, I'll provide a primer on the challenges, history, and risks of indoor climbing, as well as the must-know issues relating to your initial visits to a climbing facility. Next, I'll describe the subtypes of climbing you will encounter—bouldering, toproping, and lead climbing—and how climbers classify the style of an ascent. The chapter wraps up with a look at the human-made vertical terrain, its shapes and features, and how unique paths up the wall are defined and graded.

The Challenges and Rewards of Climbing

Climbing offers challenges and rewards that are very different from—unlike, and often more intense than— those of other sports. As you will soon discover, climbing is steeped in paradox. Yes, it's child's play—watch a four-year-old at a playground and you'll see that climbing is indeed intuitive—yet solving a climbing sequence while hanging by your fingertips on the side of a rock wall can be perplexing and stressful. Quite often your climbing attempts will end in failure as you hang on the rope pondering the difficulties of the route. It's at these times that you are faced with my favorite climbing paradox: To succeed, you must embrace and learn from failure.

If you are beginning to sense that climbing is also a process of self-exploration, you're right. To me, that's one of this sport's greatest rewards—climbing releases untapped resources, it reveals unknown potentialities, and it provides an endless series of metaphors for effective living. Most people begin climbing for the rush of the new experience, but in time they find it's the motion and emotion—how it makes them feel and grow—that hooks them as climbers for life.

A Brief History of Indoor Climbing

Technical rock climbing was born in the late 1890s as an offshoot of mountaineering; in fact, early climbers practiced roped climbing on short cliffs primarily as a method of training for expeditions to the mountains. Gradually rock climbing became popular

Portable walls are now commonly featured at fairs, shopping malls, and parks.
PHOTO COURTESY OF **NICROS, INC.**

in and of itself, and the 1950s and 1960s produced major breakthroughs in equipment and technical ability. This was the Golden Age of American rock climbing, though the first indoor climbing wall had yet to be built!

In the 1970s British climbers frustrated by their perpetually damp climate created crude indoor practice climbs up concrete block walls. But it was not until the advent of synthetic climbing hand-holds in the early 1980s that modern indoor climbing was born. Indoor walls and competition climbing exploded across Europe during the mid-1980s, but the trend was slow to spread across the Atlantic. American climbers, enamored of traditional crag and big-wall styles, viewed climbing on artificial surfaces as contrived and purposeless. Still, in 1987

the first climbing gym in the United States opened in Seattle, Washington. A major paradigm shift soon followed. Many American climbers came to embrace indoor climbing as an efficient method of training for outdoor climbing, as well as a valid activity in its own right.

Fifteen years later there are more than 1,000 indoor climbing walls scattered across the United States from Miami to Maine and from Seattle to San Diego. More than 200 walls are run as full-service commercial climbing gyms with locker rooms, retail shops, and lounges. But perhaps the ultimate endorsement of climbing as a unique source of great fun and self-development are the myriad walls recently added to high schools, colleges, churches, and rec centers from the Great Lakes to the Gulf Coast, an area basically void of mountains. Indoor climbing walls bring some of the joys and lessons of rock climbing to our urban flatlands, allowing more than five million Americans to try their hand at the sport each year.

The Differences between Indoor and Outdoor Climbing

Indoor climbing and outdoor climbing are vastly different activities, and competency as an indoor climber does not guarantee safe climbing in the great outdoors. It is vitally important that all indoor climbers recognize that there are wide-ranging complexities and dangers to rock climbing in a natural setting. Not even the most realistic indoor facility provides the experience and training needed to transition your climbing outside.

Yes, outdoor climbing can be a most gratifying progression for a skilled indoor climber, but the move outdoors must be treated as if you are beginning a new sport from scratch. Don't even ponder venturing out to the crags by yourself. More than a few novices have tried this approach and ended up with broken bones, or worse.

Rule number one of outdoor climbing is to bring a pack load of prudence. For the beginner, this means signing up for a weekend class in outdoor climbing or, better yet, obtaining one-on-one instruction from an American Mountain Guide Association (AMGA) certified climbing guide. While you can learn the basics of indoor climbing in a day or two, the many nuances of real rock climbing demand several days of quality instruction. If you find the outdoor experience pleasurable, your next step would be to join a local climbing club or find an experienced climbing partner to hook up with for regular outings. In the end, you may find the unique experiences afforded by both indoor and outdoor climbing to be equally enjoyable. I, for one, enjoy training on an indoor wall during the workweek, but I do so with the intention of pulling down on some of Mother Nature's finest on the weekends.

Your First Visit to the Climbing Gym

Your first step through the doors of a climbing gym will be eye opening, energizing, and likely a bit frightening. For an instant you may contemplate a retreat from the facility; resist this urge with the knowledge that indoor climbing is completely safe and that you are up to the challenge. Remind yourself that new experiences and pushing personal boundaries of any kind always result in some degree of anxiety and discomfort. However, you will soon learn one of climbing's great life lessons—pushing through discomfort and harnessing anxiety into productive energy is the strategy for uncommon experience and personal success.

Okay, you accept the challenge and you are ready to tie in and begin climbing. Well almost. First, you'll need to fill out some paperwork and pay your dues, literally. You will also need to make a few decisions regarding equipment and instruction, so let me take you step by step through all the key issues.

Types of Gyms and Fees

Climbing gyms come in all shapes and sizes, ranging from a modest 20-foot-high wall installed in the back of a school gymnasium or health club to a multi-million-dollar commercial facility possessing a maze of 40- to 80-foot walls. While walls at schools and community centers may be open to the public free of charge (or included as part of tuition), commercial climbing gyms require a membership or daily access fee. Expect to pay between $8.00 and $25.00 for a single day's pass, depending on the size of the gym and cost of doing business in a given city. Annual memberships typically run between $200 and $600, with fees at most full-service gyms in major cities falling near the high end of this range.

Waiver of Liability

In this age of litigation, don't expect to make it past the gym's front desk without signing a waiver of liability. Yes, indoor climbing is safer than crossing the street, but streets don't have employees, investors, and a balance sheet to protect. The waiver shields the gym, its owners, and their insurance company from potential lawsuits brought by climbers injured as a result of their own inexperience or errors. Of course, the waiver does not prevent you from seeking compensation should you get injured due to the gross negligence of the business. Again, this is all "fine print" stuff; the odds are about one in a million that you'll be seriously injured while climbing indoors.

Renting Basic Equipment

As you pay the entry fee and sign the waiver, you'll also be asked if you want to rent any climbing equipment. While I'll provide detailed coverage of climbing gear in chapter 2, I'd like to touch here on your most basic needs—a safety harness and climbing shoes.

Like a seat belt, a climbing harness is the most vital piece of safety equipment. It's the link between your body and the safety rope. Climbing shoes are also important, although the need for these specialized shoes is all about performance, not safety. While some people climb their first day in sneakers or hiking boots, I urge you to rent a pair of sticky-soled climbing shoes. The difference these shoes will make in your climbing experience cannot be oversold—it's like the difference between skiing with shaped skis versus a 2-by-4 board strapped to each foot. Rent the shoes, please!

Expect to pay between $5.00 and $10.00 to rent a harness and shoes for the day. If after your first few days of climbing you feel you are hooked, then invest the $125 to $200 needed to purchase your own harness and shoes. By the way, pass on any offers to buy used gear. If you are serious about climbing, treat yourself to a perfectly fit harness and brand-new shoes.

Climbing Lessons and Belay Tests

Most gyms require first-time climbers to go through an introductory class. Some gyms charge a fee for this basic instruction, while others build the cost into the entry fee. The typical lesson provides a crash course on the fundamentals of climbing movement, as well as on vital issues of putting on your harness, tying into the rope, and belaying. **Belaying** is a two-person rope-management technique that allows for safe ascent and descent of the walls. It's a simple process that takes only a few minutes to understand, yet most people require a few days in order to feel completely comfortable as a belayer.

Table 1.1	**What to Expect on Your First Visit to a Climbing Gym**
On Your First Day Climbing	*Fee, If Any*
Pay entry fee	$10–$25
Sign waiver	—
Rent climbing shoes and harness	$5–$10
Take introductory climbing lesson	$0–$25
Pass belay test	—
Have fun climbing	Priceless!

I'll cover all these subjects in great depth later on, though you must remember that reading is not doing. In climbing, there is no replacement for personal instruction and real-life experience. Most gyms will require you to pass a basic knot-tying and belay test at some point during your initial visits. Don't sweat the test; it's all pretty easy stuff.

An Introduction to the Climbers' Lexicon

Send. **Pumped**. **On-sight**. **Thrash**. **Flash**. Like many sports, climbing has its own lexicon of terms and slang words, which you'll hear echoing throughout the gym. While I will largely avoid using slang—you can have some fun trying to decipher the lingo you hear at the gym—I will introduce you to

the terminology needed to effectively learn, describe, and engage in gym climbing. Remember that key terms are typeset in **boldface** on first use, and you will find each term defined in the glossary.

Types of Climbing

Most commercial gyms offer three very different types of climbing: **bouldering**, **toproping**, and **leading**. A fourth approach to climbing found at some pay-to-climb facilities involves the use of an **auto belay**. Each of these activities comes with unique challenges, rewards, and safety requirements that I'll cover below. Should you settle in as a regular gym climber, you'll likely develop a preference for one of these activities, yet from the perspective of optimal learning, it's best to spend time practicing within each subdiscipline. (You'll find more on accelerated learning techniques in chapter 4.)

Bouldering

Bouldering is arguably the purest form of climbing, since all the complexities of gear and ropework are removed. The goal in bouldering is to ascend short sections of wall, called a **problem**, typically ranging from 7 to 15 feet in height. Most gyms have an area designated specifically for bouldering, and in a few big cities, there are entire climbing gyms dedicated to it. In some circles bouldering has evolved into a sport of its own, which is understandable given its highly engaging nature and the common tendency to work boulder problems with a group of comrades.

During your initial visits bouldering offers an easy way to practice footwork, develop balance, and experiment with different ways of moving in your new vertical environment. Since in bouldering you rarely climb more than several feet off the floor, it's easy to step or jump off the wall and try again. In fact, that is the beauty of bouldering: You can pick a problem and focus on solving it, even if it means jumping off and trying the problem over and over. This process of targeting your efforts on solving a specific sequence will challenge you physically, mentally, and technically, all without the distraction of a rope, belayer, or dauntingly long climb.

When bouldering more than 6 or 8 feet off the

The challenge of bouldering is to ascend a short, difficult section of rock within jumping distance of the ground.
PHOTO BY **SHAWN BRÜNNER**

floor, it's vital that you employ a **spotter**, as well as having a **crash pad** in your landing zone. Jumping off such **highball** problems is hard on the ankles, knees, and lower back. Worse yet, a surprise fall from a steep problem can send you twisting and turning out of control with little time to right yourself for a clean landing.

Most gyms possess cushioned floors and bouldering crash pads intended to soften your impact and reduce the risk of injury. Still, it's best to have a spotter (of same or greater size than you) help protect you during an attempted ascent of a steep or high boulder problem. As you climb, the spotter stands just behind you—not under you, unless your spotter wants to be pancaked—with hands reaching toward the back of your hips. Should you jump or fall from the problem, the spotter grasps near your hips and helps direct you feetfirst toward the crash pad. In the rare case of a tumbling fall, the spotter may only be able to push on your back in an attempt to prevent your head from hitting the ground first. Spotting, like belaying, is an activity that demands vigilance—your partner's safety is on the line. See chapter 3 for detailed instruction on spotting.

Toproping

Toproping is the most popular activity for beginners, since it allows safe movement up even the highest,

Toproping is the most popular form of climbing for beginners.
PHOTO COURTESY OF **NICROS, INC.**

most scary-looking walls. The name *toprope* describes the rigging of the safety line that runs from the floor up through an anchor atop the climb, then back down to the bottom. Gyms commonly have a dozen or more topropes hanging in place and ready to go—you just need to tie into one end of the rope and have someone belay you from the other end. The specifics of belaying are upcoming in chapter 3.

Like bouldering, toproping is an excellent way to practice your skills, but with a toprope it's the belayer, not a spotter, who's got your back. With a snug toprope belay, you can safely try your hand at any climb and be softly lowered back to the ground at a moment's notice. Some toprope climbs will be easy; you'll breeze up the wall on your first try. Other routes might spit you off onto the rope—called a **fall**. Fortunately, the toprope will hold you in place at the problem spot so you can hang there and work on the sequence. Sometimes it will only take a few tries to unlock the sequence and continue on to the top; other times you may be stymied and you'll need to lower off and try the climb another day.

In the earliest stages of learning, it's important to log a lot of mileage on easy climbs and to avoid difficult routes that will frustrate or demoralize you. Toproping is the ideal way to test the waters and see just what level of difficulty you are climbing on a given day (more on the grading scale of routes in a bit). What's more, toproping is highly time efficient—it lets you pack in the most climbing mileage per session. There are also specific practice drills you can perform while toproping. Chapters 5 and 6 will detail twenty powerful drills for developing good technique and accelerating your progress as a climber.

Auto Belay Climbing

Auto belay climbing is growing in popularity, especially at climbing walls located in sporting goods stores, health clubs, amusement parks, and shopping malls. These mechanical belays do not require a second individual to hold the other end of the climbing rope—in fact, the auto belay *is* your belayer. The actual belay machine is located atop or behind the climbing wall; the safety cable (not a rope) hangs

No matter what your age, auto belays provide a safe, enjoyable climbing experience.

from the top of the climb with the end dangling near the base of the route.

Using an auto belay is elementary and completely secure, as long as you properly clip into the belay cable before you start climbing. The auto belay draws in the cable as you move upward; should you fall, it will catch and slowly lower you back to the ground. While auto belays are indeed an efficient way for commercial facilities to process a large number of novice climbers, they do have drawbacks in terms of learning. If you are serious about pursuing climbing long-term, it's beneficial to leverage the partnership that a human belayer provides. An auto belay can't provide encouragement or helpful tips when you struggle on a difficult move, nor can it share the joy of a great ascent. In climbing, your greatest resource is often the human resource—the dynamic give-and-take process among like-minded climbers that accelerates learning and makes for so many wonderful experiences.

Leading

Lead climbing is the bomb! For me, nothing beats the intense game of trying to lead the **sharp end** of the rope from the ground to the top anchors of a climb. Unlike the snug belay afforded by a toprope, the hallmark of lead climbing is the dangling rope that trails from the climber's harness down to the ground. Periodically the lead climber comes upon anchor bolts to which the trailing rope is clipped,

Lead climbing is the most challenging and heady style of climbing.

while a belayer on the ground pays out rope. The upshot (or more appropriately "downfall") of this way of climbing is that a slip-up yields a true free fall until the rope draws tight onto the last anchor bolt that was clipped. The permanent anchors bolts for lead climbing are typically spaced so that such free falls are limited to just 5 or 10 feet. However, an inattentive belayer and rope stretch can turn a short fall into a 15- or 20-foot **screamer**.

Make no mistake: Lead climbing is not a beginners' activity. It is, however, a wonderfully powerful experience you should look forward to as you become a more competent and confident climber. When is the right time to get into lead climbing? Depending on your degree of natural ability and how often you climb, you could be ready as quickly as a few months or maybe not for several years or more. Most gyms have an additional competency test you'll need to take before you are lead certified. Talk to instructors about your desire to begin leading, and let them be the judge as to whether you are ready to tie into the sharp end.

Learning about the Climbing Walls

Although most indoor walls have little resemblance to real cliffs, climbing the two kinds of walls can feel remarkably similar. Climbing wall technology, both the wall surface and the handholds, has come a long way over the last fifteen years. The shape, height, and topography of climbing walls are becoming more dramatic and varied every year, so the realism of a wall tends to be a function of the age of the facility and, of course, budget. The route-creating process of placing and arranging handholds on the wall surface also contributes to the realism of the climbing movement. It's a fact that good route setting can make an average wall "climb good," while a great wall can be spoiled by poor route setting. Assessing route quality is certainly subjective, but you'll soon come to know a good route when you feel it.

Following is a primer on climbing wall features, the designation of routes, and the popular scales for rating the difficulty of a climb. The section concludes with a look at climbing style and the terms used to describe the quality of an ascent.

Wall Features

The most obvious characteristic or macro feature of a climbing wall is often its steepness. Steepness can be assessed as an angle compared with vertical—say, 10 degrees less than vertical or 30 degrees past vertical—or as the angle the wall is offset from the ground as it would be measured with a protractor. For example, the 10-degrees-less-than-vertical wall mentioned above would be called an 80-degree wall, whereas the 30-degrees-past-vertical wall would be classified as a 120-degree wall. The final, simplest method of describing wall angle is simply to refer to less-than-vertical walls as **slabs**, verticals walls as **vert**, and wall angles past vertical as **overhanging** or steep.

Three other features of steepness are **overhangs**, **roofs**, and **ledges**. An overhang is a section of wall that juts out horizontally, parallel to the floor; it's a common **crux** feature on indoor climbs. A ledge is the opposite of an overhang, in that the wall briefly cuts back in horizontally so that you can stand up on a perch as if you were standing on the floor. While ledges are a common feature on natural cliffs, they are a rarity on indoor walls. A roof is a large overhang that juts out horizontally more than a body length. For example, some indoor lead climbs conclude with a dramatic 10- or 20-foot sequence out the actual underside of the building's roof (hence the name).

Well-designed indoor walls possess a wide variety of other topographic features that add to the complexity and enjoyment of climbing. An inside corner or **dihedral** is a common feature consisting of two walls that intersect at a 90-degree angle, as in the squared corner of any room. In some cases the insider corner forms a more obtuse angle (greater than 90 degrees) called an **open book**.

Another variant that's a favorite of wall designers is the outside corner or **arête**. These prominent features possess a sharp edge formed by two intersecting walls, as in the outside corner of a building. When the walls meet to form a clean 90-degree angle, the feature is usually called an outside corner. More commonly the angle is skewed away from 90 degrees, making a more visually and technically interesting arête.

A final wall feature to recognize is a fissure or crack. Ubiquitous among Mother Nature's rock walls, cracks are a rarity on human-made walls since they are difficult to create using the typical plywood substrate of indoor walls. Some high-end gyms, however, possess a more realistic concrete-based wall system that does allow the creation of cracks. These fractures are usually oriented vertically, and they can vary from about ½ inch up to a few feet in width. Climbers typically refer to smaller cracks by how much of their hand fits into one. Thus, from small to large, cracks are classified as fingertip, full finger, shallow hands, full hands, and fist. Cracks large enough to fit an arm are called **offwidths**, while a body-sized fracture is known as a **chimney**.

Route Setting and Naming of Climbs

Since the macro features of a wall are fixed, it's the placement of modular hand- and footholds that ultimately dictate the movement and difficulty of a route. Climbing gyms employ a route setter or **forerunner** to reposition the holds and set new routes every few weeks. With thousands of different types of holds possessing nearly an infinite range of texture and relief, a skilled forerunner can create routes of amazing realism for climbers of all abilities.

In order to maximize the climbing possibilities at an indoor facility, a forerunner typically sets three or four different routes up a given section of wall. Each route is identified by the color of tape placed below each hand- and foothold. At first glance a section of wall may look like a random array of holds and a rainbow of tape swatches, but you will quickly learn to distinguish the various routes by focusing on a single color tape. For instance, in climbing a route marked with red tape, only the holds marked with red tape are considered on route, whereas holds of all other colors are off route. While it would be just fine to climb the wall using holds of any color, it's not the way the climb was designed, nor the way the indoor climbing game is played.

Upon setting a route and marking all the holds with a single color of tape, the forerunner climbs the line and then assigns a name and grade to the

open book

overhanging wall

roof

arête

"vert" wall

dihedral

Common indoor climbing wall features.
PHOTO COURTESY OF **NICROS, INC.**

Table 1.2 Comparison of the ADS Scale and the V-Scale

ADS	V-Scale
5.5	V0-
5.6	
5.7	
5.8	
5.9	V0
5.10a	
5.10b	V0+
5.10c	
5.10d	V1
5.11a	
5.11b	V2
5.11c	
5.11d	V3
5.12a	V4
5.12b	V5
5.12c	V6
5.12d	
5.13a	V7
5.13b	V8
5.13c	
5.13d	V9
5.14a	V10
5.14b	V11
5.14c	V12
5.14d	V13
5.15a	V14
5.15b	V15

creation. This identifying information is usually written on a piece of tape at the base of the route. Naming routes is a carryover from outdoor climbing; the names enable cataloging of routes in a guidebook. While not all indoor climbs are named, it's a fun practice that enables you to talk about a specific route with your friends, an instructor, or the gym staff.

Difficulty Rating Scales

Grading the severity of a climb is highly subjective and sometimes controversial. Consider that how difficult a climb feels may be affected by issues other than absolute skill—height, reach, and so on. This route may feel harder than its grade should you not be able to reach a critical hold. Fortunately, a highly skilled forerunner is able to set routes that do not penalize climbers of nonaverage build. Still, it's not uncommon for a grade to change slightly as a consensus develops based on repeat ascents by many other climbers.

The primary rating scales used in the United States are the **American Decimal System (ADS)** for roped climbs and the **V-Scale** for boulder problems. The ADS is a pseudo-decimal running from 5.0 (easiest) to 5.9, then continuing in the sequence 5.10, 5.11, 5.12, 5.13, 5.14, and 5.15 (hardest). The 5 refers to fifth-class climbing, which is the general classification for steep climbing that requires a safety rope and belay. Some gyms truncate the fifth-class designation and decimal point, and simply list the grade as, say, a 9 (instead of 5.9) or 12 (instead of 5.12). Two subdivisions of the ADS are also commonly used to help indicate subtle differences in difficulty within a given grade. Routes rated between 5.7 and 5.9 sometimes carry a minus sign (-) or a plus sign (+), indicating easy or hard for the grade, respectively. Ratings of 5.10 and harder often carry a nuance subgrade of a, b, c, or d. For instance, 5.10a is considered easy 5.10, while 5.10d is a hard 5.10.

The V-Scale has become the most popular rating system for boulder problems. Still, a few gyms prefer to use fifth-class grades or, possibly, a mix of both scales to rate boulder problems. The V-Scale is open ended, beginning at V0 and currently extending up to V15. Plus (+) and minus (-) signs are commonly appended to the grade to provide further grade distinction. Since boulder problems are short and intense in nature, the V-Scale begins at a harder absolute difficulty level than the ADS. Knowing roughly how the two scales relate will help you determine boulder problems appropriately rated for your roped climbing ability (see table 1.2, Comparison of the ADS Scale and the V-Scale). Given the brief nature of boulder problems, however, you may discover that you can boulder at least one to two V-grades above your corresponding maximum ADS roped ascent.

Classifying the Style of Ascent

Climbing is a sport in which style matters. No, I'm not talking about fashion style, but instead climbing style—the manner in which you ascend a boulder problem or route.

Climbing style has both subjective and objective elements. First, your style of movement on a climb is a quality assessment based on subjective factors such as smoothness of movement, poise, and execution of fundamental techniques. More clear-cut is the style in which you work on and come to succeed on a climb. The purest style of climbing is **on-sight**, which means you climbed the route on your first try and, literally, first sight of the route. The next best style of ascent, called **flash**, refers to climbing a route first try, but with prior knowledge of the climb. Flash ascents are common in a gym setting where you might watch another person climb the route or gain verbal **beta**, or tips, from someone as you climb.

Upon hanging on the toprope or falling on lead, you lose the chance to ever on-sight or flash the route. Still, you can make an ascent of good style by working for a **redpoint**—climbing the route from bottom to top without hanging or falling. Sometimes you can redpoint a climb on your second attempt, whereas a difficult route may require repeated attempts over the course of several days before you achieve the redpoint.

In bouldering, style of ascent also matters, and on-sight or flash is the ultimate goal. However, boulder problems of steep and intense character (common) are often tough to flash despite their short length. It's not uncommon to try a given boulder problem over and over, or to take turns working the problem with a group of friends. Such an approach is a good way to learn climbing moves, and it's great fun. As for style of ascent when working problems in this manner, most people simply count the number of attempts it takes to succeed on the problem. Thus you might say, "I sent the problem second try," or "It took me twelve attempts to do the problem." Of course, the modus operandi of some people is to work boulder problems beyond their ability, which means they'll likely lose count of the number of attempts or just not care how long it takes to succeed. This approach is completely valid, too. One of the beauties of climbing is that you can make up the rules if you choose.

While it's great to strive for the highest style of ascent, it's vital that you not obsess on *having to* on-sight or flash every route. In chapter 8 you will learn that the best mental approach for effective climbing is to focus on the process and let the outcome (on-sight, flash, or fall) just happen. Recognize that even if you're failing, you're still learning and getting a good workout. Enjoy the process of climbing regardless of the result and you'll naturally become a climber of great style.

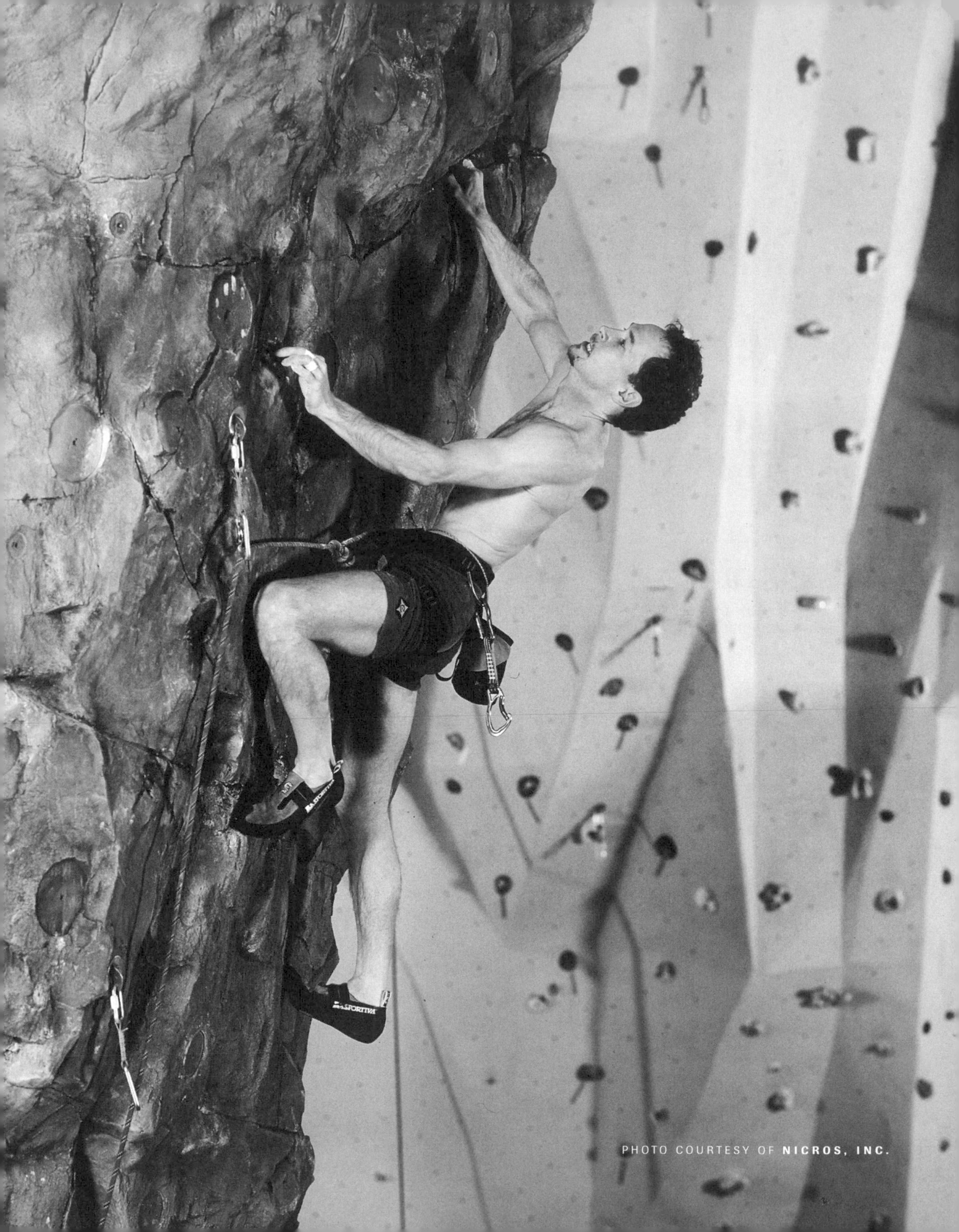

PHOTO COURTESY OF **NICROS, INC.**

2

Equipment
and Safety Gear

Climbing is a form of exploration that inspires me to confront my own inner nature within nature.

—*Lynn Hill, the first woman to climb 5.14a and the first to free climb El Capitan*

Clubs, bats, sticks, balls, and rackets—this is the equipment of most mainstream sports.

Fingers, toes, muscle, and the mind—these are the only mandatory tools for climbing.

In its essence, climbing is simply a vertical dance. The wall is the medium on which you perform; the selected route up the wall is your challenge, or partner, if you will. The need for gear arises only as you ascend to a height from which you cannot safely jump down. Even so, the necessary safety equipment will go hardly noticed as you safely rise above terra firma.

Compared with climbing outdoors, indoor climbing requires minimal equipment and only a small financial investment. Climbing shoes, harness, and a belay device are the only absolutely necessary pieces of gear, although there are a few other items you'll likely want to acquire, such as a chalk bag and a rope. During your first few visits, it's often best to simply rent this gear from the gym. Should you begin to climb on a regular basis, however, you will want to purchase a perfectly fitted harness and pair of shoes.

Following are descriptions of the mandatory equipment for indoor climbing, as well as some not-necessary yet common items you may see in use around the gym. While you can use this chapter as a sort of buyer's guide, I encourage you to do further research on manufacturers' Web sites and by visiting your local climbing store or gym pro shop.

Shoes

No one will ever mistake a climbing shoe for a street shoe—they are worlds apart in look, feel, and function. Sure, you can get away with wearing a tightly laced pair of sneakers during your initial foray at indoor climbing, but after your first day you should upgrade to wearing climbing shoes. Try out a rental pair, and I guarantee you'll be sold on the value of these sticky-soled shoes. However, exercise due diligence before purchasing a pair, because there are a wide variety of brands and designs to consider. Pull up a chair, and let's try on some shoes.

Finding the Right Shoe

The right climbing shoe for you depends on several factors, including the shape and width of your foot, your body weight, ability, and budget. With more than fifteen different brands of shoes on the market and over one hundred different styles, picking out your first pair can be daunting.

Let's begin with cost. Technical climbing shoes—not to be confused with hiking boots or approach shoes—run anywhere from $70 to $150 a pair. Since the most expensive models are designed for expert climbers pursuing high-end climbs, I suggest you not look at anything priced more than about $120. Conversely, shoes priced around $70 are typically of low quality and should be avoided. There are, however, many excellent buys in the $90 to $110 range,

Three styles of shoes by La Sportiva: lace-up (left), Velcro-closure slip-on (center), slipper (right).

so make this the price point at which to begin your search.

Within this price range you will find many models and a variety of design features. The most obvious feature is whether the shoe is a lace-up or slipper design. Lace-up models maintain a tighter fit throughout the life of the shoe and tend to have better support than slipper styles. As an indoor climber, however, you'll be switching in and out of your shoes several times over the course of a session, and the slipper designs simplify this process. Some manufacturers make a hybrid slipper that incorporates a Velcro strap-closure system. This unique design provides a snug fit similar to a lace-up, but with the ease of exit of a slipper. Give serious consideration to this style of shoe.

If the Shoe Fits . . .

Fit is everything when it comes to buying the right climbing shoe, so don't be overly swayed by what a friend or the local rock star wears. Ideally you want to visit a large outdoor store or well-stocked gym pro shop that carries six or more styles of shoes. Evaluate the quality of fit for each shoe based on three criteria: last shape, stiffness, and comfort.

LAST SHAPE

The last is the general mold around which a climbing shoe is designed and constructed. Most brands of shoes feature styles built on several different lasts—hopefully one of them will be similar to the shape of your foot.

Observe how the shape and width of the shoe compare with those of your foot. Is your foot narrow, wide, or about average? Is your foot asymmetric (longest at the big toe) or more symmetric (longest near the second or third toe)? It's these aspects that you are trying to match.

STIFFNESS

Consider the stiffness of different models and, in particular, test the flexibility of the shoe around the forefoot. Midsole thickness and whether the shoe is slip-lasted or board-lasted determine how stiff and supportive a shoe feels. The stiffness produced by board-lasted designs facilitates the use of small footholds, yet this benefit comes at the price of reduced sensitivity and feel—important for optimizing your foot placement on small holds. The heavy-duty support of a stiff-soled shoe is most important for a climber with a larger-than-normal build (in terms of weight), while an individual of average or slight build tends to perform best with a less stiff, slip-lasted shoe.

Light weight, supersensitive slipper models possess the least stiffness and are quite popular among indoor climbers. However, these minimalist shoes require significant foot strength and precise footwork, making them a poor choice for a novice. More appropriate as a first pair of shoes would be a slip-lasted model possessing a modest amount of stiffness and the snug fit provided by Velcro closures.

COMFORT

Finally, there's size and comfort to consider. Unfortunately, picking the right size climbing shoe is far more difficult than sizing a street shoe. Complicating matters are the stretch inherent to climbing shoes, size variations among manufacturers and styles, and the fact that some brands use European units of shoe size while others use the American scale. Ultimately, finding the right size shoe comes down to trial and error and a bit of luck. Also, be sure to try on shoes without socks, since that's the way you'll be wearing them to climb.

As a guideline, the right size shoe will be snug from heel to toe with no air pockets or dead space anywhere around the front half of the shoe. In fact, it's best to select a size small enough to induce a slight toe curl. A rough rule of thumb is to size unlined shoes about two full sizes smaller than your street shoes; lined shoes need only be one size smaller, since they will stretch much less. You can easily determine whether a shoe is lined or unlined by looking inside the shoe toward the toe box—the shoe is lined if you see a smooth white material and unlined if you see only brushed leather.

Some stores and gyms allow you to test the shoe out on a climbing wall. If that's not an option, take a walk around the store to determine whether you can wear the shoe for ten to fifteen minutes without severe pain. The shoe should be tight and somewhat uncomfortable to walk in—they are climbing shoes, not hiking boots!—yet you should not be wincing in pain with every step you take. Bottom line: It's best to err on the side of half a size too small rather than half a size too big, since most shoes tend to stretch more than you would expect.

Harness

The harness is the link between your body and the climbing rope. The fit should be snug and secure, yet the harness should not inhibit movement or feel bulky. As in selecting a pair of climbing shoes, it's best to try on several different midpriced harnesses ($40 to $70). Here are the three criteria to consider.

1. Is the harness a full-feature model or a minimalist, bare-bones design? Avoid purchasing one of the overdesigned, highly padded models, which are primarily designed for the rigors of climbing outdoors. For indoor climbing, a sleek, lightly padded harness is the ideal choice—you definitely do not need all the bells and whistles found on high-priced harnesses.

2. Does the harness feature adjustable leg loops and waist belt, or just an adjustable waist belt? The rental fleets of most gyms are filled with fully adjustable harnesses with buckles on both legs and waist, but such designs can be bulky and bother-

A standard seat harness by Black Diamond Equipment.

some. In purchasing a model, look for a harness with leg loops sewn to the proper size and possessing only a single buckle to adjust the fit around the waist. Many designs incorporate small elastic straps to keep the leg loops comfortably snug to your body—a nice feature to look for.

3. Many manufacturers now make women's harnesses that are uniquely proportioned around the legs, hips, and waist. While some women can find a good-fitting unisex harness, others swear by the perfect fit afforded by the women's styles.

As a final note, kids under the age of ten (or less than seventy pounds) should wear a specially designed full-body harness. Even the smallest

Kids under the age of ten should use a full-body harness.

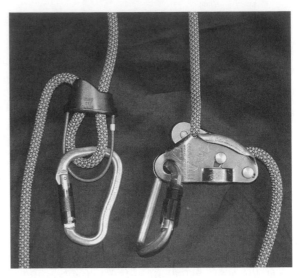

Popular belay devices: ATC (left) and Grigri (right).

adult-style harness will not properly fit around the legs, hips, and waist of a small child. However, a full-body harness with its legs, waist, chest, and shoulder straps is supremely secure and will allow parent and child to climb with peace of mind.

Belay Devices

After buying shoes and a harness, a belay device is your next likely investment. There are two basic types of belay devices—a belay plate and a self-locking device such as a Grigri—and it should be your goal to become proficient in using both pieces of equipment. Interestingly, gyms tend to have an affinity for

one device or the other, so inquire about this before you make a purchase.

A belay plate, and the more modern Air Traffic Controller (ATC) and Tuber, are the belay devices traditionally used for both indoor and outdoor climbing. These basic belay devices are available at any climbing store and most gyms for between $15 and $25.

Increasingly popular among indoor climbers are self-actuating belay devices such as the Petzl Grigri. As you will learn in chapter 3, these self-locking devices are more foolproof than the traditional belay plate. As the Cadillac of belay devices, however, they come at a higher price: $60 to $80.

Carabiners and Quickdraws

In addition to a belay device, you will also need a large safety-pin-like climbing link called a **carabiner**. Carabiners are made of an extremely light and incredibly strong aluminum alloy. Climbers use them in a number of different ways, but none is more important than the link between their belay device and harness. While a closed carabiner will never fail, there is always the remote chance that the

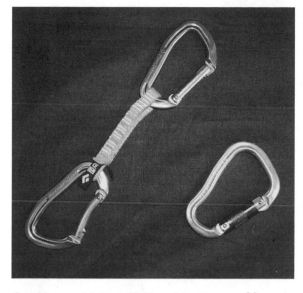

Carabiner quickdraw (left) and locking carabiner (right).

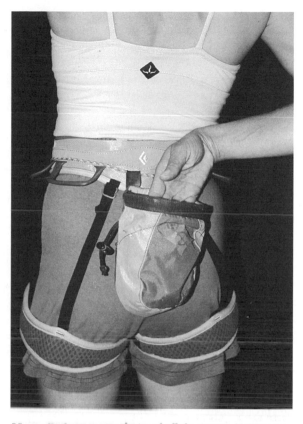

Most climbers agree that a chalk bag is an indispensable piece of equipment.

carabiner's gate could open and come unhooked from the rope or harness. As a safeguard, most manufacturers make a specialized locking carabiner, which possesses a twist-locking gate that secures the closed position. Purchase one locking carabiner ($8.00 to $15.00) for use with your belay device. Never use a nonlocking carabiner to belay.

Initially you will need only a single locking carabiner to engage in toprope climbing and belaying. If you someday delve into lead climbing, you may need to purchase some additional biners. As discussed in chapter 1, lead climbing involves leading the rope up the wall and clipping into anchor bolts with **quickdraws** as protection against large falls. A quickdraw is a couplet of carabiners connected with a short sling of nylon webbing. Most gyms affix permanent quickdraws to all anchor bolts on lead climbs. However, some facilities may have a few routes without them so that you can practice clipping into the bolts as you would when climbing outdoors. This is actually a good thing to practice if you plan to venture onto real rock, but you will need to invest in eight or ten quickdraws ($15 each).

Chalk

Just the thought of climbing likely makes your palms sweat, so imagine how your sweat glands will react when you are actually up on the wall hanging by your fingertips! To combat sweat and improve grip, climbers use magnesium carbonate, better known as gymnastics chalk. The chalk is carried in a small pouch or chalk bag ($15 to $20) attached to the back of your harness so that you can easily dip the fingers of either hand into the chalk in the midst of a climb. It won't be long before you discover that chalk is almost as important to effective climbing as sticky-soled shoes.

One downside of chalk use at indoor facilities is the dust it creates. In poorly ventilated gyms, you can often see a haze in the air during peak hours. Furthermore, the dust eventually settles out, producing a fine accumulation of chalk on all flat surfaces. In an attempt to control this problem, many gyms disallow use of loose chalk. Instead, the chalk in your bag must be contained inside a panty hose-like nylon sleeve that yields a slow release of chalk but no spillage. Many gyms sell premade Chalk Balls ($3.00 to $5.00) that provide a controlled release of chalk onto your hands. Tite Grip antiperspirant lotion is a chalk alternative available from www.cut melon.com.

Rope and Rope Bag

A climbing rope is unlikely to be an investment you'll make anytime soon, since climbing gyms supply and pre-rig topropes on most of their walls. Still, it's good to know about the equipment to which you trust your life, so let's cover the basics.

Climbing ropes are made of extremely strong and durable nylon, so straight up we can dispel any fears that a climbing rope might ever break. That said, a mistreated rope will wear out prematurely, and a rope that is drawn tight across a sharp edge may be damaged or cut. Consequently, there are three critical rules of rope care:

1. Keep the rope clean.

2. Never step on it.

3. Prevent the rope from touching anything sharp—whether it's a sharp edge on a climbing wall or a sharp object in the trunk of your car.

There are two basic types of climbing ropes: dynamic and static. A rope is dynamic if it stretches under the load of body weight or the force of a fall. In catching a falling lead climber, the rope's stretch absorbs energy, making for a soft catch and reducing peak forces on the climbing anchors, belay device, and belayer. Consequently, a dynamic rope is mandatory for all lead climbing.

Conversely, static ropes stretch very little. Their use for indoor climbing is limited to toprope routes, where there's little force generated by the very short

falls. Some gyms use static ropes on all of their toprope routes, since static line wears better and lasts longer than dynamic rope. Other gyms only use dynamic rope as a safeguard in the case the rope somehow finds its way onto a lead climb. The bottom line: There's no reason for an indoor climber to ever purchase a static rope.

When you begin lead climbing, however, you will likely need to purchase a dynamic rope. Most climbing gyms do not supply dynamic ropes for lead climbing, but even if they did, I'd prefer to use my own versus a heavily used communal rope. Dynamic ropes are available in a variety of thicknesses ranging from 9.5 to 11 millimeters (with 10 to 10.5 millimeters being the most common) and lengths of 50, 60, and 70 meters. Given that most indoor walls are less than 25 meters (80 feet) in height, a 50-meter rope is plenty long to lead and then lower off almost any indoor walls. However, if you plan to climb outdoors or patronize a gym with a lead wall more than 80 feet tall, it would be wise to buy a longer rope. Upon determining length and thickness, most people select a rope based on color preference and price. Expect to pay between $150 and $200 for your lifeline.

You should also consider purchasing a rope bag ($25 to $45) to protect your investment and extend its effective life. Most rope bags are designed to open up into a small tarp at the base of a climb. The opened rope bag makes a more visible no-step zone, and it also serves as a barrier between the rope and any foreign matter native to the floor of the facility.

Belay Gloves

I've been climbing for nearly thirty years, and I've rarely used belay gloves. Out of all the equipment needed for climbing, these are the most unnecessary. Still, some folks feel that leather gloves facilitate rope handling and belaying. Metolius makes a nice pair of fingerless gloves with reinforced palms ($25). Or you can buy a pair of high-quality leather work gloves at Home Depot and cut off the fingertips (necessary for good dexterity when handling gear).

Helmet

Helmets are not required equipment at most gyms, although some instructors and facilities recommend their use. While head protection is extremely important when climbing outdoors (where rockfall is a very real danger), the risk of a head injury indoors is minuscule. The only imaginable risks are a swinging fall into an adjacent wall or the remote chance that you might invert while falling and hit a surface headfirst. Ultimately it's a personal choice, and for many climbers the comfort and freedom of climbing hat-free predominate. I suggest discussing the matter with a few instructors and then making an educated decision as to whether a helmet is right for you. Don't make cost the determining factor—a good brain bucket only costs between $40 and $75.

Clothing

Unlike most traditional sports, there is no uniform or dress code for climbing. All that really matters is that you don comfortable clothes that won't inhibit your movement. Well-fitting athletic sweatpants or shorts along with a T-shirt or tank top will serve you just fine. Lightweight, cotton-based fabrics with a small amount of Lycra usually provide the best combination of fit, function, and comfort. Most important,

avoid anything that's overly baggy or oversized—a loose shirt can get stuck in your belay device, and baggy pants will get in the way of your view of footholds.

If cost is not an issue—and if you like a trendy, fashion-conscious look—you might want to shop for a few pieces of climbing-specific togs. There are several excellent apparel lines designed by climbers for climbers, such as prAna, Verve, The North Face, and Mountain Hardwear. While a single shirt-and-pants outfit can run upward of $100, in most cases you do get what you pay for from these companies. The designs are thoughtful, tested, and generally quite attractive. And you certainly can't blame a lackluster day of climbing on your clothing!

A final consideration in dressing for indoor climbing is that some facilities are not well climate controlled. In winter the gym may be a little colder than you'd like, while in summer it can be hot and humid, especially as you near the top of the climbing wall (remember, warm air rises). If conditions are uncomfortably warm, wear a cotton shirt, drink lots of water, and consider just bouldering for the day so as to stay close to the floor where the coolest air resides. In cold conditions, however, dress in layers that can be removed as your core temperature rises.

Table 2.1 An Equipment Checklist

Indoor Climbing Gear	Approximate Cost	Bouldering	Toproping	Leading
Technical climbing shoes	$100	x	x	x
Harness	$50		x	x
Locking carabiner	$10		x	x
Belay device	$15–$80		x	x
Chalk bag	$15	x	x	x
Belay gloves	$10–25		optional	optional
Rope and rope bag	$150–200			x
Quickdraws	$15 each			x
Helmet	$50	optional	optional	optional

Learning
the Safety Systems

Reaching the summit is always the goal, but the biggest victory is living to try again.

—*Steph Davis, top all-around American climber*

Climbing gyms offer an awesome setting for an amazing workout. A multitude of routes blazed up sheer walls are the apparatus, and your mind and body are the only tools for performing the exercise. One of the beauties of indoor climbing is the simplicity of engaging the rock wall with just your fingertips, toes, and mind, while all the complexities of life are left behind on the ground. Still, to engage in safe climbing requires use of the safety system called belaying that will guarantee you live to climb another day.

While you will spend many months learning all the subtleties of climbing technique and movement, the must-know safety information is something you'll pick up during your first few visits to the gym. This chapter presents an overview of the most fundamental safety techniques for bouldering and roped climbing. You must recognize, however, that reading about belaying is not a replacement for personal instruction. The bottom line: Use this section as a primer on these safety techniques, but vow to participate in a formal belay class to learn—and then perfect—the system.

Putting on Your Harness

Putting on your harness is not much more difficult than pulling up and buckling a pair of pants. Of course, the consequences of not properly securing your climbing harness are much greater!

Although the dozens of different harnesses on the market vary slightly in design, the one common feature is a master buckle on the waist belt. Upon stepping into the leg loops, pull the waist belt up over your hips and wrap it around the narrowest part of your waist. Be sure to tuck in your shirt so it lies smoothly underneath the waist belt. Thread the loose end of the waist belt through the buckle and pull until it's comfortably snug. Now the most vital step—take the loose end of the waist belt and double it back through the master buckle. Although the harness may feel secure with just a single pass through the buckle, it is nowhere near full strength without this second pass. Thus it's critical to double-check the master buckle every time you tie into the rope.

Tying Into the Rope

The vital link between your harness and the end of the rope can be established in a couple of different ways. The most popular method is the simple retraced figure-eight knot in which the rope ties directly to your harness. Consult the instruction booklet that accompanied your harness to determine the exact place through which to tie the rope. With most designs, the rope passes under the piece of webbing connecting the leg loops and then up under the waist belt. You do not want to tie into the belay loop that connects the waist belt and leg loops.

Some gyms prefer use of a figure eight on a bight and a locking carabiner as the junction to your harness. Such gyms usually have permanently tied

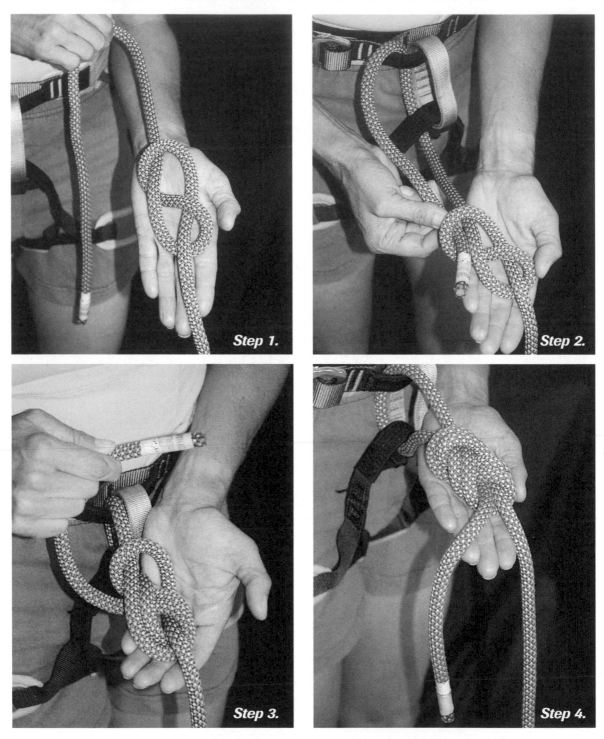

Step 1.

Step 2.

Step 3.

Step 4.

Strong and secure, the retraced figure eight is the best knot for tying into a harness.

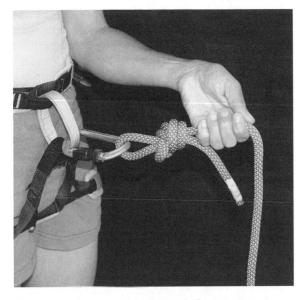

Some toprope rigs and all auto belays possess a permanent knot or connect point, which is clipped to the belay loop of the harness with a locking carabiner.

figure-eight knots at the end of all their topropes. This way you need only clip the knot to the belay loop of your harness with a locking carabiner.

Gyms with auto belays have a similar setup that's presumably foolproof. A locking carabiner is affixed to the end of the belay cable, so you need only clip the carabiner to your harness and then begin climbing. Sounds simple, right? Alarmingly, I've heard of climbers starting up the wall only to realize halfway up that they had forgotten to clip into the auto belay cable! Most gyms have an employee working as a wall monitor to check knots and keep an eye on the auto belays, but it's ultimately *you*, the climber, who's responsible for your own safety.

While these tie-in techniques are indeed simple and quick to perfect, there is obviously zero room for error. Accidents have occurred due to a botched knot or an unbuckled or misclipped harness. Make it a habit to inspect your connection to the rope before starting up every climb. Make "Double-check everything" your preclimb mantra.

Learning How to Belay

Roped climbing takes two people—a climber and a belayer—working in concert. As the climber ascends the wall, the belayer pays out or takes in rope according to the climber's movement. And should the climber slip from the wall, it is the belayer who arrests the fall and lowers the climber back to the ground. Fortunately, there are specialized belay devices and techniques that make catching a fall a relatively easy endeavor.

Who Should Belay?

Belaying is a solemn duty of highest importance. It is not an activity for an immature or flighty person of any age, nor should kids under about the age of fourteen be permitted to belay. Each gym has its own

Belayer using an ATC.

rules as to who is allowed to belay and what is required to be belay certified.

Ultimately, a climber must have complete faith in the belayer and the system—any doubts make it difficult to climb effectively or have much fun. Select a belayer whom you can trust and forget about while climbing. Similarly, you should strive to be a focused, world-class belayer when it's your turn to hold the rope.

Belay Techniques

Proper belay technique is dependent on the type of belay equipment you select: a self-actuating device or a one-piece passive device. The two are equally effective as belay tools, but each requires different skills and places different demands on the belayer. It should be your long-term goal to become proficient at both.

Self-actuating units, such as the Petzl Grigri, are widely used by both indoor and outdoor climbers. Assuming the rope is correctly fed through the device, it will clamp down on the rope and instantaneously arrest a falling climber, even if the belayer lets go of the rope or isn't paying attention. This nearly foolproof device is the obvious choice for climbing gyms.

Belay plates come in several different styles, the most common of which are the ATC and Tuber. These old-school devices place a much greater onus on the belayer, since letting go of the rope for even an instant could have dire consequences. Learning to use a belay plate demands more instruction than, say, the Grigri, and a novice belayer using a belay plate needs to be monitored for a longer period of time. Still, use of a belay plate is something all

Belaying with a Grigri

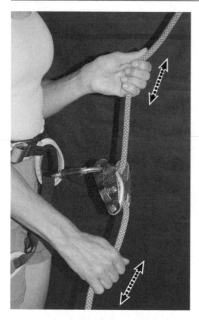

Feed out or take in rope by slowly pushing/pulling the rope through the Grigri.

Feeding out rope rapidly, as in belaying a lead climber, is best accomplished by lightly pressing down on the release handle with the middle and ring fingers of the right hand.

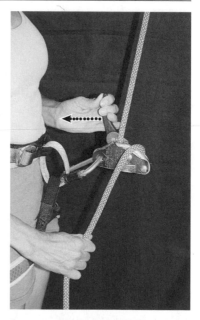

Lower a climber by slowly retracting the release handle, while the right hand guides the rope over the rounded right side of the Grigri.

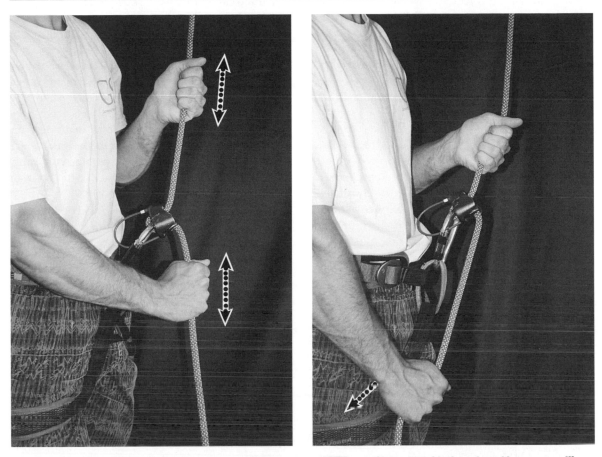

There are several different techniques for belaying with an ATC or other type of belay plate. Your gym will demonstrate its preferred technique. Two fundamentals: (1) Keep both hands on the rope at all times. (2) Keep the right hand low and pull the rope to your hip to lock the device.

climbers should learn, especially if they plan to climb outdoors, where its versatility can come in handy.

Some gyms require belayers to be anchored to the floor, while others allow the belayer to roam around the base of the climb to find the best position for a secure belay (which may change as the climber ascends the route). We'll take a closer look at catching and lowering climbers later in this chapter.

Belay Commands

There is a unique "belay-speak" that facilities unambiguous communication between the climber and her belayer. This is a universal language that you can use at any climbing gym in America to ensure a safe climbing experience. Here's a sample exchange between a climber and belayer.

Upon tying into the rope, the climber asks the belayer, "Am I on belay?" If the belayer has the rope threaded through his belay device and is ready to go, he responds, "Belay on; climb when ready." The climber then responds, "Okay, I'm climbing." As the climber moves up the wall, she will occasionally instruct the belayer regarding her rope-management needs. For instance, a request for "tension" tells the belayer to pull the rope tight, whereas "slack" asks for the rope to be loosened. The dialogue continues as needed until the climber returns to the ground and unties from the rope. To conclude, she instructs, "Take me off belay"; the belayer responds "Off belay" upon removing the rope from his belay device. See table 3.1 for a complete list of belay commands.

Catching Toprope Versus Lead Falls

Catching a falling lead climber and catching a falling climber on toprope are significantly different experiences. While the way in which the rope locks in your belay device is the same, the force generated in the two cases is vastly different. A toprope fall onto a snug rope induces very little force onto the belayer, whereas a 10-foot lead fall can pass on hundreds of pounds of force.

In the belay system, the belayer serves as a counterweight while catching a falling climber. Should the force generated by the falling climber exceed the weight of the belayer, then the belayer will be pulled off the ground. This is rarely an issue when toproping (unless the belayer's body weight is much lighter than the climber's), but it's the norm when catching a falling lead climber. Short lead falls may just pull you along the ground or upward a few inches, while larger lead falls could lift you a couple of feet off the ground. This is only a concern should you get pulled into another climber or the climbing surface itself. In rare instances, belayers have been hurt in this way. As prevention, some climbing gyms require belayers to be anchored to the floor via a piece of permanently fixed webbing or rope. Ultimately, you can provide a superb belay with or without being anchored to the floor.

Lowering Off a Route

Quite often you will climb a route to the top without falling onto the safety rope. Still, you will need the service of the rope to gain a ride back to the ground floor. For some beginners, lowering down a route is actually scarier than falling off the climb. This difference in fear factor is a function of the time you have to ponder the prospect of having to trust the rope—

Table 3.1 Common Belay Commands

Speaker	Command	Meaning
Climber:	"Am I on belay?"	Are you ready to belay me on this climb?
Belayer:	"Belay on; climb when ready."	Yes, the belay is ready; you may begin climbing.
Climber:	"Climbing."	I'm going to begin climbing now.
Climber:	"Up rope."	The rope is hanging too loose, so please take some in.
Climber:	"Slack."	The rope system is too tight; please loosen it a little.
Climber:	"Tension" or "Take!"	Pull the rope tight and hold me here.
Climber:	"Watch me."	I'm in a tenuous position, so please keep an alert belay.
Climber:	"Clipping."	I'm pulling the rope upward to clip an anchor bolt.
Climber:	"Falling!"	I'm coming off the wall—lock off the rope!
Climber:	"Lower" or "Dirt me."	I'm done climbing, so you can lower me to the ground.
Climber:	"Off belay."	I'm on the ground and done climbing, so you can take me off belay.
Belayer:	"Belay off."	I have taken you off belay.

A toprope belay provided off the belayer's harness. Some gyms require the belayer or belay device to be anchored to the floor.

PHOTO COURTESY OF **NICROS, INC.**

Lowering from a climb. Place your hands on the knot, sit back, and bend at the hips to form an L-position. Relax and walk down the wall while keeping your feet roughly level with your hips.

a fall happens in an instant, so there's little time to worry. Of course, any fears about the trustworthiness of the rope are unwarranted, given that the entire system is indeed bombproof.

In any case, upon topping the route you simply need to command the belayer to "take," at which time he will draw the rope snug. With your feet on good holds, ask the belayer to begin lowering you. As the rope initially begins to loosen, keep your feet on the holds and allow your rear end to drop down until your torso and legs form an L-position (with legs nearly straight and hips about level with your

feet). As the rope continues to pay out, simply walk down the wall with your feet about shoulder-width apart and your body maintaining the L-position throughout. Soon enough your feet will be back on firm ground.

Safe Bouldering and Spotting

Spotting is to bouldering as belaying is to roped climbing. Both types of climbing have inherent risks, and it's the spotter's or belayer's job to help mitigate these risks for his partner.

In recent years bouldering has become exceedingly

popular among indoor climbers. Bouldering is an excellent way to warm up and train for roped climbing, not to mention a terrific activity in and of itself. Hanging out in the gym's bouldering area and working some problems with friends can be great fun. But to participate in the good times, it's vital that you become a competent spotter.

There are two steps to effective spotting: determining and preparing the landing zone for a given problem, and the actual act of providing a trustworthy spot. Let's look at each.

Landing Zone and Crash Pads

Compared with the highly variable landing zones common to outdoor bouldering, the level base inherent to indoor climbing provides an excellent landing surface. Furthermore, most gyms have shock-absorbing flooring and copious crash pads in the bouldering area; this alone makes indoor bouldering vastly safer than doing it outdoors. Still, an unexpected fall onto a padded floor can be injurious. Thus it's best to boulder with a partner and take turns playing the roles of spotter and climber.

Working as a team, examine each boulder problem to determine the landing zone and best location for the spotter. Every problem is different, so visualize the fall line from different points on it. In the case of an overhanging problem, the landing zone will be changing as the climber ascends the wall. Make your best guess as to the footprint of the landing zone and position a couple of crash pads along this line. Of course, sometimes a best guess may be wrong and a falling climber will surprisingly land off the edge of the pad. For this reason, it's vital to proceed with caution on the initial attempt on a problem. You might even consider climbing partway up and then cautiously jumping off to determine the exact landing spot.

In any case, it's your goal to position the crash pads so that the falling boulderer will land as near the center of the pad as possible. Many climbers have injured their ankles and knees because they landed on the edge of a crash pad or in the gap between pads. Another possible risk is landing on a foreign object lying in the landing zone. Common objects to watch out for are water bottles, street shoes, and backpacks—make sure the area is cleared of such objects.

How to Become a World-Class Spotter

If you've ever participated in gymnastics, you're already familiar with the core demands on a spotter. If not, here are the solemn duties of a spotter and the techniques you need to learn to fulfill your duties!

1. Fix your eyes on the boulderer's hips throughout the duration of the climb. You can only provide an excellent spot if you can react quickly and apply force near the climber's center of gravity. It's a common mistake to watch the climber's hands or feet, instead of the hips—being a good spotter demands acute attention and resistance to distractions that may surround you.

2. Keep the boulderer upright to prevent his head from hitting the floor. This is paramount, and it is quite possibly the only thing you will be able to do in the rare case of a tumbling fall from a steep boulder problem. In this situation, you need to push forcefully on the boulderer's upper back near the shoulder blades or, possibly, grab under his armpits. Either way, you want to use the palm of your hands and not be shy about being forceful in your application of the spot. Executed properly, this technique slows downward movement of the head and shoulders just enough so that the feet reach the ground first.

3. Help break the fall by absorbing some of the energy with your arms and legs. Most often the boulderer will fall from a route feetfirst and in a relatively controlled manner. In these cases your primary duty is to serve as a shock absorber. The technique is simple: As the climber begins to drop, simply grab him at the hips and help slow his fall to the floor. Two important subtleties of this technique are to maintain a slight bend in your arms and legs (which allows your muscles to absorb more energy) and to keep your thumbs folded against the side of your hands (to prevent your thumb from getting hooked and bent backward).

A spotter is a boulderer's "belayer," so he must dedicate complete attention until the climber tops out or achieves a safe landing.

PHOTO BY **ERIC J. HÖRST**

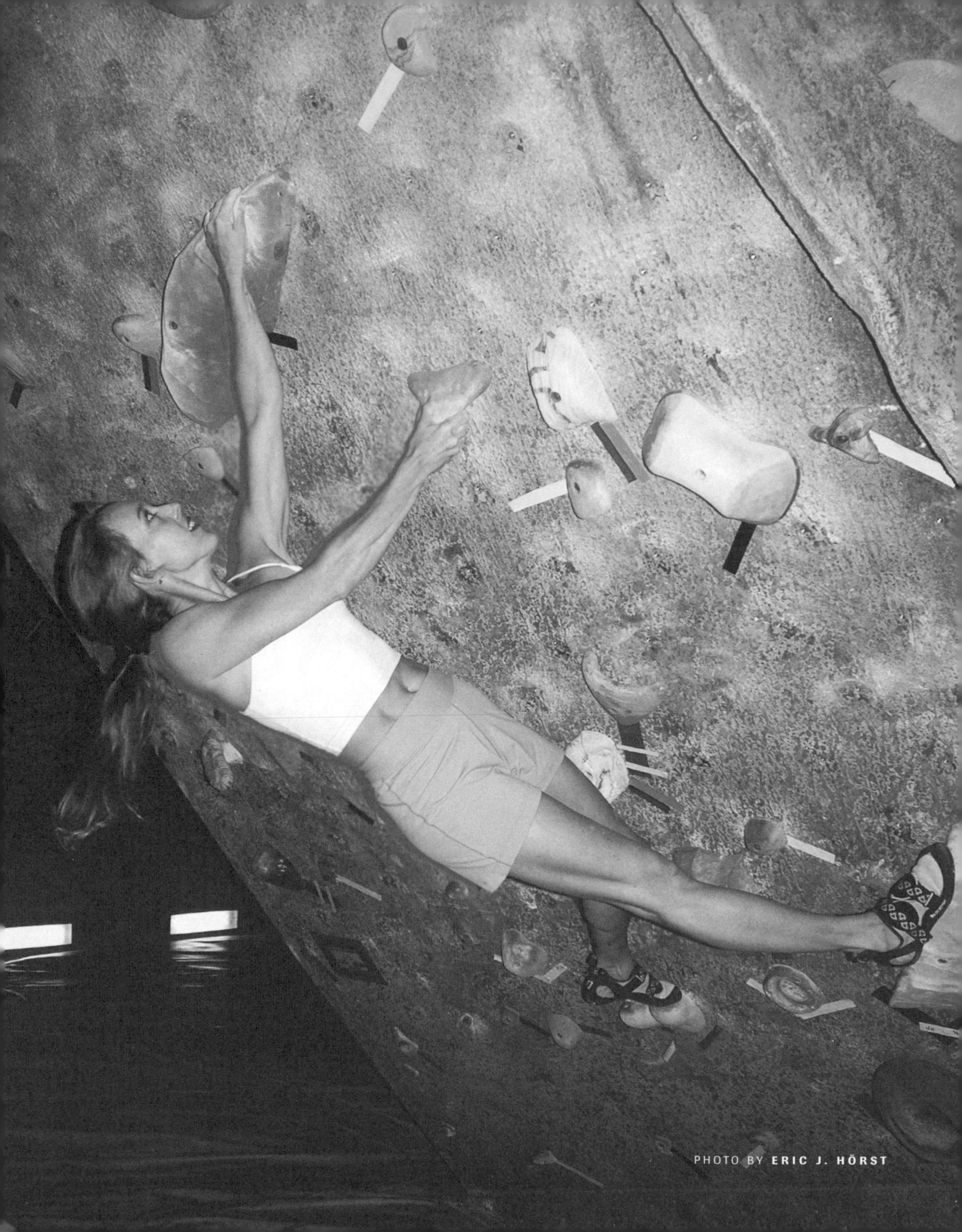

PHOTO BY **ERIC J. HÖRST**

The Keys to
Rapid Learning of Skills

It's very important to climb for yourself; if you do, your enthusiasm and motivation will allow you to progress faster than the rest.

—Catherine Destivelle, top all-around European climber

What could be simpler than climbing? Watch kids swarming over playground equipment and you will quickly recognize that climbing is as intuitive and natural as walking and running. In fact, it may be an inborn, primal need to climb that draws adults to a different sort of playground—the cliffs and climbing gyms of the world!

You will soon discover, however, that these adult playgrounds yield a remarkably complex and demanding activity. Consider that the climbing gyms and crags of the world offer a playing field of infinite variation, along with endless potential to discover and learn. Compound this with the adrenaline-releasing risks and perplexing challenges of ascending a steep wall, and you'll come to realize that climbing is indeed one of the most complex—and rewarding—forms of recreation.

Thus the goal of this chapter is to provide guidelines and expert tips for accelerating your learning of climbing skills. While the majority of new climbers stumble slowly through the maze of trial-and-error learning, you can take a more direct path to improvement by leveraging known absolutes of climbing performance. Following are eight powerful strategies that you can put to work beginning today.

Hire a Climbing Coach

The basic instruction you receive on your initial visit to a gym is but a first step in your long journey of learning to climb. The wealth of remaining knowledge is something you can try to discover on your own little by little—or you can hire a coach to tutor you on the critical skills and techniques. Sure, playing around on boulder problems and on a toprope is a fun and invaluable way to test skills and develop feel, but targeted, interactive instruction shifts learning into high gear.

Begin by taking a few of the optional classes your gym offers. Most gyms have several tiers of instruction, with each one- to two-hour class typically costing $20 to $40. In these sessions you'll learn much more about the subtleties of movement, mental preparation, and refining your skills as a belayer. Group classes are also a great way to meet other climbers of similar ability—you just might find a good training partner and climbing companion!

After a few months of climbing, your skills will advance beyond the level of typical "climbing 101" classes, so a personal coach is your new ticket to higher learning. Unlike the basic instruction provided in the group classes, a climbing coach will shape his lessons around your current skills and performance goals. For instance, he could help you learn very specific moves and tactics, or prepare you to test the waters of lead climbing. A good climbing coach can also develop an appropriate strength-training program to enhance your capabilities.

Given the pricey nature of hiring a climbing coach ($30 to $50 per hour), you might consider a modest commitment of one lesson per month. This way, the coach can observe your development on a more macro scale that makes it easier to spot the development of bad habits or poor technique. Such objective evaluation and a proactive approach to correcting weaknesses is part of the prescription for steady improvement and, ultimately, climbing excellence.

Warm Up Properly before Every Climbing Session

Climbing is a rigorous activity that places unique strains on your body. For example, consider the way you lock onto small handholds and pull a large portion of your body weight on only a few fingertips. The acute strain placed on the tendons in your fingers and arms is unlike anything your body has likely experienced before. To compound matters, over the weeks and months ahead your muscles will grow stronger at a faster rate than will the tendons that connect them to the bones. This simple fact of human physiology is a primary reason so many climbers experience tendinitis in the fingers and elbows.

A thorough warm-up is a good first step in preventing such injuries. The resultant increase in blood flow and core temperature enhances muscular function and flexibility, and it may help make tendons and other connective tissues more resistant to strain. Furthermore, you will climb and feel noticeably better after a brief warm-up than you would just jumping on the wall stone cold. The bottom line: Warm up before you go vertical.

The perfect warm-up would begin with a few minutes of light aerobic activity. The goal is to do just enough to produce a light sweat, but not so much that it tires you out. A few possibilities would be going for a short jog, riding a stationary bike (found in some gyms), or at the least doing fifty jumping jacks. Next, perform some gentle stretching of the forearms, shoulders, torso, and legs (see chapter 9 for details). Complete your warm-up with a non-maximal single set of push-ups, pull-ups, and abdominal crunches. This will bring your muscles to a simmer, and you'll be ready to rock!

Focus on Developing Technique and Mental Skills over Muscular Strength

Struggling on a climb almost always produces a muscular pump, so the seemingly obvious conclusion is that you were not strong enough to do the route. In climbing, however, things are not always what they seem.

The fact is that pumped muscles (and failure) most commonly result from improper sequences of moves, poor technique, and mental anxiety. Inefficiencies in these subtle areas multiply physical exertion and accelerate energy use in a way that induces premature failure of the muscles, most commonly in the arms. Thus it's important to view deficiencies in the areas of technique and mental control as a deadweight you are hauling up the climbing wall. Given this paradigm, do you think it would be best to engage in strength training (so you can continue to haul this extra weight around)—or to improve your mental and technical skills so as to permanently eliminate this weighty baggage? Hopefully, you agree that the latter approach is more intelligent, especially given that you can improve technique faster than you can strengthen your muscles.

Make refining technique and mental control the hallmark of your climbing gym workouts. When you fail on a climb ask yourself *How can I climb this route more efficiently?* not *How can I get stronger?* During your initial months your upper-body muscles will naturally adapt to the stresses of climbing and grow stronger simply by climbing a few days per week. There's really no need for a large commitment of time to strength-training exercises. Instead, invest your gym time on learning new moves, conquering your fears, and developing smooth, fluid technique. Strive to climb like a fuel-efficient Honda, not a gas-hogging Hummer, and you'll soon be tearing up the walls!

Strive to develop foot focus—
a master skill of efficient climbing.

PHOTO COURTESY OF **NICROS, INC.**

Model Advanced Climbers to Learn New Techniques and Tactics

An excellent way to learn new skills is to mimic the movements and tactics of more advanced climbers. This learning strategy, known as **modeling**, is highly effective for opening your eyes to new body positions and techniques that you might not discover on your own. One caveat to modeling, however, is that you must always practice the new move on a route of your ability, not on the route the advanced climber was on.

Here are some specific things to model from a more advanced climber: How did she prepare for her ascent? What did she do to warm up and how did she

Modeling the techniques and tactics of advanced climbers is a powerful method of learning.
PHOTO COURTESY OF **NICROS, INC.**

scope the route before beginning to climb? How fast did she move on the route, and how did her pace vary with the steepness of the climb or size of the holds? What unusual body positions did she use? How often did she stop to chalk up, shake out, or catch a rest? If she hit a sticking point on the route, how did she work the problem moves and how long did she spend on this crux before calling it quits (if, by chance, she couldn't solve the move)? All of these are actions you can test out on a climb of your own ability. Use what works, and modify or discard what doesn't.

It's important to point out a few things you should *not* model from advanced climbers. First and foremost, do not try to mimic their training routines. Experienced climbers possess muscle and tendon strength that takes years to develop, so attempting to copy their training program may get you hurt. Similarly, don't attempt the severe routes or sheer volume of climbing performed by these elites—this would yield little learning and might even lead to poor technique and bad habits of movement.

One thing you will quickly come to appreciate is beta, a verbal explanation of a specific move or crux sequence. In the sometimes festive gym environment, it's not uncommon to have one or more persons providing (maybe even yelling) beta as you are in the midst of a climb. In the earliest stages of learning, beta can indeed be quite helpful, because it helps you see critical holds and unlock complex sequences that you might never figure out on your own. It's best, however, if you have just a single person—your belayer or climbing coach—providing beta; overlapping or conflicting beta will only confuse you. Of course, it's also important to experiment with moves that differ from the beta you receive— you just might find a better way.

As your technical ability improves, you must shift to a more autonomous approach to working routes. While beta might help you solve a crux more quickly, it does somewhat shortcut the learning process. Remind yourself that learning to problem solve on the fly is a big part of becoming a better climber. Therefore, you will gradually need to begin saying no to beta. Make your intentions known to your belayer and others around you; if you don't want beta, express this in no uncertain terms before you leave the ground.

Embrace a Practice Perspective and Resolve to Always Have Fun

We get into climbing because it's an enjoyable activity that diverts attention from the serious or stressful aspects of daily life. Ironically, some climbers gradually come to take climbing too seriously. They create a self-imposed pressure to perform that generates stress and anxiety—and ultimately ruins the fun of climbing.

As a wide-eyed beginning climber excited at the prospect of simply playing around on the walls, you may find it hard to believe that climbing could ever not be fun. Well, just look around the gym and you'll likely observe a couple of climbers (or more) losing their cool when they fall from a boulder problem or climb. Sure, it's natural to be disappointed and frustrated when you fail on a route, but to throw a tantrum or spew expletives as some climbers do is a sure sign they are taking the activity too seriously. Interestingly, the more pressure you place on yourself to climb well, the more difficult it becomes to think and climb proficiently. Another great paradox of climbing is that it's easier to climb harder by not needing to!

The same goes for the process of learning to climb. Optimal learning of skills comes when you embrace a carefree practice perspective, as opposed to a more serious performance perspective. The neuromuscular system is most effective at coding new motor skills, called **schemas**, when you are in a fresh, relaxed state. As fatigue and tension grow, it's harder to either learn new skills or perform up to your current ability.

Another vital distinction for effective learning is that you must strive to perfect technical movements, not just get by with them. This is true regardless of the difficulty of the climb you are on, but it's most important when climbing near your limit. The common approach is to call an ascent successful when you solve the crux and successfully ascend the route from bottom to top without falling. In doing this redpoint ascent, you might struggle and fight through the hardest moves—a good mental success—but

with less-than-perfect technique. Becoming an outstanding technical climber, however, comes only by means of a constant resolve to master every sequence with perfect economy. This goal may take a few more attempts or even a few more days to achieve, but in striving to meet this high technical standard, you will develop true climbing excellence.

Finally, make it a goal to foster a constant self-awareness of your changing mental and physical state throughout your climbing gym workout. Strive to break new ground—technically and mentally—during the first part of your session when you are feeling fresh. When you sense a growing level of fatigue or frustration, it's time to redirect your efforts to another climb more within your capabilities. The bottom line: Resolve to always have fun, regardless of the quality of your climbing on a given day, and you'll maintain the requisite disposition for developing uncommon ability.

Regularly Experiment with New Techniques and on New Terrain

Most climbing gyms possess a wide range of wall terrain, and the person serious about learning to climb should commit to exploring every square foot of this climbing surface. In the earliest stage of learning, you'll obviously need to practice on the lower-graded, nonimposing sections of wall until you develop some of the basic skills. As your confidence and ability increase, however, you must gradually progress to the more novel, daunting features such as arêtes, overhangs, cracks, and steep faces. Continued technical growth comes only when you consciously push yourself onto foreign and uncomfortable-feeling sections of wall.

Consider that climbing is a highly complex sport with an infinite variety of moves and crux situations. Mastery comes only to those who pursue the long-term goal of doing it all. That means gradually exposing yourself to every wall feature a gym has to offer, and eventually traveling to different gyms and maybe outdoor crags to expand the learning even further. In a technical sense, climbing is similar to golf—both sports require many years to develop a high level of competence, because both have playing

Regularly test yourself on new terrain to expand your abilities.

sense of your current level of climbing. While your first day at the gym may be spent learning the basics on a beginners' section of wall (commonly not given an ADS grade), you'll no doubt venture onto other routes during subsequent visits. Most beginners quickly gain comfort in ascending routes graded between 5.4 and 5.8. Let's assume, for example, that 5.8-rated routes are the highest level you can successfully climb bottom to top without falling. My rule is that you should spend 70 percent of your climbing time on routes between your limit and two grades below your limit. In this case, you'd spend most of your time practicing on routes rated between 5.6 and 5.8. The other 30 percent of your session should be spent on routes up to one full grade above your maximum ability; in this case you'd want to work on one or two 5.9 routes.

Climbing a route more than two grades below your limit is useful as a warm-up, but not for advancing your technical abilities. Similarly, flogging yourself on a climb more than a number grade beyond your limit is generally not productive. It might also be demoralizing and tempt injury.

The best plan is to break a climbing session into three parts. Begin by warming up on several routes that are two or more number grades below your limit. Strive to develop rhythm and smooth movement. Next, get on a couple of routes that are at or just above your limit. The goal here isn't necessarily to succeed on the routes—though it would be great if you did!—but instead to stretch your boundaries and gain exposure to new moves and situations. Finally, spend the last third of your session on routes that are roughly a number grade below your limit. Your goal is to reinforce control and poise while elevating confidence with a few solid, no-falls ascents.

Follow this plan long-term and you will obtain uncommonly good results. Many climbers do not operate in accordance to this training principle, as they spend most of their time climbing—or, more correctly, flailing—on routes way over their head. While they may occasionally beat a route into submission, there's little learning going on. In fact, I've seen climbers behave this way for years, and many end up getting injured or simply burned out on climbing. The

fields of infinite variety. Thus becoming excellent at either sport is not something that just happens—it's something that happens by way of intelligent, disciplined practice in a wide range of settings.

Push Yourself, But Know When to Call It a Day

Just as it's important to explore new terrain, it's also fundamental to regularly push the boundaries of what you feel is possible. Given the ADS and V-Scale grading used at most gyms, this is a strategy that's fairly easy to execute. Here are some guidelines to testing the waters of more difficult climbing.

During your first few weeks of climbing, you'll come to understand the ADS scale as well as gain a best approach is to gain a high win-to-loss ratio: Spend most of your time winning on routes close to your maximum ability, with only limited exposure to testing the waters of the next higher grade.

Get on a Regular Climbing Schedule

As in learning any skill sport, you need to engage in a regular schedule of climbing in order to realize gains in ability. Consider climbing once or twice per week the minimum commitment if you want to improve. Climbing less frequently can still be great fun, although you will see little improvement.

If you are serious about improving, you can maximize learning by practicing your climbing three or four days per week. Enthusiastic individuals may ponder going to the gym more than four days per week—this is not wise! While you can play golf or, say, practice the piano seven days per week, it's a flawed and dangerous practice strategy to apply to climbing. Climbing is an uncommonly rigorous activity that requires copious rest for the neuromuscular system to recover and **supercompensate** to greater capability. The bottom line: Climbing too frequently is the ultimate bad investment in terms of developing skill, since you will eventually succumb to overtraining syndrome, a plateau in performance, and quite possibly injury.

A good two-day-per-week practice schedule is to climb once during the midweek (say, Wednesday) and then one day over the weekend. The most popular routine among gym climbers may be the three-day-per-week schedule of climbing on Tuesday, Thursday, and Saturday. This can be upgraded to a four-day-per-week program by adding a Sunday session as well. However, you do not want to climb on more than two consecutive days—another common pathway to **overtraining** and injury.

How long should you climb on a given day? Your goal for actual time on the wall should be thirty to sixty minutes. Obviously you'll take many breaks between climbs (resting, socializing, and belaying), so you may only log about fifteen to twenty minutes of climbing per hour in the gym. Given this ratio, you need to plan on two to three hours at the gym in order to accomplish an effective workout.

The Keys to Rapid Learning of Skills

1. Hire a climbing coach. Obtain the objective evaluation and sage guidance of a climbing coach to get on the fast track to climbing excellence. Even just one session per month will be extremely beneficial.

2. Warm up properly before every climbing session. Perform a progressive warm-up to reduce injury risk and modulate your neuromuscular system for optimal learning and performance. Spend twenty to thirty minutes on easy climbs and doing various warm-up activities.

3. Focus on developing technique and mental skills over muscular strength. Refining movement and mental skills is shortest pathway to climbing stronger. Invest most of your gym time on climbing, not strength training.

4. Model advanced climbers to learn new techniques and tactics. Stretch your imagination for climbing movement and strategy by observing and mimicking the techniques and tactics of top climbers.

5. Embrace a practice perspective and resolve to always have fun. Optimize learning of new skills by maintaining a curious, carefree disposition and having fun regardless of climbing outcomes.

6. Regularly experiment with new techniques and on new terrain. Challenge yourself on a wide range of wall features to expand your skill set and develop confidence. Avoid the rut of always climbing known routes and training in the same familiar ways.

7. Push yourself, but know when to call it a day. Spend about one-third of your climbing time on routes just beyond your limit to effectively stretch your boundaries. However, focus the majority of your practice on routes just below your limit to fortify skills and confidence.

8. Get on a regular climbing schedule. Climb two to four days per week (never more) to maximize learning and improvement. Only disciplined, regular practice over the long term will yield consistent improvement and climbing excellence.

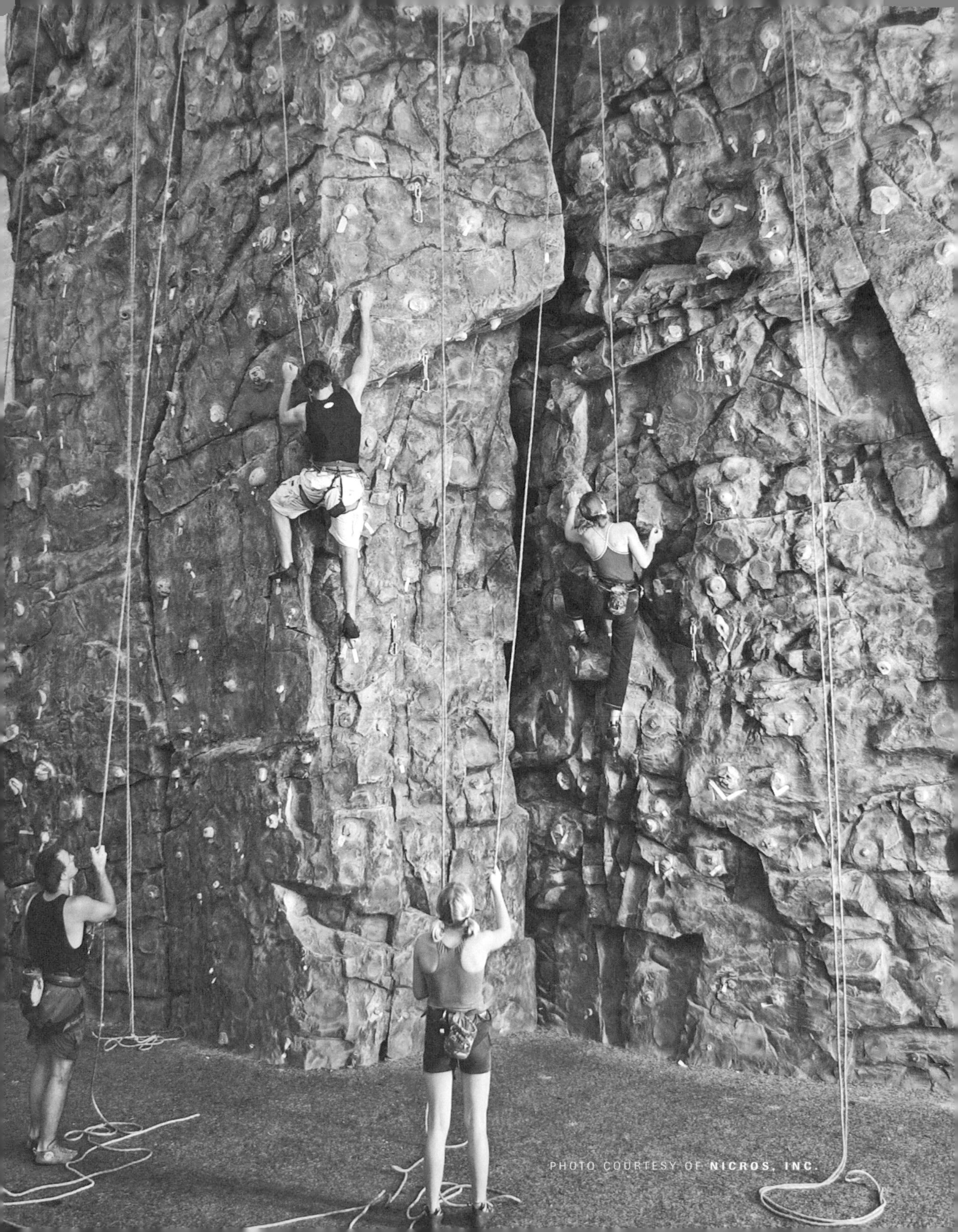

PHOTO COURTESY OF **NICROS, INC.**

CHAPTER FIVE

Basic
Skills and Drills

*Climbing relies more on technique
and balance than brute strength,
so there is no reason an enthusiastic
climber cannot carry on at a top
level until old age, as many do.*

—*John Long, legendary California climber,
adventurer, and author*

This is where the rubber meets the road—or,
more correctly, where your shoe rubber and fingertips meet the rock.

Almost all climbing movement results via the
four points of contact that your hands and feet
afford, and thus nothing is more fundamental for
effective climbing technique than the ways in which
you engage the rock with your fingers and toes. A
wise beginning climber will learn and make habit of
optimal hand and foot contact early on, or risk
developing poor techniques that could stunt
improvement for years to come. Same goes for your
body positions and methods of movement, the quality of which directly affects your energy consumption and apparent strength on the rock. Therefore,
the following pages of instruction on basic skills and
drills are as important and powerful as any other
portion of this book. Don't skip over this material
because of its seemingly basic content.

Four Points of Contact

There are countless ways in which your hands and
feet can make contact with our infinitely varying

playing field. However, the majority of finger grips
and foot placements you execute will be but slight
variations on a more finite number of basic methods
of contact.

Detailed below are the six most common fingergrip techniques and the five basic arm positions you
will utilize in leveraging off a handhold. Following
this you will learn the four most common methods
for securely positioning your feet on holds of any
shape or size.

It's important to recognize that the hand and
foot positions covered in this chapter are the staple
techniques of face climbing. There's a completely
separate class of hand and foot placements used for
climbing crack; these involve inserting and **jamming** your appendages into a vertical fissure in the
wall. Given that crack climbs are a rarity at climbing
gyms, it's not necessary that you learn the jamming
techniques at this time. Chapter 10 does provide a
primer on crack climbing since you will eventually
want to expand your skill base to cover all novel
types of climbing.

Finger Grips

The basic finger-grip positions are full crimp, half
crimp, open hand, pocket, pinch, and palm. You will
find some of these grips to be more intuitive and
comfortable to use than others. Many climbers simply use the comfortable grip positions and ignore the
rest—do not fall into this trap! As you execute the
drills presented later in the chapter, strive to regularly practice each grip position. In doing so, neuromuscular adaptations will gradually make you
stronger and more comfortable in using all the grips.

45

Basic Finger Grips

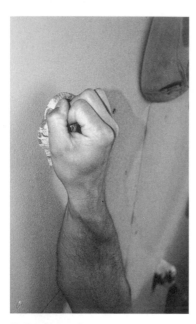

Full-crimp grip.

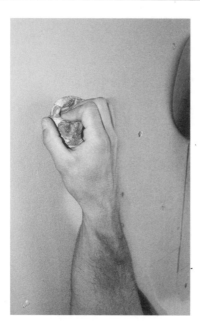

Half-crimp grip.

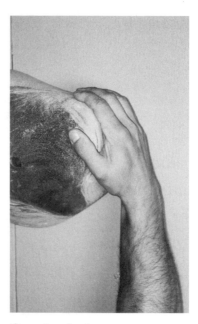

Open-hand grip.

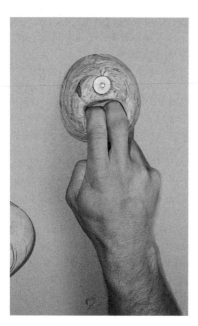

Pocket grip.

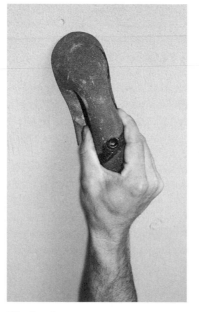

Pinch grip.

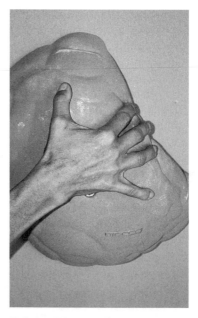

Palm or friction grip.

It's this kind of attention to the subtle details of effective practice that will pay huge dividends in ability in the months and years to come.

FULL CRIMP

The full crimp is favored by many climbers since it provides what feels like the most secure lock onto small handholds. The hallmark of the full crimp is the hyperextension of the first joint of each finger and the sharp **flexion** of the second finger joint. The full-crimp grip is then secured by locking your thumb over the end of the index finger.

Unfortunately, this grip position places the highest force load on the joints and tendons, and **overuse** can result in nagging finger injuries. While it is absolutely necessary to use and train the crimp grip, the best approach would be to limit it to holds that cannot effectively be gripped any other way. The full-crimp grip excels on small, square-cut edges, shallow flakes, and any hold that possesses a small incut or recessed edge.

HALF CRIMP

The half-crimp grip is just a variation on the full crimp in which you do not thumb lock over the index finger. This reduces slightly the aggressive angles on the first and second joints of the finger, thus making the grip a bit more ergonomic. The trade-off is that the half crimp often feels less secure than the full crimp, although you can develop strength and comfort in the half crimp through regular use.

Once again, it's important to use the practice drills to experiment with the half-crimp grip. Initially it's a good practice to compare the full- and half-crimp grips on a given hold. Which feels more secure? Can you use the half crimp even though it might feel less secure than the full crimp? If so, use the half crimp, and save the full crimp only for holds that absolutely demand its use.

OPEN HAND

The open-hand grip, also known as the extended grip, has distinct advantages over the crimp grip. First, the open-hand position is kinder to the finger tendons and joints since it softens the joint angles and may allow the rock to provide some tendon support (as your fingers wrap naturally over a curved hold). Furthermore, despite its frequently less secure feel, the open-hand position can be trained to become your strongest grip position on all but small, incut holds (which require a crimp grip). Use this knowledge to fuel diligent practice, and you will gradually develop amazing open-hand grip strength. Make the open-hand position your first choice on all medium to large handholds with smooth, rounded features.

POCKET

Pocket holds are exceedingly common on indoor climbs, and they are quite often part of the recipe for a frustrating crux sequence. Pockets can range in size from a small dimple barely big enough to fit a single fingertip to a large hole in which you can stuff all four fingers. Of course, it's the little pockets that fit only one or two fingertips that are most disconcerting. Fortunately, regular practice will increase your strength and confidence in being able to hang on to even the smallest pocket hold.

A subtle but important difference in how you grip pocket holds relates to whether the fingers used are clinging to the pocket via an open-hand (extended-finger) position or with more finger flexion, as in the half-crimp grip discussed above. As a rule, the depth and sharpness of the pocket will be the determining factors. For instance, if a pocket is shallow and possesses a sharp edge, you'll almost always want to grip the pocket with your fingers in a half-crimp position. A deeper, more rounded pocket will generally feel better with your fingers in the open-hand position.

Finally, there's the matter of which fingers to insert into pockets too small to fit all four. Pockets that only fit two fingers, commonly called two-finger pockets, are most securely gripped with the index and middle fingers or the middle and ring fingers. The ever-scary, one-finger pocket is best avoided—but if you must, the middle finger tends to work best. Comparatively, the pinkie is a wimp in terms of strength; however, it is useful when it can be stuffed into a small three-finger pocket along with the middle and ring fingers. A large three-finger pocket can best be gripped with the index, middle, and ring fingers working as a powerful team.

PINCH

The pinch grip is vital for grasping protruding holds such as pebbles, ribs, "bread-loaf" holds, or opposing edges. Due to the protruding nature of indoor climbing holds, use of the pinch grip is far more common indoors than on natural rock faces.

The good news is that our hands were designed to excel at pinching motions. Difficulties in using this grip tend to relate more to the smoothness or shallowness of the gripping surface—as always, there are many possible shapes, ranging from a small, shallow pencil-sized rib to a giant bread-loaf blob. Like all the other grips, strength at pinching holds is specific and requires regular practice. You can best increase strength in this slippery grip by seeking out and working on boulder problems possessing a variety of pinch holds.

PALM/FRICTION

This final grip is hardly a grip at all, since your point of contact is simply the friction created by pressing or wrapping your palm over the rock surface. Although the palming technique isn't needed for the typical beginner-level climb, it is extremely valuable when attempting more complex routes that feature corners, arêtes, or large featureless holds. The bottom line: While the positive grip provided by all the other grips will almost always exceed that of the palm grip, you still need to have the palm grip in your bag of tricks as you advance to more difficult climbs.

Arm Positions

Regardless of how you grip the rock, it's the arms that utilize this point of contact to create torque, leverage, and upward movement. Therefore, it's vital to distinguish between grip position—the point of contact—and arm position, which connects this point of contact to your torso. You will soon discover that you'll be using your arms in countless different ways and directions, yet every arm position is but a slight variant on one of five basic positions: the down pull, the **mantle**, the **undercling**, the side pull, and the reverse side pull or **Gaston**.

It's important to recognize that each arm position places your hand in a different orientation with respect to your center of gravity. In viewing the photos, note how the different arm positions place the palm—and therefore the application of force—facing either downward, upward, inward, or outward. Which arm position you choose for any given move will be determined by whether the role of the arms is to provide balance, locomotion, or both. Initially, you'll need to make this determination through sometimes clumsy experimentation. With practice, however, you will rapidly develop the ability to intuit the proper arm position for almost any novel move.

DOWN PULL

The down pull is by far the most common arm position used in climbing, as it's the arm position you would use in climbing hand-over-hand up a ladder. With each grip on the rock, the arm begins in a position above your head with the palm facing downward. From this starting position you can either hang straight-armed in a static rest position or you can pull downward to aid in upward movement. When used to aid in locomotion, the down-pulling arm often concludes its work in the lock-off position typified by the arm bent at an acute angle with the elbow pointing downward and your hand pulled in tight against the side of your chest. This range of motion from the above-the-head, straight-armed position to hand-against-chest lock-off is the single most fundamental arm movement in climbing. Consequently, your strength and endurance at this pulling motion will increase simply by climbing a few days per week.

MANTLE

The mantle, or press-down, position is essentially the opposite of the down-pull position in that your arm begins in a bent position near your torso and then pushes palm-downward. An ordinary-life use of mantling is the simple act of pushing yourself out

Basic Arm Positions

Down pull.

Mantle.

Undercling.

Side pull.

Gaston.

of the water at the edge of a swimming pool—both hands contact the edge of the pool palms-downward as they push down from near your chest to below your waist. In climbing, the mantle move is significantly more difficult since there's no water to provide the lightening effect of buoyancy. Furthermore, in climbing it is rare to come upon a large, flat surface on which to mantle (except at the top of a boulder problem). Instead, you will often need to mantle on the top of a large handhold, a shallow edge, a pocket, or in extreme cases even press down with only your thumb resting on the top edge of a hold.

UNDERCLING

An inverted, downward-facing handhold demands gripping the usable surface palm-up while contracting the arm muscles with the arm bent in an elbow-down or elbow-back position. Your palm-up contact with the handhold is usually a half-crimp, open-hand, or pinch grip. Underclinging a hold above your head is a difficult feat that provides little more than balance; leverage increases exponentially, however, as the handhold nears your center of gravity. Therefore, the most common use of this arm position is to utilize a downward-facing handhold located somewhere near your torso. What's more, combining this undercling with an opposing foot placement makes for a winning combination that's both stable and powerful.

SIDE PULL

The more difficult a climb, the more likely it becomes that you'll need to use side-pull arm positions. As the name implies, this position involves grabbing a hold that faces sideways and away from your body, not upward or downward. As in the down-pull and underclinging arm positions, you can execute a side pull by grasping a handhold using just about any grip position. The primary difference is the lack of locomotion that you can create by simply pulling with your arm in a side-pull position. Consequently, the side-pull arm is less intuitive and more technical to use effectively.

Although you will come to use side pulls in a wide range of positions, the most common is to grab an outward-facing hold somewhere off to the side of your body and then pull inward to gain leverage and balance. A side pull can also be used in pairs, with both the right and left arms pulling inward toward the torso. This is a method of attaining balance when the rock is void of upward- or downward-facing edges, but you'll need your feet to provide locomotion from this body position. This leads us to the important idea that the hands and feet *must* work together in unison—this is, in fact, a fundamental concept, and it's something we'll look at later in the chapter.

REVERSE SIDE PULL OR GASTON

The reverse side pull, also known as a Gaston, is a more difficult arm position used on inward-facing holds located near your body. The Gaston position is typified by a bent-armed, elbow-out position with the hand gripping the hold thumb-down. Force is applied in a sideways pull away from your body—the arm position is similar to that of grabbing the edge of a sliding door (in front of your face) that you intend to fling open. Of course, it's also possible to use opposing Gaston holds such that both hands are positioned thumbs-down in front of your face as if getting ready to separate two window curtains.

Most people are naturally stronger and more comfortable using a standard side pull, where you grab a hold off to the left or right and pull inward toward your body. However, the more difficult reverse side pull must be used on many side-facing edges that are located in front of your body. For instance, imagine a left-facing vertical edge in front of your face. The best use of this hold would often be to grab it with your right hand (thumb down) and pull outward to the right. This is the classic Gaston technique.

As with the side-pull arm position described earlier, it's next to impossible to glean upward movement exclusively from the Gaston. Gaston arm positions are most commonly used for balance or to help maintain a static body position as you advance a foot placement.

Foot Positions

You have four points of contact while climbing, and it is vital that you make the most of each. The hand contact points just discussed will be easy to learn and experiment with, especially given the close proximity of the handholds to your eyes. You can inspect each handhold close-up and determine exactly the best way to grab it. This, unfortunately, is not the case with foot placements. Trying to optimally stick the edge of your shoe to a small nubbin several feet from your eyes can be surprisingly difficult. And to make matters worse, "feel" with your feet is greatly diminished due the layer of rubber and leather that separates your feet from the holds.

Consequently, developing solid footwork demands pinpoint focus and lots of deliberate practice. The goal is to place each foot in a way that maximizes the area of contact between the shoe rubber and rock, while also placing your foot in a stable position that doesn't shift as you stand up on it. Ultimately, lots of real-life experience on the walls is the only way to develop such feel skills. You will want to experiment with the four basic foot positions described below and assess how the security of each varies with the shape and size of different footholds. You will find that certain footholds demand use of a specific foot position, whereas other times it will be your body position or direction of movement that determines how to best place your foot on the hold.

TOE-IN (AKA FRONT-POINTING)

The toe-in foot placement is the same one you'd use to position your foot in climbing a stepladder. The front part of your shoe is contacting the foothold while your heel extends straight out from the wall. This style of foot placement is indeed most natural to the novice climber, but it is rarely the optimal method when climbing. In standing toe-in on a hold, your foot becomes a long lever; this requires significant calf muscle strength to maintain. Thus climbing toe-in on small footholds will quickly fatigue your calf muscles. Below you'll learn how using the inside or outside edge of your shoe reduces the lever length of your foot, and also brings the best part of the climbing shoe—and most rubber—into play.

Pockets and other recessed holds are the one situation where the toe-in foot position excels. You can gain the best purchase inside a pocket if you simply stick the tip of your shoe straight into the hole. Some asymmetric-style climbing shoes possess a more notable point at the big toe and thus provide an even more secure placement on pockets.

EDGING

The most secure foot placements usually come from positioning the inside or outside edge of your shoe on the top edge a foothold. Although every foothold—and therefore foot placement—will be different, the goal is to maximize the area of contact between the edge of your climbing shoe and the hold. With the more common inside-edging, you'll want to utilize the sharp rubber edge that runs from the ball of your foot to the end of the big toe. Climbing shoes are designed to provide tremendous support and feel through this area, and you'll soon learn to use this portion of your shoe like a finely tuned instrument.

Outside-edging is a less instinctive yet still vital foot technique, especially on tricky moves with the holds spaced far apart. In these situations you can increase reach and stability by turning your foot inward and placing the outside edge of your shoe on the foothold. There is a definite sweet spot on the outside edge of your shoe—usually near the side edge of your little toe—that can provide excellent purchase in some difficult situations. Experimentation and practice will eventually yield an instant sense of how to best use your outside edge on any given climbing hold.

Two rules of effective edging relate to the stability and angle of foot placement. First, keep your foot steady on the foothold throughout its use. Readjusting or shifting your foot in the slightest way may cause the shoe to pop off the edge. This underscores the importance of precise foot placement from the get-go. Paste the shoe rubber on the edge, then stand on it with no doubts or foot wobble. Second, since not all footholds possess horizontal surfaces to stand on, you need to try to match the

Basic Foot Positions

Toe-in or pocket.

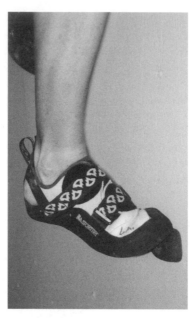

Inside-edging.

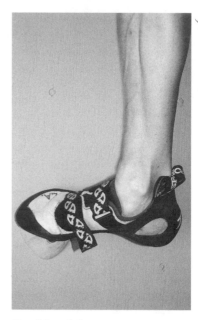

Outside-edging.

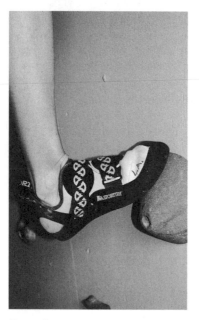

Smearing.

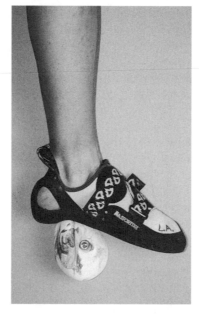

Rest step.

Foot-stack rest step.

angle of your shoe edge to the angle of the hold in order to maximize contact area. For example, an edge that angles downward toward the centerline of your body is best used by lowering your heel and trying to match the inside edge of the shoe to the angle of the hold.

As a final tip, strive to develop a sense of foot feel with every step you take. As a true novice, you may have no idea what I'm talking about; you will, however, gradually develop a heightened awareness of foot-placement quality. You can develop this important sense most rapidly with focused practice of footwork, either on toprope or while bouldering. Try to feel each hold—it helps to visualize the hold and the shoe's positioning on it—and then exert a slight "press" down on the edge as you stand on the foothold. While this press should not actually move or reposition the foot, it does help solidify the placement.

SMEARING

Many climbing holds lack crisp, distinct edges on which to place your feet, and thus present you with the challenge of standing on a rounded, sloping surface. Use of the smearing technique will usually provide a secure point of contact, although the act of smearing is more subtle and heady than edging.

The name *smearing* describes the process of using the shoe sole to smear onto the surface of the foothold. Smearing is all about maximizing friction between the sole of the shoe and the hold. Depending on the angle of the climbing wall and the size of the hold, you may need to smear with your foot turned inward, outward, or in the toe-in position. No matter which orientation you use, it's vital to flex at the ankle and place as much of the shoe sole on the hold as possible. More rubber contact means more friction and less chance of slippage.

As in edging, effective smearing comes only with an acute sense of feel and attention to each placement. View each foothold as unique and determine the ideal place to smear for maximum security. Some footholds possess a few different surfaces on which to smear, so you'll need to make a quick assessment of which spot looks most promising. Consider the texture of the surface and whether there is an irregularity or rugosity that might dig into the shoe rubber and provide more grip. As you step onto the smear, do so with confidence and a firm pressing feeling. Many climbers do the exact opposite—and their doubt in the smear and tentative placement often result in slipping or skidding feet.

The climbing shoes you choose to wear also play a role in how well you can smear on a hold. Flexible slipper-style shoes tend to smear better since they will conform to the surface of sloping holds as well as providing superior feel. Smearing with stiff-soled shoes is far more challenging and will likely lead to a higher frequency of foot slips.

REST STEP

In learning to climb you will surely be surprised by how much foot and calf muscle strength is required to stand on small footholds. You will discover firsthand that standing on a particular foothold too long will pump out the calf muscles of your lower leg and possibly lead to shaky leg (aka sewing machine or Elvis leg). To help prevent the pump, it is important to regularly utilize the rest step.

The rest step can be performed on any medium to large hold with a reasonably flat-topped surface. Just place your heel on the foothold and stand with a straight leg so that your weight is supported by the bones, not muscular contraction. In some cases you may be able to place the heels of both feet onto holds and cop a super rest! You can further speed recovery by wiggling your toes and deliberately trying to relax the calf muscle.

While relatively easy climbs will feature lots of opportunities for the rest step, the smaller holds found on more difficult climbs makes getting a rest step more difficult. One trick for *making* a rest-step hold is to stand toe-in on a hold with one foot, then place the heel of the other foot on top of the laces part of the supporting shoe. This foot-stack rest step is just one example of the many clever moves you will learn—or discover—to excel on more difficult routes.

Fundamental Techniques

The essence of climbing is a dance up the wall using the four points of contact as your dance steps. Since each climb possesses a novel configuration of hand- and footholds, your challenge is to unlock the perfect sequence of moves and leverage your points of contact into this dynamic dance.

In executing any physical skill—whether it's shooting a basketball or simply running—there are fundamental techniques that represent optimal use of body position, leverage, and physical energy. While the specific techniques may be hard to observe with an untrained eye, just about any novice can spot an athlete steeped in the fundamentals: Her movements are smooth, crisp, and confident, and her demeanor reveals a poise and ease of execution, despite inherent difficulties of the situation. The bottom line: Fundamentally sound movement affords perfect economy and looks "easy."

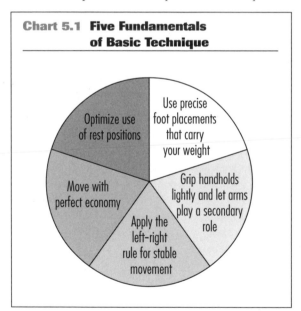

Chart 5.1 Five Fundamentals of Basic Technique

- Optimize use of rest positions
- Use precise foot placements that carry your weight
- Move with perfect economy
- Grip handholds lightly and let arms play a secondary role
- Apply the left-right rule for stable movement

In climbing, achieving perfect economy of movement is the Holy Grail that few individuals ever realize. You can become the exception, however, by means of a constant focus on climbing in accordance to the fundamentals of this sport. Please recognize that becoming a well-skilled climber is a conscious decision that takes a plan and disciplined long-term follow-through.

Let's consider the two basic modi operandi of climbers at a gym. Most individuals tie into the rope and just climb. They move in ways that feel easiest based on their experience. However, beginners' lack of experience will often lead them down a road of clumsy movement and poor technique that can solidify into bad habits.

The more effective, but less common, second mode is to climb with the intent of doing each move and every route in accordance with the fundamentals. It's this attention to detail that imparts technically sound skills and leads to rapid gains in ability. These results are indeed remarkable, and they are achieved only by an individual who is uncommonly effective in his practice and training. Okay, it's time to learn the first of five fundamentals for effective climbing.

Precise Foot Placements That Carry Your Weight

Given that your legs are stronger than your arms, the first fundamental of climbing is that the legs should do the majority of the work. The exceptions to this rule are overhanging routes, which demand greater use of the arms. Coming up in chapter 6, you will learn six additional fundamentals for climbing difficult overhanging routes.

The process of effectively using your feet begins with spotting the footholds and positioning your feet on the best part of each hold. Directing your foot placement demands attention to detail beyond that given to hand placements. Whereas handholds are easy to inspect, the greater eye-to-foot distance commonly leads to less-than-ideal foot placements. Furthermore, your feet don't provide the same degree of feel as the hands, making the quality of each foot placement more difficult to assess. For these reasons, developing good footwork isn't something that just happens—it's an attribute you *make* happen via constant foot focus and practice.

Upon spotting a foothold and positioning your foot for optimal purchase, you want to shift some body weight over the hold before standing up on it.

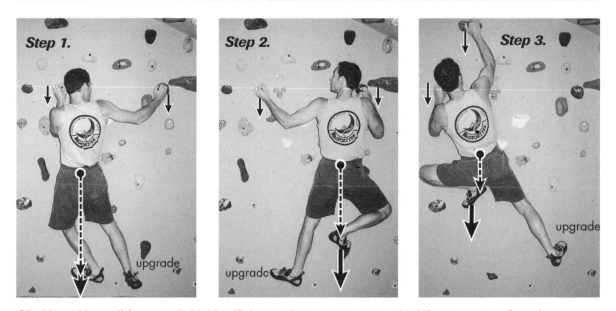

Climbing with small footsteps is highly efficient, as long as you constantly shift your center of gravity over the weight-bearing leg.

It's this downward pressure that helps the shoe rubber stick to the hold, so not properly weighting a hold often leads to the foot slipping off it. Of course, the location of your other three points of contact will dictate a unique balance point and weighting for every new foothold.

In many cases you will be able to advance both feet so they can push in unison. However, it's more intuitive to climb with one foot pushing at a time (as in climbing a ladder), so you'll need to make a conscious effort to develop this important foot skill. To this end, use the practice drills at the end of this chapter to step up your performance.

The final aspect of fundamentally sound footwork is proper alignment of your center of gravity directly over a foothold. Balance, stability, and application of force are optimized when your center of gravity is positioned directly over your feet, forming a line perpendicular to level ground. On a less-than-vertical wall or slab, this requires a hip position out from the wall and over the foothold. On a near-

Pushing with both feet is another highly efficient foot technique.

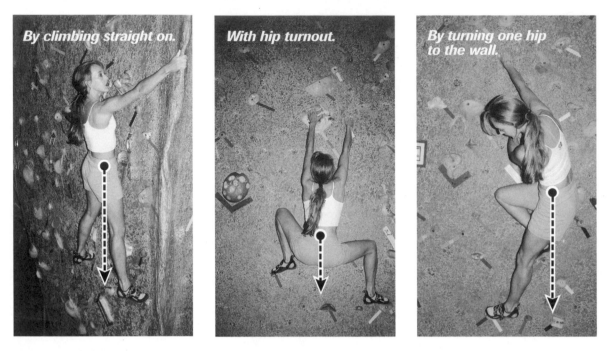

By climbing straight on.

With hip turnout.

By turning one hip to the wall.

Balance, stability, and application of force are optimized when your center of gravity is positioned directly over your feet, forming a line perpendicular to level ground. Depending on the wall angle and position of the hold, there are several ways to accomplish this.

vertical climbing surface, you simply need to keep your body position straight and over the feet as much as possible. When the climbing wall overhangs, it becomes impossible to position your weight over your feet, so new fundamentals take over (to be discussed in chapter 6).

Grip Handholds Lightly and Let Arms Play a Secondary Role

In a sport where anxiety and fear often rule, it's understandable that many climbers hang on with their hands for dear life. This tendency manifests itself with overgripping of the handholds and unnecessary muscling of moves with the arms. The end result is rapid fatigue, pumped forearms, and an eventual need to hang on the rope in order to rest and recover. You will no doubt experience this scenario during your initial days learning to climb.

You can avoid this outcome by practicing—and making habit—the fundamentals of proper hand and arm use. These critical skills include gripping each handhold with the minimum force required, using the arms mainly for balance and not as a primary source of locomotion, and pushing with the feet in unison with modest arm pull.

Begin by making each hand contact a conscious process. Whereas many climbers just grab a hold with little thought and continue with the process of climbing, you must make each hand placement a thoughtful act. First, consider where the best place is to grab the hold. It's not always on the top of the hold, and it often relates to the location of your last foot placement. Now as you grab the hold, focus on using a light touch that yields soft forearms. Sure, certain holds will demand that you bear down hard on them, but most don't. Your goal must be to try to

Grip each handhold with the minimum force required, using the arms mainly for balance and not as a primary source of locomotion.

use each hold with a light touch, and then increase the gripping force only as much as is required for the move at hand. This process of minimally gripping each handhold takes but a split second, yet it's a master skill that separates the best from the rest. Commit to making this skill a habit through targeted practice with the drills detailed later in the chapter.

Beyond gripping the rock, you need to decide just how much you need to pull down on a given handhold. As discussed earlier, it is imperative that you push with your feet and let the leg muscles carry the load. Think of your arms as points of contact that simply prevent you from falling backward off the wall. In climbing a ladder, for example, your legs do all the work while the arms mainly provide balance. While rock climbing is far more complex, hold this model in your mind as the ultimate goal—the arms maintain balance while the legs drive movement.

Still, there will be occasions in which your arms

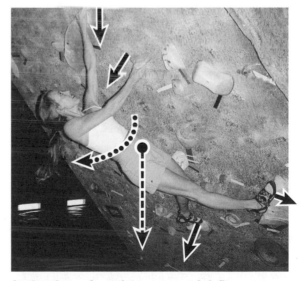

In situations where the arms must briefly carry much of your weight, it's imperative to maintain straight arms.

will need to briefly carry much of your weight. In these situations it's imperative that you maintain straight arms. This way the bulk of your weight is supported by the skeletal system of your upper body and not by your muscles.

The Left–Right Rule for Stable Movement

The magic of efficient climbing movement comes from the synergistic interaction of the arms and legs and a constant transfer of force and torque through your body. To this end, the Left–Right Rule states that maximum stability and ease of movement comes from the pairing of a left hand and right foot (or a left foot and right hand) into harmonious action.

Let's again use climbing a ladder as our model. Ascending a ladder with opposing hand–foot combinations (say, the left hand pulling and right foot pushing at the same time) is so intuitive that it's almost impossible to climb a ladder any other way.

The Left–Right Rule

Use of just a right hand and right foot (or left hand and left foot) creates instability and can result in an uncontrolled swing away from the wall known as "barndooring."

A left-right hand-foot combination maximizes stability and allows for better center of gravity positioning over the feet.

Suppose you tried to climb a ladder with non-opposing hand–foot combinations, such as a right hand and right foot working together; you'd immediately begin to **barndoor**, or rotate sideways off the ladder. Thus, the Left–Right Rule is a fundamental for balanced, stable movement.

While you don't need to even consider the Left–Right Rule in ascending a ladder, formulating movement up a climbing wall is much more complex since the position and shape of the hand- and footholds wreak havoc with your intuitive sense of movement. Thus, in seeking to reposition your hands and feet on the wall, it's helpful to ponder which holds will provide the best opportunity for a left–right combination. Easy climbs will often provide a pulling right hand that can combine with a pushing left foot (or vice versa). More difficult climbs tend to be more devious, because the holds are smaller, farther apart, or displaced off to the side of the route line. Later in the chapter you will find several toprope drills to develop skill in using left–right combinations.

Move with Perfect Economy

The technical paramount is to climb with perfect economy. Make these two words—*perfect economy*—your mantra every time you touch the rock.

Perfect economy means discovering the way to do each move, and an entire route for that matter, with minimal energy expenditure. If you have a cat, you can observe highly economic movement firsthand. Most of the time a cat moves in a slow, smooth, deliberate way; however, sometimes a situation demands a powerful, dynamic leap to maintain perfect economy. Catlike movement should be your technical model for efficient climbing: smooth, quiet, leg-driven movements, but with an unhesitating shift to an arm-pulling, dynamic movement when it is required to most efficiently execute a difficult move. Here are five attributes of economic movement that you should aspire to acquire.

QUIET FEET

Quiet foot movements are one of the hallmarks of a climber with great technique. Conversely, feet that regularly pop off footholds or skid on the wall surface are typical of an individual possessing lackluster footwork and poor economy.

For many climbers, noisy footwork is just the way they climb—it's a habit that developed over a long period of time, as well as a flaw in their technique that will prevent them from ever reaching their true potential. Your goal, of course, is to learn to climb with good foot technique from the start. This means concentrating on each foot placement, holding the foot steady and firm to the hold, and standing up on the foot with confidence as you proceed smoothly to the next hand- or foothold.

RHYTHM AND MOMENTUM

Like any dance, climbing should have a natural rhythm that utilizes momentum and inertia. Climbing in a ladderlike motion yields the rhythm "step, reach, step, reach." However, a better rhythm for effective movement is often "step, step, reach, reach," since it allow the legs to direct and drive the movement. There are obviously many other rhythms, such as "step, reach, step, step, reach, reach" and "step, step, reach, step, reach, reach." Consider that every unique sequence possesses a *best* rhythm of movement, and you'll eventually learn to intuit this on the fly. As a beginner climber, however, it takes a conscious effort to avoid leading with the hands in a strenuous and inefficient "reach, reach, step, step" rhythm. Strive to tap into the rhythm of each route, and climb accordingly.

Similarly, you want to utilize momentum in a way that helps propel successive moves. This is especially important on difficult climbs with large spacing between holds. Think of how you would move hand-over-hand across monkey bars at a playground, each movement blending with the next in a perfect continuity of motion. This style of smooth, continuous motion is critical when climbing through crux sequences. Interestingly, many folks do just the opposite, engaging the crux sequence with measure and caution. In doing so, they not only lose upward movement but also have the inertia of stillness to overcome. Hopefully you can avoid this tendency by consciously directing a steady rhythm that maintains forward momentum through the most difficult parts of a climb.

SMOOTH MOVES AND RELAXED BODY

Smooth, fluid movement is another sign of high economy. A climber appears to flow up a route when only the muscles necessary for stability and upward motion are contracting and all other opposing, or **antagonist**, muscles remain relaxed and relatively passive.

Unfortunately, many climbers wrought with anxiety, fear, or the need to perform find themselves contracting most all their muscles from head to toe in an attempt to hang on or fight through a crux. Such tension in the antagonist muscles forces the prime movers to work harder than needed and leads to inefficient movements and rapid energy expenditure. You can spot climbers suffering from this afflic-

tion by their stiff, rigid, and forced movements, which will likely soon have them hanging on the rope in frustration. And if they somehow succeed in fighting up the route, it will be at the expense of a great amount of energy and further ingraining of bad habits of technique.

The key to smooth, efficient movement is to maintain a high level of relaxation throughout the climb. You can best achieve this with a two-pronged approach. First, think about contracting only the muscles necessary for engaging the rock, maintaining stability, and directing movement; usually these will be the muscles of your forearms, shoulders, core, thighs, and calves. Next, switch your focus to the antagonist muscles and scan for unnecessary tension that might be developing in your upper arms, hips and legs, neck, and face. While taking deep, slow breaths, visualize this tension escaping

Smooth, fluid movements that look relaxed and easy are a sign of optimal technique and high economy.

like air from a balloon—such mental imagery really helps the process. Now return your focus to executing the next climbing movement, but continue alternating your focus back and forth between *directing movement* and *directing relaxation*.

Developing a habit of relaxed, fluid movement is something that takes time and awareness. This is largely a mental endeavor, because anxious thinking rapidly manifests itself in muscular tension. To help you on this journey, chapter 8 presents several effective strategies for preventing or mitigating mental tension.

PACE

Pace is another aspect of climbing economy that becomes increasingly important as a route gains in steepness and difficulty. While an easy climb with large holds allows you to ascend at a leisurely pace, a crux sequence or overhanging terrain will demand that you kick into high gear and surmount the difficulty in short order. When climbing near your limit, it must be your intention to move as briskly as possible without any drop-off in technique (skidding feet, botching sequences, and such). Reduce the pace at the first sign that your technique is suffering. It helps to identify obvious rest positions ahead of time, and then make it a goal to move from one to the next as fast as possible. Ultimately, knowing just the right pace on a given route is a sense you will develop with experience. Practice climbing at different speeds and on different types of routes, and you'll quickly foster the subtle skill of proper pace.

STEADY BREATHING

Breathing is the essence of life. Steady breathing is essential to sustain the life in your climbing. Conversely, restricted breathing is akin to tightening your muscles, constraining your thinking, and fostering failure.

Obviously, a steady flow of oxygen to the muscles is important for energy production and recovery, and it's the slow, deep, steady belly breaths that best get the job done. Many climbers, however, have a tendency to shift into shallow, rapid breathing as fatigue and mental anxiety grow. Worse yet, some climbers unknowingly hold their breath at times of high stress. These are two tendencies that you must be aware of and proactively counteract if you are to climb your best.

Before every climb, pause to close your eyes and take several slow, deep breaths. Feel your belly expand outward as you slowly inhale, and then allow the air to escape sparingly through pursed lips in a slow ten-second count (count in your mind). Visualize calmness washing across your body—this sets the stage for optimal performance. As you commence climbing, strive to maintain the same slow, steady breathing that you initiated on the ground. This is, of course, often difficult since a dicey sequence or strenuous move can trigger irregular breathing patterns. Consequently, it is critical that you use every rest position as an opportunity to reset your breathing cycle with a few slow, deep belly breaths. Such proactive breath control is like topping off your gas tank—do it frequently, and you'll rarely hit empty.

Optimize Use of Rest Positions

Finding efficient rest positions is as important as finding the best way to do a crux sequence. If you miss a good rest stance, you miss an opportunity to physically recover as well as mentally "read" and prepare for the next section of the climb. Consequently, locating rest positions on a climb should be viewed with the same sense of importance as locating all the key holds.

This process begins with on-ground visualization of the route (to be discussed in depth in chapter 7) in an attempt to estimate the location and body position of rest stops. Upon reaching a rest step, assume a body position that will allow the most fatigued muscles to rest (usually the forearms, biceps, and calves). An optimal rest position would consist of your feet in the rest-step position, legs straight, and hips over the legs or in a position midway between the feet (should they be on holds more than shoulder-width apart). If the climb is less than vertical, your upper body can relax completely, and in some cases you might even be able to assume a no-hands rest position. Such a casual stance places

Ideal rest positions consist of a straight-legged stance that largely unweights the arms and positions the center of gravity over the feet. Here's the stem rest with the center of gravity positioned evenly over both feet.

This position is known as the foot-stack rest step with straight arms and legs.

no time limits on how long you can remain parked there—although this luxury is rare on more difficult routes.

Rest positions on vertical to overhanging climbs make complete weighting of the feet more difficult and often impossible. While you still want to place as much weight as possible on the footholds, a significant amount of weight will remain on your arms. In this case it's absolutely vital that you hang with straight arms, so that the bones are providing the

support, not the muscles of the upper arm. It is also advantageous if you can obtain a heel hook above your center of gravity from which you can hang a high percentage of body weight. Still, your forearm muscles will need to contract in order to maintain a grip on the handhold. The best strategy, then, is to attain a stable stance and shake out alternate arms every ten to twenty seconds. This way, both arms take turns resting. At some point, however, hanging out at the rest begins to cost more energy than you can recover. It's at this time that you need to begin climbing toward the next rest spot.

Fortunately, there's a recovery technique that I

A corner stem yields a classic no-hands rest.

On overhanging walls, heel hooks are often the key to attaining a good shakeout position. Notice the straight (right) arm position and hip turn that shifts the climber's center of gravity closer to the wall.

developed called the **G-Tox**, which can markedly accelerate recovery of finger strength while at a marginal rest position. Instead of simply hanging the resting arm by your side, alternate the arm position every five seconds between the normal dangling position and an above-your-head raised-hand position. This simple technique has been shown by a British researcher to increase recovery by 50 percent or more over the standard dangling-arm shakeout. This should be evidence enough to make the G-Tox a regular part of your climbing stratagem.

A big part of becoming a fundamentally sound climber is learning to gain brief rests in the midst of even the most difficult routes. Practice and unbridled creativity are the only two requisites for solving dif-

ficult sequences and finding vital rest positions. Remember that the best climbers are not always the strongest; their prowess instead comes from uncommon mastery of climbing economy and effective resting.

Seven Basic Drills

Practice drills are the backbone of training for increased performance in sports. Consider that in practicing soccer, golf, or almost any other traditional sport, execution of certain drills helps develop fundamental skills, techniques, and mental control. Strangely, however, most climbers *just climb* for practice. In doing so they miss out on many powerful methods of developing the critical climbing skills.

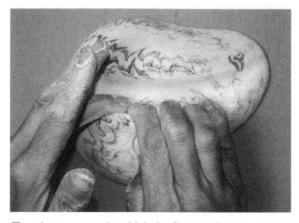

The piano move—in which the fingers of one hand are lifted off one by one to allow the fingers of the other hand to latch on to the hold one by one—is a useful technique for matching hands on a narrow hold.

Following are seven skill-building drills to make a staple of your climbing gym workouts. Use these drills as warm-up exercises or integrate them throughout your climbing session as a reminder of proper technique and the good habits of effective climbing. The long-term aggregate effect of performing these drills will be exceptional technique grounded in the fundamentals, as well as a level of performance that's above and beyond the average climber (who just climbs).

Traverse Training Drills

Perform these drills in the designated bouldering area or along the base of a roped climbing wall that is not in use. Traverse drills are ideal for experimenting with techniques and refining your movement skills, but it is vital that you hold yourself to a high standard of quality. As the saying goes: "Practice doesn't make perfect; it's perfect practice that makes perfect." To this end, make it your goal to foster these six subtle yet fundamental skills:

1. Pinpoint focus on each foot placement.

2. A sense of feel as you weight each foothold.

3. Maximally weighting each foothold by shifting your center of gravity over the leading foot placement.

4. A relaxed grip that uses the minimum amount of force required to stick each handhold.

5. Quick, smooth movement through thin sequences.

6. Anticipation of rest position locations and a commitment to stop and rest *only* at these spots.

SHUFFLE DRILL

In this most basic drill, you simply shuffle your hands and feet sideways as you move horizontally across the wall. The key lesson to be learned is the importance of leading with your feet and letting your legs do the bulk of the work. In traversing to the right, for example, you should initiate each horizontal move with the right foot stepping ahead onto a hold, and then shifting your hips over the right foot. In doing this, your hands play a subordinate role in providing only stability and balance. Let your feet run the show—this should always be the goal in striving to climb with perfect economy. Continue traversing for ten to fifty total foot moves.

MATCHING DRILL

This practice drill zeroes in on the important technique of hand–foot matching or sharing. Traverse across the wall with your feet in the lead, as above—but now your hands and feet must match on every new hold. For example, in traversing to the right, your left foot will always come to share a hold with your right foot before the right foot advances to the next hold. In the case of a very small foothold, you will need to do a "jump match" in which you switch feet in a single small "jump." The hands will similarly match left onto right before the right hand advances to the next hold. Matching onto a narrow handhold is difficult and may require use of the piano move (see photo above) in which the fingers of the right hand are lifted off one by one, allowing the fingers of the left hand to latch on to the hold one by one. Continue for ten to fifty moves.

ISOLATION DRILL

Use this drill to isolate and strengthen a specific grip or arm position. For example, if you find the open-hand grip insecure and unnatural to use (common for beginners), practice doing an entire traverse using only the open-hand position. Similarly, you could do traverses exclusively using the side-pull arm or undercling arm position, or using only two fingers of each hand! Be inventive and have fun contriving all kinds of restrictions in the "rules" for traversing. Such constraints will demand optimal footwork, and ultimately make you a more complete climber.

Toprope Drills

The two modi operandi in roped climbing are *climbing for performance,* and *climbing for practice.* Performance climbing is all about attempting routes at your limit, in the hope of breaking new ground and learning new skills. Climbing for practice, however, is the important act of climbing less difficult routes with the intention of fortifying fundamental skills and techniques. Use the following drills when climbing in the practice mode. Select routes that are two or more number grades below your limit.

FROG-FOOT DRILL

This drill teaches the important technique of pushing with both feet simultaneously, much the way a frog would extend its legs in jumping. Beginning with both hands and feet on the wall, step up with one foot and then the other until you are in a sort of squatting position with your knees out to the side and crouching into the wall. Now press down with both feet and in a continuous motion advance one hand, then the other. The hands should be used primarily for balance, not pulling—let the legs do most of the work. Repeat this process while subvocalizing the mantra "step, step, push, reach, reach." Continue up the route, striving for smooth movement and a steady rhythm in advancing the hands and feet.

HIGH-STEP DRILL

On more difficult routes, you will often need to step high onto a hold near your thigh or hip level. Initially this will feel awkward and difficult, especially if you lack flexibility and hip-flexor strength. You can improve in these areas, however, by regularly performing the high-step drill. On a relatively easy route (one that would surely not require the use of a high step), force yourself to ascend using only high steps. With hands and feet on the wall, begin by high-stepping with one foot onto a hold near hip level. Now rock over this foot—think about moving your crotch over the hold—and then drive downward with that foot and advance your hands until you reach a straight-legged position. Continue the process, but this time high-step with the opposite foot. The rhythm of movement for this drill is "high-step, rock, push, reach, reach" and repeat.

TENNIS BALL DRILL

A common technical flaw that kills climbing performance is overuse of the arms and overgripping of handholds. You won't be able to do this if you climb with a tennis ball in the palm of both hands! Consequently, this is a great drill to develop the vital skill of optimizing use of the feet. Rope up on an easy route with lots of large holds, and then begin climbing by using the tennis balls to hook on to the handholds. Clearly, your hands will only be useful for maintaining balance, so relax and allow your legs to do all the work. Concentrate on shifting your weight from one foot to the other while attempting to keep your upper body relaxed and tension-free. Don't get frustrated if you frequently need to hang on the rope. Persevere and try to make it to the top of the route—this drill *will* make you a better climber.

STRAIGHT-ARMED DRILL

Use of straight-armed positions is critical for conserving upper-body energy. Thus the goal of this drill is to climb a route while trying to maintain straight arms at least 90 percent of the time. Strive to use straight-armed positions anytime you aren't moving, such as when resting or scanning the wall above you. Practice maintaining straight arms when stepping up or adjusting your feet. In the case of a foot placement out to the side, you may even be able to leverage off a straight arm that's clinging to a side-pull hold. Continue upward using mainly straight-armed positions, despite that fact that it will feel contrived at times. In forcing this overuse of the straight arms, you will learn to move and rest with high economy.

CHAPTER SIX

Advanced Techniques
and Drills

The best climber isn't necessarily the one who climbs the hardest, he's the one who's most in tune with their body and the rock.

—*Chris Sharma, the first American to climb 5.15*

Steeper, blanker walls are your destiny as an indoor climber. Such terrain will tap into the very core of your being—physically, mentally, and emotionally—and demand an entirely new set of techniques and tactics.

As you progress into routes rated 5.10 and above, you'll notice a decrease in the frequency of large holds and a likely increase in wall steepness. Succeeding on these more challenging climbs requires a modified approach from that used on entry-level climbs. Not only are these difficult climbs more strenuous, but they also demand technical and mental acumen that can take many months or years to develop. Thus it's important to assume a long-haul mind-set and not to expect mastery of these skills and success at the lofty grades to come easily. If you are a true novice, then you should probably hold off on testing these techniques for a few months. Upon gaining competence and confidence in climbing 5.9 (or bouldering V1), however, you should begin using some of the practice drills detailed below.

In the previous chapter you learned five fundamentals of basic climbing movement. While these rules are valid in just about every type of climbing situation, they must be appended with several fundamentals for climbing more severe terrain. For instance, as hold sizes diminish and hold spacing increases, you'll need to leverage a new set of skills in order to surmount these difficulties. Furthermore, steeper climbs accelerate energy drain, so learning to move with high efficiency is tantamount to being a successful steep-wall climber. Let's take a look at six fundamentals of advanced-level climbing.

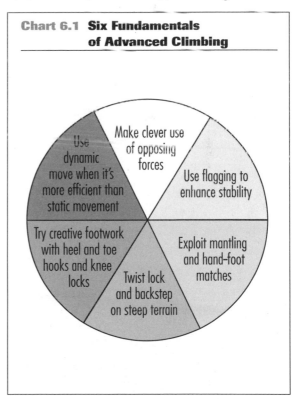

Chart 6.1 Six Fundamentals of Advanced Climbing

- Make clever use of opposing forces
- Use flagging to enhance stability
- Exploit mantling and hand-foot matches
- Twist lock and backstep on steep terrain
- Try creative footwork with heel and toe hooks and knee locks
- Use dynamic move when it's more efficient than static movement

Clever Use of Opposing Forces

You have already learned the importance of the Left–Right Rule for enabling stable movement. On easy climbs this left–right combination is usually a pulling right hand along with a pushing left foot (or vice versa). More difficult climbs tend to be more devious, however, so you'll need to consider all the other possible arm positions—side pull, undercling, and Gaston—and figure out how to match one of these with an opposing foot placement.

Detailed below are a few of the most common left–right combinations called into use on difficult climbs. You should practice each of these on the bouldering wall in order to develop its unique motor skills. Vary your hand and foot placements as much as possible to acquire a broad range of use for each hand–foot combination.

Side-Pull Arm and Outside Edge of Opposite Foot

Side-pulling hands are a staple move on almost every moderate to advanced climb. While this move is a bit less intuitive than down pulling, you will quickly gain comfort in its use. Most important is the foot position you select to oppose the side-pulling hand. In most cases it's best to use the outside edge of the opposing foot, not the inside edge. Doing this may feel awkward at first, but you'll find a natural sense of stability once you learn to appropriately set your hips over the outside-edging foot. The key is to concentrate on rotating your hips so that the hip opposite the pulling hand is turned into the wall—that is, your face and chest will rotate toward the side-pulling hand. This very stable position will allow you to step up your free (nonoppos-

Side-pulling right hand combined with the outside edge of the opposite foot. Note hip turn over the left foot.

Gaston arm position in tandem with an inside-edging opposite foot.

ing) leg and quite possibly your free (nonopposing) hand as well.

Occasionally a move will dictate that a side-pulling hand must be combined with use of the inside edge of the opposing foot. While this, too, is a fairly stable body position, it provides less reach upward with the free hand. Therefore, anytime you are struggling to reach a handhold, try using the outside edge of your shoe to maximize reach.

Gaston and Inside Edge of Opposite Foot

The Gaston (aka reverse side pull) is the most unnatural and weak arm position for beginners, yet it's a fairly common move needed to unlock many crux sequences. Use of the Gaston is best opposed by the inside edge of the opposite foot. Combining a Gaston with an outside-edging foot is strenuous but doable if absolutely needed. Practice this move in a variety of ways to gain comfort and strength in its use. As with all these advanced moves, the bouldering area is the ideal proving ground to experiment with and learn the skills.

Undercling and Inside or Outside Edge of Opposite Foot

Often overlooked by beginner-level climbers, undercling hand positions are actually quite easy to perform. What's more, an underclinging hand helps maximize your reach with the free hand, and it positions your arm and body in a naturally strong position. Therefore, the undercling is a move you want to practice and put to frequent use.

Typically you will undercling a hold somewhere near your torso while you press with an opposing foot. This foot can edge with either the inside, outside, or toe portion of the shoe, although use of the outside edge is best for maximizing your reach. Remember that in edging with the outside of your foot, it's best to turn the hip opposite the pulling hand to the wall. In extreme situations you may even need to use a foot smear to oppose the underclinging hand. This is a very powerful but important move that you can practice on the bouldering wall.

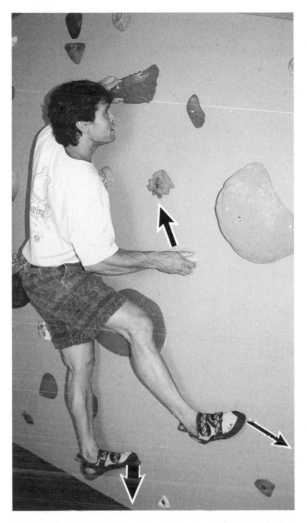

Underclinging right hand working effectively with the opposite foot in the toe-in position.

Side-Pulling Left and Right Hands

Use of opposing handholds is a key move for unlocking a sequence that lacks any usable down-pull or underclinging handholds. Most common are two opposing side pulls that you'll draw inward to create tension through your arms, shoulders, and upper body. While you will be unable to create much upward movement, this opposition will allow you to upgrade one or both feet. Ideally, you'll want to

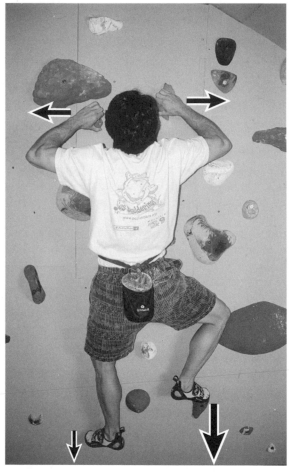

Use of opposing handholds is often necessary to unlock a sequence that lacks a good down-pull or undercling. This photo shows opposing side pulls.

This photo illustrates opposing Gastons, an advanced move that requires a great deal of base strength.

upgrade the foot that opposes the better of the two side pulls, so that it sets up a stable left–right combination. This will enable you to release the other side-pulling hand so as to upgrade it to the next hold.

Another possibility is opposing Gaston holds. Though strenuous, you may occasionally need to grab two Gastons at or just above head-height and pull outward in order to support your weight while upgrading a foot position. This is a most advanced move that requires a high level of base strength. A word of caution, however: Using a Gaston hold on an overhanging wall places great force on the shoulder joint and in rare cases can cause injury. Proceed carefully.

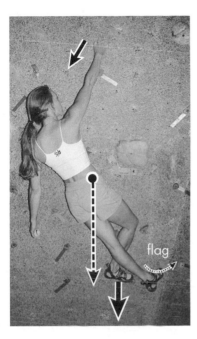

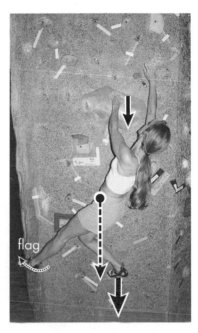

Foot flagging is an important technique for maintaining optimal balance and center of gravity positioning when a left–right hand–foot combination is not possible. Here you see outside cross flagging.

Inside cross flagging. This requires an aggressive hip turn and moderate body tension. Flag the inside leg until you find the balance point.

Side flagging. With a straight arm and hip turn over the weight-bearing leg, flag the leg out to the side to find the balance point.

Use Flagging to Enhance Stability

Flagging is the alternative technique for maintaining stability when a left–right hand–foot combination is not possible. Suppose you are attempting to use a right hand and right foot combination to propel upward movement. Upon releasing your left hand to make a reach upward, you will immediately begin to barndoor (see the photo on page 58). This sideways rotation is hard to fight, and often results in a fall. However, a simple flagging of the free leg (in this case the left) significantly improves stability and balance by shifting your center of gravity more directly over the supporting (right) foot and under the supporting (right) hand.

Let's take a look at the two methods of flagging;

which one you use depends on whether your supporting leg is edging with the inside or outside edge of the shoe. For example, consider a move in which you are edging on the inside of your right foot and pulling with your right hand. In order to avoid barndooring, you would flag the left leg across the right leg. However, if your supporting leg is edging with the outside edge of the shoe, it's best to flag the free (left) leg out left along the wall surface in an effort to find a balance point. If you're lucky, you'll find a foothold or wall feature on which to splay the flagging foot. Practice using these flagging techniques on a vertical wall and then expand their use onto overhanging terrain.

Fingertip press-down with foot match.

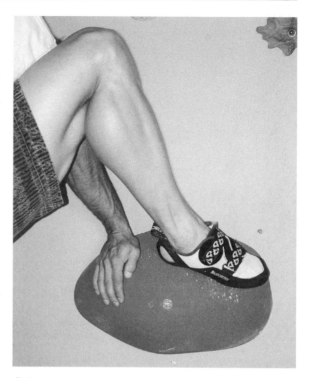

Palm mantle with foot match.

Exploit Mantling and Hand–Foot Matches

As described in chapter 5, mantling is the act of pressing downward on a handhold. The mantle move is often called upon to overcome a long reach between holds. In such a situation, first consider the possibility of using an undercling handhold; if none is available, you may have no choice but to mantle with one or both hands.

Let's consider the most common scenario of needing to mantle with one hand while the other hand is pulling. The pulling hand will usually be positioned above your head while the mantling hand will contact a hold somewhere near your torso. Depending on the size of the hold to be mantled, you may be able to press your entire palm onto the hold or, possibly, just your fingertips. The left–right combination of pushing and pulling hands provides great

stability, so you will be able to upgrade one or, possibly, both feet. Quite often you'll need to match a foot to the handhold on which you are mantling. Regardless, the mantle is complete when you are able to weight your feet, gain balance, and upgrade your hand from the mantle.

Twist Lock and Backstep on Steep Terrain

The twist lock and backstep are the bread-and-butter moves of a steep-wall connoisseur. As a climbing wall tilts back past vertical, it becomes increasingly difficult to place a high percentage of weight on your legs. Consequently, a greater portion of body weight must be supported by the arms—which, of course, possess less absolute strength than the legs. Use of the twist lock and backstep together helps draw your body in toward the surface of the overhanging wall.

Difficult: Without the twist lock the climber's neutral, straight-on body position places the center of gravity well out from the wall. This makes for strenuous, inefficient movement.

The twist lock is a vital go-to move when a route gets reachy and/or steep. Notice how the climber twists and locks her body with an aggressive hip turn and side-pulling hand drawn in to her torso. This shifts the center of gravity very close to the wall and nearly over her weight-bearing foot.

Easier: The twist lock, with its hallmark hip turn, draws the center of gravity into the wall, thus improving weighting of the feet, increasing reach, and enhancing grip on handholds (thanks to improved force vector of arm pull).

Twist locking in a steep corner often allows for an exaggerated backstep foot position—called a drop-knee—that greatly reduces weighting of the arms and optimizes the center of gravity among the three points of contact.

This changes the force vector on the handholds, making them feel more positive and secure. More important, this drawing-in of the body places more weight onto the footholds. However, proper execution of these moves requires practice and a significant amount of strength through the core muscles of the torso. See chapter 9 to learn exercises for strengthening these core muscles.

The twist lock is typically used to ease the upgrading of a hand on an overhanging section of wall. For example, consider the situation in which your left hand is on a good hold and you'd like to reach up high with the right hand. While you could attempt this move straight-on—chest facing toward the wall in a neutral position—it's far less strenuous to turn your right hip to the wall before making the reach upward. Proper positioning of the feet is critical for making this move work. Since the right hip is turning to the wall, you'll need to use the outside

edge of your right foot on a hold somewhere below or in back of your body (hence the term **backstep**). Usually you'll find a complementary left foothold to help maintain the twist-lock body position. The feet then press in unison while the left arm pulls down and in toward your torso, creating the twist lock. Finding just the right body position is the key to providing a secure twist lock; when you do, you'll notice that a surprising lack of effort is needed to reach up and acquire the next right handhold. This amazingly efficient locomotion over steep terrain is the magic of the twist-lock technique.

Granted, superlative use of the twist lock and backstep is something that will take many hours of practice. In fact, during your initial attempts at using these moves, you might swear that they require more energy than basic straight-on moves. Trust that with practice you will develop the necessary motor skills to make these moves feel quite easy. Initially limit your practice of the twist lock and backstep to boulder problems that overhang about 20 degrees past vertical. As you acquire skill, expand use onto even steeper boulder problems as well as onto overhanging toprope climbs.

Use Creative Footwork with Heel Hooks, Toe Hooks, and Knee Locks

So what do you do when you run out of handholds? Consider using one of your feet as a hand! Heel hooks, toe hooks, and knee locks are real difference makers when it comes to surmounting overhangs. Given the strength of the leg muscles, a good heel hook is often *better* than a handhold in helping turn the lip of a difficult overhang. Similarly, toe hooks and knee locks provide terrific support when attempting a series of inverted moves out a large roof. Let's kick into the details of these critical moves.

Heel Hooking

Your primary use of heel hooks will come when turning the lip of a roof, topping out on a bouldering problem, or copping a quick shakeout while on steep terrain. In these cases, you'll likely have your hands on holds at or above face level and intend to place one of your heels on a hold off to the side near

Heel hooks are remarkably effective as a "third arm" on steep walls and overhangs. Here the right heel is pulling in unison with the left hand (Left-Right Rule), enabling the climber to easily upgrade her right hand.

PHOTO BY **RANDY LEVENSALER** © 2005,
WWW.LEVENSALER.COM

shoulder level. Which heel you choose to hook with depends on two factors: the availability of a decent-sized hold on which to place your heel, and the location of the next handhold that you hope to acquire. This next reach up is best made with the hand on the same side as the heel hook. So if it looks like the next attainable hold is set up for the right hand, it would be best to use a right heel hook. Once set, pull with the heel hook as if it were a third arm and, of course, pull with both arms as well. Often it helps to think about *pulling your heel toward your rear end*; this will maximize use of the leg muscles and help shift your center of gravity toward the heel hook. Meanwhile, the other foot should inside-edge or smear on the wall to help contribute to the upward motion. As you gain elevation, make a quick reach to the next handhold and then switch your heel hook into a standard step-down foot placement.

Toe Hooking

Toe hooking is a foot move used mostly in pulling overhangs or in navigating roofs. This technique involves simply hooking as much of the top (laces) side of your shoe as possible on a large protruding hold. Sometimes you will toe hook onto a hold with a bent leg, and then straighten that leg as your hands move out the roof. Ideally you'll have one foot toe

Toe Hooks: Another "Third Arm"

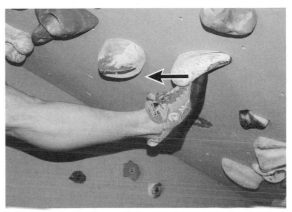

Toe hooks are another example of creating a "third arm." This solid toe hook provides a powerful opposition with a pulling arm and prevents body swing off the steep wall.

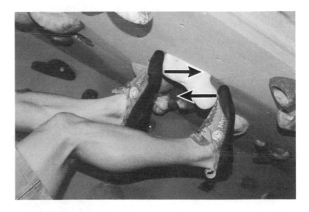

Combining a toe hook and a pressing foot creates excellent stability on a severely overhanging wall.

hooking while the other foot pushes off a nearby hold. This opposing push–pull combination enhances the foot purchase on the holds and lowers the chance your feet will come swinging off the roof (a common problem). Strive to keep your arms and legs in the straight position as much as possible so that your body weight is being supported more by bone than by muscles. Done properly, you can navigate a surprisingly large roof with the limiting factor being forearm endurance. Experiment with this foot technique in the bouldering area, and you'll gradually gain skill and confidence in climbing with your back to the ground!

Knee Locks

Knee locks are a boon on overhanging walls and roofs with large protruding holds—that is, if you know the technique and can find a position to exploit this "thank-God" move. Consider a severely overhanging climb with no obvious rest positions. Chances are the forerunner has positioned two holds in just the right way so that you can place your toe on one hold and then lock your knee against a larger opposing hold. Such a knee lock provides surprising purchase; it will allow you to drop one hand at a

time to shake out and chalk up. Occasionally you will come upon a knee lock that's so solid you'll be able to cop a rare, no-hands inverted rest! Of course, miss the knee lock and you have no choice but to sprint up the climb in the hope of reaching the anchors before the pump clock runs out.

It's unlikely that you'll ever run across a knee lock on a route much below 5.10 or V2. On high-end climbs and boulder problems, however, look for knee locks and toe and heel hooks with the same resolve you'd give to searching for handholds. Practice knee locks on a steep bouldering wall, and you'll soon learn to leverage this technique like the pros.

Seven Advanced Drills

Regularly performing these drills is like taking skill-building steroids. Each drill focuses on a specific technique or move that will be repeated for the full length of a climb. Such repetitive practice of a specific technique enhances motor learning and fortifies skills faster than random climbing. Incorporate a few of these drills into every gym session, striving for smooth, controlled execution. Perform each drill on a toprope climb of moderate difficulty—two or three number grades below your maximum ability.

A knee lock on a protruding hold can provide a merciful rest on a steep wall.

INSIDE/OUTSIDE FOOT EDGE DRILL

Turning a hip to the wall and edging with the outside edge of your inside foot is a simple move. The goal of this drill is to climb an entire route in this hip-turned position. For example, beginning with your left hip to the wall, the outside edge of the left foot and the inside edge of the right foot will do all the work. Your hands can use down-pull or side-pull holds for balance and stability. Repeat this drill with your body turned in the opposite direction—in this example, with your right hip to the wall.

FINGER-PRESS DRILL

Climbers typically consider their hands as tools for pulling. Ironically, it's often a hand pushing downward that helps unlock a crux. While you will rarely need to mantle or finger press on beginners' routes, it is an important skill to have in your arsenal for your advance up the grading scale. Use this drill to foster confidence and intuitive execution of the finger press. Attempt to climb an entire route by using a pulling hand and pushing hand in unison. Begin with both feet on the wall and one hand grabbing a hold above your head, while the other hand grips a hold somewhere between your chest and waist. Now step up with one or both feet and then focus on pulling with the high hand and pressing down with the lower hand as you extend with your legs. Ideally all four points of contact will contribute to the upward movement. Try to achieve a balanced, relaxed stance, and reposition your hands with one above your head and one again near your waist. Alternate the pushing and pulling hand as you repeat this process in ascending the wall.

UNDERCLING DRILL

Undercling holds are often the secret to unlocking impossible-feeling moves. Perform this drill to gain competence and confidence in using underclings in just about any situation. Try to climb an entire route with nothing but undercling handholds. Granted, this may be impossible on a route lacking enough downward-facing edges or large holds, so select a climb that appears to possess a large number of high-profile holds. In climbing, you'll find that your hands are mostly underclinging holds between your face and waist. Progress and energy conservation will depend on your ability to find and use footholds in ways that oppose the underclings. Let the feet do most of the work, and remain open to all possible body positions: hip-turn right, hip-turn left, or neutral. This drill can be performed on vertical and overhanging walls, but not on slabs.

FOOT-FLAGGING DRILL

This drill emphasizes the flagging technique, which provides stability when a left–right hand–foot combination is not possible. Your goal is to climb an entire route by alternating the flagging leg with every move upward. For example, begin with the right hand pulling and right foot pushing, in which case you will need to flag the left leg to maintain stability. Remember that it's the position of the right foot (inside edge or outside edge) that determines whether you are better off with a crossed-leg flag or just an extended side flag. Upon finding a balance position, upgrade the left hand, upgrade the left foot, and then begin upward movement on these new points of contact. Notice that you will begin barndooring the other direction; you now need to flag the right leg to oppose this barndooring effect. Continue this dance all the way up the wall. Yes, it may look strange and it will feel contrived, but trust that in doing this drill you are coding important motor skills. Select a vertical route with modest-sized holds—the goal is not to get pumped, but instead to practice flagging on relatively nonstressful terrain.

TRACKING DRILL

Tracking is a challenging elimination-type drill where the feet are restricted to using only the exact holds used by the hands. Performing this drill will develop a variety of important skills, including high-stepping, finger presses and mantles, hand–foot matches, and balanced stand-ups. Begin with your hands staggered—say, the left arm fully extended to grip a hold above your head while the right hand grips a hold near shoulder level—and work your feet up so that you can high-step your right foot onto your right handhold. Such matching of hand and foot (see page 72, for example) takes practice, but you'll eventually learn to make a smooth transition or hand–foot switch. Now upgrade the right hand and use three points of contact (right foot, and left and right hands) to enable a step up with the left foot onto your current left handhold. Repeat this process for the full length of the climb, remembering that the feet can only use holds occupied by your hands. This is a challenging drill that will yield a big payoff in ability!

DOWNCLIMBING DRILL

When leading or toproping indoors, it's rare that I climb a route to the top and lower off without trying to downclimb as much of the route as possible. There are benefits to this practice drill beyond the obvious one of doubling the pump. First, in knowing that you plan to downclimb a route, you become a more observant and focused climber on the way up. Furthermore, since poor footwork is a leading handicap for many climbers, there's much to be gained from practice that demands intense concentration on footwork. Initially you'll find downclimbing to be difficult, awkward, and very pumpy. As your hold recognition and fluidity improve, however, you may discover that downclimbing actually feels easier than ascending. Make it a practice to downclimb all warm-up routes as well as any other route that's one or more number grades below your maximum ability. Occasionally test yourself by attempting to downclimb a route at your limit. While you will likely get a vicious pump, you'll also be forced into making the most of your footwork in order to conserve upper-body energy.

FAST-PACED CLIMBING DRILL

When the rock gets steep and the moves hard, it becomes crucial that you increase your pace of ascent. Climbing quickly is primarily a function of skill, not strength or power (we're not talking about lunging wildly up a speed-climbing route). In fact, the less strength and endurance you possess, the more important it is that you can climb swiftly and efficiently. Practice fast-paced climbing on routes

you already have **wired** or climbs two or more number grades below your maximum ability. Begin by climbing the route at your normal pace. If available, use a stopwatch to time your ascent. Rest for a few minutes until you feel recovered, then climb the route again but at a slightly faster pace (say, about 10 percent faster). Repeat the climb one or two more times, with each successive lap about 10 percent faster than the last. Ease off the accelerator at the first sign of degrading technique or botched moves. Perform this drill once or twice per week for several months, and you'll find yourself naturally moving faster when bouldering, toproping, and even climbing on-sight. This new fast-paced style of climbing may very well elevate your ability by a full number grade.

Dynamic Moves

In chapter 5 you learned the importance of climbing with economy—the goal being to climb a move, a sequence, and an entire route in a way that requires minimal energy. In most cases the hallmark of economic climbing is smooth, relaxed movement that utilizes the feet and legs over the muscles of the upper body. Such controlled, fluid movement is referred to as static climbing.

The opposite of static style is dynamic or explosive movement. As a beginner, you will naturally find yourself grabbing quickly or lunging for handholds in a dynamic way that is not very economic. As you gain skill, however, you will naturally come to move in a more static, economic way. Still, there are certain moves and sequences that demand dynamic movement. In particular, vertical routes with tiny handholds and overhanging routes with long reaches often require dynamic movements in order to maintain high economy.

The key is to know which moves are best attempted dynamically versus statically, and this is a recognition skill that will take years to fully develop. Often you will need to attempt a crux in both a static and dynamic way in order to determine which style yields the most economic passage. The strategy of trying a move or sequence both ways is vital—if you are satisfied to simply struggle through the crux once, you'll never know if there was a more effective method and you'll miss out on an important learning opportunity.

The two primary forms of dynamic movement are **deadpoints** and **lunges**. Although it's a rarity to need either move on a beginner-level climb, you will eventually need to call these moves into action as you progress onto more difficult terrain. As in learning all advanced skills, you can best practice and experiment with these dynamic moves in the bouldering area. Employ some of the bouldering drills described later on in this chapter to help accelerate your learning.

Deadpoints

Consider a situation where both hands cling to poor holds and you would fall off the wall if either hand let go for more than an instant. It's in just such a predicament that the deadpoint move will save the day, because it allows you to make a rapid hand

Deadpoint Moves

Deadpoint moves are invaluable for upgrading hands on extremely thin, vertical to overhanging walls. 1. Begin with a slight droop down and out from the wall.

2. Pull in with the arms and press only lightly with the feet. Reach quickly to the next hold at the peak or deadpoint of the motion.

3. Catch the hold firmly and immediately tense through your body to establish a left-right hand-foot connection.

upgrade despite the fact you can't hang on to the wall statically with a single-hand contact point. How's this possible? It's the magic of the deadpoint!

Envision a basketball player making a jump shot. He jumps straight up and shoots the ball at the peak of his flight, a moment of apparent weightlessness before gravity returns him to the floor. This instant of weightlessness and stillness is the deadpoint. Climbers can similarly exploit the apparent weightlessness of the deadpoint to upgrade a hand position as in the desperate situation described above. But instead of jumping as in the basketball example, the climber needs to use a smaller, more controlled motion to facilitate the delicate upgrading of a hand from one small hold to another.

For example, imagine a tenuous move on a vertical or slightly overhanging wall in which you want to upgrade your right hand, but you can't make a static reach for the hold. Initiate the deadpoint movement with a small droop downward (or a release outward in the case of an overhanging wall) immediately followed by a firm drawing inward of the handholds toward your torso. This drawing-in of your body is akin to—but less dramatic than—the basketball player's jump, and there will be an instant when the motion peaks and you'll be able to flash your hand up to snag the next hold. A well-executed deadpoint is calculated and controlled in a way that it flows naturally in perfect economy. In extreme cases you may need to execute several deadpoint moves in a row in order to climb through a series of small handholds that you could never hang on to for a static movement.

Practice the deadpoint move at the base of a vertical climbing wall and initially by using large holds that you can easily stick. You will rapidly develop a feel for the deadpoint motion, at which time you should begin to practice the move on smaller holds and slightly overhanging walls. Upon gaining a high rate of success and a sense of confidence, you can begin utilizing this move on roped climbs.

Lunges

Unlike the careful, controlled movement of a deadpoint, the lunge (or **dyno**, as it's often called) is a full-

The Lunge

lunge

The lunge move is best saved for making a desperately long reach on an overhanging wall. 1. Droop downward to "cock" the lunge; one or two bounces may help generate beneficial momentum.

on leap for an out-of-reach hold. In lunging, the arms and legs explode in unison to propel your body upward toward the next good hold. Lunges typically end in one of two ways: Ideally you latch on to a hold and regain control of your body; however, it's also possible that you will fail to catch the target hold and end up falling on the rope or the bouldering crash pad.

Lunging is like any other skill in that it takes practice and a high level of confidence before you will be able to exploit the move in severe situations.

catch

2. Explode simultaneously with the legs and arms and slap for the target hold. You must believe in the lunge in order to stick it!

It's also a strenuous and stressful move that has led to many shoulder injuries. Consequently, it's best to view lunging as a last-resort move that you only pull out of the bag when nothing else appears possible. In the heat of a crux sequence, though, it often comes down to a gut feeling as to whether you should try to throw a lunge or attempt a static sequence. Ideally it would be best to lunge only when climbing statically would require more energy. In fact, a perfectly executed lunge in just the right situation is a classic example of climbing with high economy, despite the apparent burly nature of the move.

Executing a lunge is very physical, but also requires good timing and a belief that you can reach the next hold. Much like a gymnast attempting her hardest move, throwing and sticking the perfect lunge requires laserlike focus and an intense belief in a successful outcome. Begin by locking your eyes on the target hold and visualize exactly how your hand will hit—and stick!—the hold. Next, look down and concentrate on maximizing an explosive launch off your four points of contact. In some cases it may help to "cock" your lunge by drooping or bouncing before you catapult upward. As you go airborne, your eyes will naturally return to a pinpoint focus on the target hold. Now stick it!

Bouldering Drills and Games

A bouldering wall is the ideal platform for practicing all the advanced skills covered in this chapter—by challenging yourself in focused drills or challenging partners in bouldering games.

Steep-Rock Bouldering Drills

Bouldering on steep walls provides an excellent physical workout in addition to effective practice of technical skills. It's this one–two punch of training strength and technique that makes bouldering such an effective all-around training strategy. Select a section of wall with many large holds for your initial practice sessions, but graduate to boulder problems with fewer and small holds as you gain confidence in each new technique.

TWIST-LOCK BOULDERING DRILL

Your goal is to execute a sequence of four to ten consecutive twist-lock moves. Locate a section of overhanging bouldering wall (20 to 45 degrees past vertical) that's littered with large holds. Forget working a set boulder problem; your mission here is to use any hold needed to pull or leverage on in order to gain a solid twist-lock position (see page 73, for example). As described earlier, the most secure twist-lock position is with one hip turned to the wall and the opposite hand pulled in tight near your torso, creating the lock. After reaching up with your inside free hand, try to upgrade your feet and rotate your body 180 degrees so as to gain a new twist lock with the other hip against the wall. With practice, you will be able to gracefully ascend a steep wall with consecutive twist-lock moves—at a surprisingly small energy cost.

DEADPOINT DRILL

Perform this drill on a section of wall that overhangs between 5 and 25 degrees. The ideal setup would consist of two small footholds to stand on (just a foot or so off the ground) and four nontweaky medium-sized handholds, two in front of your face and the other two about 2 feet above that. While standing on the small footholds, pull in with both hands to draw your body inward and quickly reach up to the high hold at the moment of the deadpoint. After latching on to the high hold, immediately drop that hand back down to the starting hold. Now perform a deadpoint with the opposite hand to complete the cycle. All the while your feet remain fixed as you continue this drill for a total of four to six cycles.

ONE-ARM DEADPOINT TRAVERSING

This exercise requires a vertical or slightly overhanging wall with enough room available to traverse 10 to 20 feet using medium- to large-sized holds. The goal here is to traverse the wall using quick but controlled sideways deadpoint moves with your leading hand. In the case of traversing to the right, it's the right hand that deadpoints from hold to hold while the left hand dangles by your side (or is held behind your back). Use your arm and torso to initiate the movement—this drawing-in of the body produces a brief deadpoint during which you make a quick grab at the next hold. Attempt to traverse for a total of ten to twenty deadpoint moves, with each move traveling between 6 and 18 inches to catch the next hold. Rest for a few minutes, and repeat this drill using the other hand to traverse back across the wall.

Bouldering Games

Who needs a rope to get a good workout? An hour or two of playing in the bouldering area can provide a superb technical and physical workout. While some climbers prefer to simply send boulder problems, engaging in some of these bouldering games adds competitive strategy and challenge to the workout.

ADD-ON

Like a wild mix of chess and gymnastics, Add-On blends skill and strategy with power and strength. Select a challenger of similar ability and agree on a section of bouldering wall to play on—most people prefer a steep section. Determine who will go first. If it's you, step up to the wall and create a two-move sequence. Now step off the wall and allow your challenger to climb this exact sequence; however, he must add on one more move to the sequence before jumping off the wall. Now it's your turn to climb the three-move sequence but with the task of adding on a fourth move. Continue in this add-on fashion until one person fails to climb the complete sequence. The strategy of this game centers on your ability to add on moves that are too difficult for your challenger, but still doable for you. You can also add on moves that focus on a known weakness of your challenger—two-finger pockets, long lock-off moves, or whatever. Have fun!

STICK GAME

This popular game is great for learning to quickly assess and execute an unknown move on-sight. The drill requires at least two players, who take turns using a broomstick to point out a sequence of impromptu bouldering moves. Begin by identifying the starting hand- and footholds for the climber; the course setter then uses the stick to point to the next hold to be used. Continue in this fashion until the climber falls or the problem is completed. The game is usually played with open feet, meaning the climber can use any holds for foot placements.

SEND ME

Similar to the Stick Game, this drill has one climber dictate a bouldering sequence for the other climber to perform. Typically, the course setter will point out a sequence of six to ten hand movements out a steep bouldering wall. The climber then attempts to climb this exact sequence of handholds; once again, this game is best played with open feet. If the climber sends the problem, he gets one point—but now the course setter needs to attempt to climb her creation! If she succeeds, then she also gets a point. Now switch roles and attempt a new problem. You will soon discover that playing Send Me for an hour is an excellent workout in and of itself.

PHOTO BY **ERIC J. HÖRST**

CHAPTER SEVEN

Lead Climbing
and Success Strategies

Mastery lies not in the capturing of a summit, but in a oneness with each detail of the experience.

—*John Gill, legendary boulderer and the first person to climb V10*

Life with the nerve endings hanging out—that's how it sometimes feels when lead climbing. Given the relatively safe setting of a climbing gym, however, the acute sensations of lead climbing are something that you should aspire to, not avoid. It is on the sharp end of the rope that you fully experience what recreating in the vertical extreme is all about.

With the snug security of a toprope gone, you will tap into a whole new level of experience on lead. All aspects of climbing are magnified: the challenge, the fear, the risk, and the reward. Clearly the step up to becoming a leader is a big one that shouldn't be rushed. With the toprope gone you can—and will—catch some air time. Fortunately, lead climbing indoors can be an extremely safe activity given proper training and an intermediate skill level. In this chapter you will learn the crucial techniques and mental skills needed for beginning your adventures on the sharp end.

Climbing strategy is another skill set you need to develop as you advance in ability. Regardless of whether you are leading, toproping, or bouldering, formulating a unique success strategy for every climb is tantamount to performing your best on an on-sight attempt or when working to redpoint a project. To this end, you'll learn proven strategies for reading a route, solving perplexing crux sequences, and programming your mind for success.

Learning to Lead Climb

Learning to lead climb will definitely add some spice to your life as a climber. Clinging to tiny holds with pumped muscles, you will look downward and see a seemingly pencil-thin rope dangling from your harness and running through only a few scrawny carabiners. This adrenaline-releasing sight—and any thoughts of falling—will either refocus you into continuing upward or freeze you in place with fearful thoughts of how you got into this predicament. Of course, learning to lead is a roller-coaster-like process that will surely have you operating in both modes from day to day or even climb to climb. With experience and knowledge of lead-climbing strategies, however, you will gain confidence and comfort in being a lead climber.

Just when you are ready to begin lead climbing is a matter you should discuss with an instructor or a few of your more experienced climbing companions. If you are a quick study and a mature individual, you might be ready to test the lead-climbing waters with a few months' experience. However, many folks spend a year or more toproping and bouldering before they tie into the sharp end. Ultimately, you must take 100 percent responsibility in making the move to lead climbing. As the name implies, you are the *leader*.

When you do decide to begin lead climbing, you will need to develop several technical and risk-management skills that are not needed in toproping. Learning to efficiently clip into the quickdraws that hang from the lead-climbing anchor bolts is essential. Furthermore, you'll need to become familiar with the potential hazards unique to lead climbing and learn how to mitigate each. Upcoming are the nitty-gritty details on these skills and much more.

Clipping Quickdraws

Unlike in toproping, your safety in lead climbing requires clipping the rope into a series of anchor bolts along the path of the route. Most climbing gyms affix a permanent quickdraw to each anchor bolt so that you only need to clip the rope into a carabiner as you pass each bolt placement. Sounds simple, right? Well, if your forearms are pumped or if you are quaking in your boots, this simple task can be frustrating and stressful. Therefore, it's important that you gain lots of practice clipping quickdraws on moderate lead climbs and initially resist the urge to attempt climbs at your toprope limit. After a few weeks of ticking easy lead climbs, you'll find that clipping quickdraws becomes an automatic event, instead of the trembling *I-can't-get-the-darn-rope-into-the-carabiner* epic likely common to your formative efforts.

FIND THE OPTIMAL CLIPPING POSITION

Efficiently clipping each anchor bolt starts with a stable body position from which to act. Good forerunners typical set a specific clipping position—that is, a combination of hand- and footholds that

Clipping

Poor clipping position with the bolt far above head level and a bent, straining arm.

A better position for clipping with a straight arm and the quickdraw near head level.

LEARNING *to* CLIMB INDOORS

A heel hook provides an excellent clipping position on steep rock.

provide a steady stance to pause and clip the rope. A common mistake of novice leaders is attempting to clip too soon. Often you'll see such a climber struggling to clip the rope into a quickdraw at arm's length above his head. This is usually a bad idea, for a couple of reasons. First, such reachy clips tend to be strenuous, since you'll need to pull with one arm in order to reach high with the other. Worse yet, you'll need to pull a greater length of rope to make the clip, meaning a longer fall should you fall while attempting the clip.

A better strategy is to climb high enough so that the anchor bolt is near the level of your head or, better yet, your chest. Usually you will be able to find a high handhold from which to hang straight-armed while the free hand makes the clip. Furthermore, you'll need to pull up less rope in order to complete the clip, making for a faster clip and a reduced fall distance should you come off in the process.

Make a game out of trying to find the perfect body position for each clip. Assume the role of a "clipping position detective" searching to find the least strenuous, most stable position for every clip. Sometimes a large hand- and foothold will greet you upon arriving at a bolt, thus making the task a no-brainer. As the difficulty of the route increases, however, you'll need to be more creative and insightful in order to discover the clip position the forerunner

Finger-Grab Clip

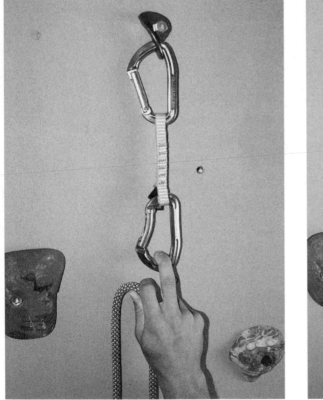

1. Pinch the rope between the tip of your index finger and thumb, and then hook the carabiner with the middle finger to hold it steady.

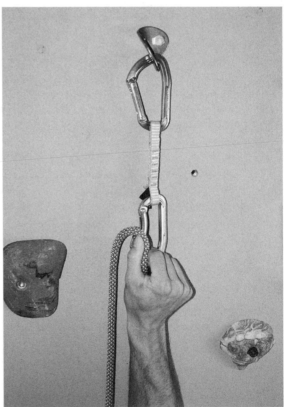

2. Push the rope through the gate with your thumb.

LEARNING *to* CLIMB INDOORS

created. Rule nothing out—consider the possible benefits of a twist lock, stem, heel hook, or flag in facilitating a casual clip. Ultimately, it's the experience you accumulated over dozens and hundreds of leads that will make you an ace at gleaning the optimal position and making a quick, efficient clip.

CLIPPING TECHNIQUE

Clipping the rope into the free carabiner of a quickdraw is a one-handed task that many beginners fumble through. To avoid this affliction, you must practice clipping quickdraws just as you practice any other important skill. There are two different techniques that you must learn, since both will be called upon depending on the direction of the carabiner gate in relation to the clipping hand. Practice both techniques with both hands until clipping becomes second nature and automatic.

Let's first consider the situation where the carabiner gate is facing the opposite direction of your free hand. Reach down and grab the rope by pinching it between the tip of your index finger and thumb. Grab the rope as far as possible below its tie-in spot with your harness, so as to maximize the length of rope available to pull upward toward the quickdraw. Now pull the rope up and hook the carabiner with your middle finger to hold it steady while you push the rope through the gate with your thumb.

Pinch Clip

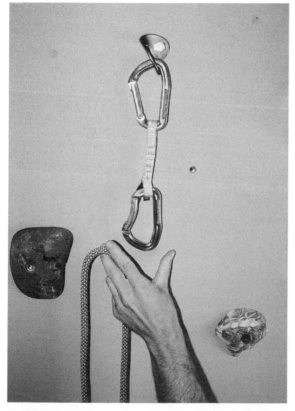

1. Grab the rope between the tips of your index and middle fingers.

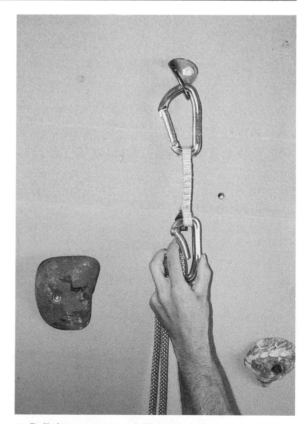

2. Pull the rope up and place your thumb against the spine of the carabiner while your fingers push the rope through the gate.

Lead Climbing and Success Strategies

The above technique will not work if the carabiner gate is facing to the same side as your free clipping hand. In this case you'll need to reach down and grab the rope between the tips of your index and middle fingers. Now pull the rope up and place your thumb against the spine of the carabiner while your fingers push the rope through the gate. Strive to hold the carabiner still by thinking about *squeezing* it between your thumb and forefingers.

If the anchor is above eye level, you may not have enough slack to clip the rope with a single pull. Here you'll need to pull the rope up and hold it in your teeth while you reach down to pull up more rope. Holding the rope in your teeth may seem like a dicey proposition—what if you fall?—but it's actually a very common technique that hasn't

caused anyone serious injury (to the best of my knowledge). Of course, climbing a move or two higher so that the bolt is at chest level eliminates the need for a double pull. When in doubt as to the optimal clipping position, explore climbing a move or two higher in an attempt to avoid a reachy clip that requires a double pull and bite on the rope. Most often you'll be rewarded with a shorter, more casual clip.

PROPER ROPE PLACEMENT THROUGH A CARABINER

One subtle but important nuance of clipping the lead rope into a quickdraw is that the sharp end of the rope (the end tied to your harness) should exit the outer side of the carabiner. If the lead end of the rope

Rope Running

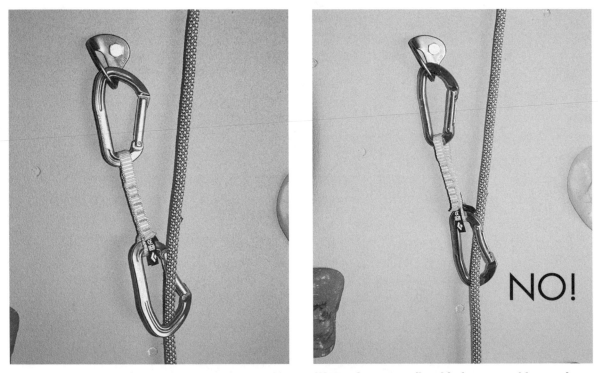

Right: Proper rope path through the carabiner, with the lead end of the rope exiting outside the carabiner.

Wrong: Improper clip with the rope exiting on the wall side of the carabiner.

LEARNING *to* CLIMB INDOORS

exits on the biner's wall side, the rope may pull across the gate as you climb past the bolt. Though extremely rare, the rope could unclip itself as you climb above—or, in the worst case, unclip as you fall past the anchor bolt. Don't take chances—learn to clip it right every time!

To make a correct clip, observe how the carabiner naturally hangs along the wall surface and estimate how the quickdraw is likely to move as you climb past it. By visualizing this, you will be able to determine the proper way to clip the rope so that the lead end exits the outside of the carabiner. A good belayer will keep a keen eye and quickly notify you if she observes a backward clip. If possible, try to correct the clip before climbing higher.

PRECLIPPING THE FIRST BOLT

On high-end climbs with difficult starting moves, some climbers choose to preclip the first anchor bolt. In doing so, they essentially gain a toprope for the first section of the climb—not perfect lead-climbing style, but widely viewed as acceptable. Getting the rope preclipped into the first bolt can be achieved three ways. First, you could climb the starting moves to the first bolt, clip the rope, and then downclimb or jump off. Another option is to have a friend or your belayer preclip the rope for you. If you promise to return the favor (or pay cash), you should have no problem finding a volunteer. Finally, you could use a specially made **stick clip** that enables you to extend a loop of rope up through the quickdraw.

Unless the route is at your absolute limit, I suggest you pass on the preclip and send the route in ground-up style, making all the clips yourself. Ask your belayer to give a spot until you clip the first bolt and, if available, place a crash pad at the base of the climb. Think of it as a boulder problem to the first bolt, and then assume a lead-climbing mentality upon making the clip.

Trusting the System and Learning to Take Lead Falls

Excelling as a lead climber demands that you trust the belay system completely and focus your attention on the act of climbing. Should your mind wander to whether the rope, bolt, or belay might fail—ridiculous thoughts, but common among beginning leaders—you will become paralyzed with fear and make lead climbing far more stressful than it need be. The fact is, proper use of the safety systems described in this book make climbing statistically safer than driving a car or riding a bicycle. In chapter 3 you learned the fundamentals of belaying, and now in this section you will learn to evaluate the potential weaknesses in the system as well as the proper way to fall. Yes, falling is an unavoidable part of lead climbing, and there are a few things to keep in mind as you come to take air on lead.

KNOW THE SYSTEM'S WEAKNESSES

The belay system itself—the belay device, the rope, the anchor bolts and quickdraws, the knot, and the harness—is essentially bulletproof given no human error. As covered in chapter 3, there can be no error in tying the rope to your harness; similarly, the belayer must be vigilant in his duties. Given all this, there are just a few remaining weaknesses or hazards that you need to be aware of and thus manage as you engage in lead climbing.

The first such hazard is the unprotected climbing up to the first bolt. As mentioned earlier, you can mitigate the risk of injury by obtaining a spotter or stick clipping the rope. The next potential hazard comes when you pull the rope to clip the second bolt. In the case of a high second bolt (or unnecessarily loose belay), the slack in the system as you pull the rope to clip the second bolt may be sufficient that a fall before completing the clip would drop you dangerously close to the ground. The best strategy here is to find an absolutely secure clipping position—one that you couldn't possibly fall from—and have a belayer who doesn't pay out any more rope than necessary. The bottom line: Falling while clipping is extremely rare, but in recognizing the hazard you can take actions that will prevent you from getting hurt should it happen.

Another concern is getting your leg looped over the rope while falling—not an uncommon occurrence, and one that often yields a nice rope burn on your leg to remember it by. To avoid this affliction,

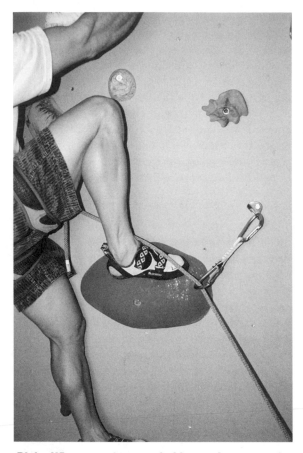

Right: When stepping on a hold near the rope path, it's crucial to always step on the outside of the rope.

Wrong: Never step over the rope to engage a foothold.

it's vital to note exactly where the rope is located each time you advance a foot. Your foot (and leg) should never pass between the wall and the rope; instead step up in a way that positions the leg outside the rope. Sequences that take a diagonal or sideways path are most problematic, so sharpen your awareness in these situations.

The final hazard in lead climbing is the slight chance that you might strike a protruding hold or wall feature while falling. Fortunately, most lead climbs that are hard enough to cause you to fall are void of large, protruding holds or steep enough that you mainly fall through air with little or no wall contact. Still, it's best to climb with an eye out for high-profile holds and recognize when they might be in your fall line. For example, in entering the crux section of a climb—a sequence from which you might fall—visualize the likely distance and trajectory of the fall and assess whether any objects present a risk. Consider whether the fall would be straight down or swinging, and feetfirst or otherwise. Should you envision a potential risk, you will need to decide whether you want to retreat from the climb or push on and assume the risk. If you decide to climb on, continue with prudence and consider downclimbing out of a hard move rather than risking the fall.

It's important to recognize that the large holds and vertical wall angle common to beginner-level climbs often present the greatest hazard to a lead climber. Consequently, such routes are rarely set (as lead climbs) at most commercial gyms, since forerunners are mindful of the risks. Still, should you find yourself struggling on such a route, always attempt to downclimb out of a hard move rather than risk a lead fall that could result in striking a protruding hold.

LEARNING TO FALL

Early ventures at lead climbing will likely have you in the midst of a crux pondering whether to retreat from the difficulties or push yourself to the point of falling (or possibly a success without falling!). No doubt, there will be many mental battles waged as your desire to do a route conflicts with a primal instinct to avoid falling. The result will be a high level of anxiety that feeds back and disrupts your ability to climb smoothly and confidently. Recognize, however, that this is a battle that all would-be lead climbers must persevere through. Given a committed, disciplined effort, you will eventually conquer the fear of falling and reveal a whole new level of ability. What's more, winning over fear is a process of self-development that will enhance your capabilities in other challenging areas of your life.

To become accustomed to falling, however, happens only via real-life experience at taking lead falls. Therefore, you must force yourself to fall despite what your instincts dictate. Such practice at falling is something that might occur simply by pushing yourself to the limit on a difficult lead climb. Many novice leaders find this to be an impossible task, because it's just too scary to push upward on a hard climb not knowing if they will fall or what the fall will be like. Interestingly, most of the fear evaporates once they do fall—experiencing the uneventfulness of the typical lead fall dispels the illusion of danger.

If you can't bring yourself to fall trying, you will

Overcome the fear of falling by taking a few practice falls on a safe, overhanging route.
ILLUSTRATION BY **MIKE TEA**

need to stage some intentional falls in order to beat the fear. Select a slightly overhanging route void of high-profile holds, and climb up to the third or fourth bolt. Confirm that your belayer is ready, and then take your first fall with the last bolt you clipped just a foot or two below your harness. In this case letting go will turn out to be rather anticlimactic: You'll drop only a few feet before the rope arrests the fall. Upon taking the fall, analyze how well the belay system worked. It is trustworthy after all! Now climb back up a foot or two higher than before and take another intentional fall. Repeat this process one or two more times, with the goal of taking your final practice fall with the bolt at or just below your feet.

At first, performing this falling drill will feel much like taking bitter medicine. After a few weeks, however, your conscious and subconscious will acclimate to the feeling of falling. Then, as you begin to pursue on-sight and redpoint ascents, you'll notice a decreasing fear of falling and a new instinctual desire to risk and embrace falling in the attempt of a worthy goal. Recognize this new disposition as a major breakthrough, and pat yourself on the back!

Learning to Read Boulder Problems and Routes

Climbing strategy isn't confined to the things you do while actually climbing; in fact, a big part of effective strategy involves the things you do in preparing for the ascent. In this section you will learn how to analyze and mentally climb a route without ever leaving the ground. You will learn how to preprogram the ascent with visualization, as well as discover how you can leverage yesterday's successes in helping you climb better today.

Anticipating Moves and Developing a Strategy

The best performers in sport are usually masters at anticipating upcoming difficulties (or the opponent) and developing novel strategies for winning. Climbing is no different. To just climb a route as it comes at you is akin to playing chess one move at a

time. You *can* play chess that way—you can even win—but the best chess players think many moves ahead, anticipate the challenger's actions, and constantly visualize a successful outcome. In this way, you must learn to think like a chess player in the vertical extreme.

The first step is to gather information about the route relating to the location of holds, anchor bolts, and rest positions. View the route from three different perspectives—straight on, from the left, and from the right—and scan for hidden holds in corners, around arêtes, above and below bulges, or anywhere else they might hide. Next, identify the location of each bolt you will need to clip and try to surmise the body position you will assume to make each clip. Finally, locate rest stances and try to figure the ideal position in each case. Consider the possibility of a heel hook, knee lock, stem, or any other trick position that the forerunner might have slyly built into the route. While none of these moves or rests is guaranteed to be correct, the act of mentally assessing the situation empowers you to climb with more confidence and a greater sense of "knowing" what's likely ahead.

Most important, it's your goal to be able to identify the crux portion of the route and then determine the ideal sequence of moves. As you decipher the best-looking sequence, keep an open mind for alternative possibilities. You may even want to memorize two sequences through the apparent crux section, and then make the choice of which to use when you get there. Finally, don't get stuck in the bottom-up paradigm when figuring sequences. Often you can unlock a puzzling sequence by mentally downclimbing from an obviously good hold or rest.

This skill of reading a route is one part visual intelligence and one part climbing experience. Over time you will develop the ability to see the correct sequence of moves up most, if not all, of the climb. Commit to reading every route, regardless of grade, and you will eventually become a chess master on the rock!

Visualization

The route-reading strategies covered above are but simple mental rehearsal. You can compound the positive effects of such preprogramming by taking a few minutes to engage in detailed visualization of the upcoming ascent.

In previewing the route, you likely pictured yourself on the wall in different body positions and, possibly, testing moves and rest positions. This disassociated, on-TV perspective of envisioning yourself on the route does little to program your nervous system and subconscious for peak performance. To be maximally effective, you must be associated, or get in your body, as you mentally climb the route. You need to see the holds and feel the moves as if you were actually on the wall. Such vivid, realistic visualization programs your nervous system as if you were actually climbing the route and thus increases the odds you'll succeed on the route when you get on it for real.

Using visualization in a noisy gym environment can be difficult—ideally you'd like to find a quiet spot where you can close your eyes and relax for a few minutes while engaging in associated visualization. More likely, you'll be standing with closed eyes at the base of the climb trying to create an associated state. Take a few deep breaths and allow any tension to drain from your body. Now begin climbing the route in your mind's eye. Feel your arms and legs performing the sequence exactly as you read the route a few minutes earlier. See each hand- and foothold as you use them, and feel yourself moving with precision up the route. Finally, feel yourself successfully completing the route. Now open your eyes and return your focus to the present moment. Begin climbing with the same flow as your previous mental ascent.

As a final note, it's important to avoid any negative imagery or thoughts of falling during your visualization. Feeling yourself struggle or fall, while in the associated state, will equally program these outcomes. This explains why worry and fear are often self-fulfilling—such thoughts are usually accompanied by associated visualization of negative outcomes and thus increase the likelihood they will come to fruition.

Leverage Past Experience

Another powerful strategy is to compare the climb you are about to attempt to a similar route you've

Mental Preparation Tips for Lead Climbing

1. Scope the route from three different angles to locate holds, determine clipping positions, anticipate moves, identify rest positions, and develop a climbing strategy.

2. Scan the route for potential risks—high-profile protruding holds, the chance of taking a diagonal fall, ground fall potential, and such—then determine how to best mitigate the risks.

3. Mentally rehearse the climb. Consider taking a few minutes to close your eyes and engage in associated visualization of the ascent.

4. Elicit a peak performance state via slow, deep breathing, a narrowing of focus, and an intense knowing of your true ability. Visualize a past successful ascent of a similar route to fortify confidence and foster positive emotions.

succeeded on in the past. For example, suppose the desired climb features a large overhang with what appears to be a difficult stand-up past the lip. Close your eyes and think back to a successful past ascent through a large roof—how did you attack the route, what techniques or specific moves were required, and, most important, how did you feel upon sending the route? This process of vividly visualizing all the details and feelings of a past success will recycle these resources for use in the present. This strategy only takes a minute or two to execute, but it's exceedingly powerful in helping program your mind for peak performance.

Working a Route

Projecting, or working a route, is a common mode among gym climbers. Whether it's an impossible-looking boulder problem or an inspiring lead climb, working to solve the rock puzzle engages the mind and body in a way unlike other life tasks. Projects that take hours or days to complete are often the most gratifying, as you progressively realize tangible improvement from session to session and eventually experience the rapture of success. While no trophies or Super Bowl rings are to be won, projecting provides the priceless payoff of self-exploration and self-improvement.

Following are several powerful strategies for efficient projecting. You will learn how to chunk down a difficult route into manageable parts and then reassemble the chunks into a successful redpoint ascent. Next, you will learn several crux-busting strategies that you can leverage in solving the hardest moves of a boulder problem or route. You will then learn how to rehearse the climb for a stylish, ESPY-deserving redpoint ascent!

Chunking Down a Route

The benefits of chunking down a difficult climb into parts are both mental and physical. Psychologically, it reduces the burden of a long, hard route by allowing you to consider its parts as several shorter, doable climbs. Physically, chunking lets you dedicate full energy to solving the hardest chunk first, as if it were a route of its own. Only when this is sent do you begin working on other easier parts of the climb.

Before you can chunk down the route, it helps to have some firsthand knowledge. Take a quick reconnaissance run up as much of the climb as possible to determine its logical parts. On a project with multiple cruxes, you might chunk down the route into four or five sections defined by the obvious stopping points (rest positions or bolt clips). A boulder problem, however, might be broken into three chunks: the section up to the crux, the crux itself, and the final section to the top. After your first run on the route, classify each part according to apparent difficulty. For example, the third and fourth chunks might be the hardest, the first chunk the next hardest, and the second and final chunks the easiest. Solving the hardest part(s) is top priority, so get to work on solving the chunk you deem most difficult. Once it's sent, move on to the second most difficult chunk, and so forth.

Upon solving each chunk, it's time to begin work on linking the chunks into a complete redpoint ascent. While the natural approach would be to simply begin attempting the redpoint from the ground up, it's actually more effective to practice climbing

Hangdogging is the common practice of working a hard route section-by-section with liberal hanging on the rope between attempts.

ever-increasing lengths of the route beginning with the top section. In the above example of a route broken into five chunks, you would lower from the top anchors and attempt to link the fourth and fifth chunks. If successful, you'd again lower from the anchors and attempt to link on toprope the third, fourth, and fifth chunks. Continue adding chunks until your starting point is the ground.

This process of linking chunks might seem superfluous, but it is truly the most effective strategy for completing a project that's stretching your capabilities. Linking from top down makes you extremely familiar and confident in the final chunks of the route. On redpoint, it's here that you will want to be super dialed in due to increasing mental and physical fatigue. Conversely, the straight-from-the-ground approach may leave you thrashing to rediscover the sequence through the final chunks as lactic acid and anxiety compromise your technique and memory of the proper sequence.

Deciphering a Crux Sequence

It's inevitable that you will occasionally reach a point on a climb where all hope seems to be lost. Suppose there's a blatant lack of good holds, you don't have a clue what to do, and your confidence is tanking. What will you do in such a frustrating situation? Fish or cut bait—or, in climbers' lingo, climb or take dirt?

Hopefully you'll decide to give it a proud effort, realizing that even if you don't succeed in winning you will still succeed in learning. Climbing is a never-ending cycle of success and failure, and the down phase of the cycle is as important as the up phase for self-development and absolute improvement. The following section details several problem-solving techniques for use on projects that are resisting your best efforts.

EMBRACE THE ROUTE'S FEEDBACK

Many climbers fail on routes they are physically capable of doing because they ignore the feedback the route is providing. Avoid this mind-set by embracing the feedback of failed attempts as clues toward your inevitable success. For instance, if you are tending to barndoor off the crux move, recognize that a flagging leg will increase stability. Or if you can't reach the next critical hold, look for an undercling and hip turn to extend your reach. If you still can't solve the move, the route may be hinting that there is a hidden hold or specific body position that you have yet to discover.

No matter what, believe that the route wants you to succeed regardless of your current struggles or the apparent impossible feel of the climb. In this way, view each failed attempt as a signpost directing you toward a better course of action instead of becoming obsessed with a single way the route must be done. A creative, thinking-out-of-the-box approach is most valuable.

THINK OUT OF THE BOX

To break through a sticking point on a climb, you must get outside your current mind-set. The first key strategy is to exercise a flexibility of perspective. For a moment, detach yourself from the situation and visualize the problem spot from a perspective outside yourself. View yourself attempting the crux from a disassociated, on-TV perspective. See yourself trying a wide range of possible solutions, and in particular sequences that you have yet to test out in reality. It can also help to visualize how some great climber you know would attack the route—what tricks and tactics do you see him employing? Maybe a dyno past a long reach, a sequence of small foothold upgrades, or possibly a clever rest position that would provide a more rested attempt on the crux?

Another good strategy is to try a series of ridiculous, improbable moves. For example, try doing a heel hook, a twist lock, a deadpoint, a mantle, and any other move you can think of. Disregard the fact that a given move doesn't seem to be the solution—give it a try without prejudice. In attempting a variety of different techniques, you may very well stumble onto a workable sequence that you would have never surmised while climbing with the blinders on. Be creative and have fun, and above all maintain a belief that the route is possible. You might not send the climb that day, but you will make an important stride toward future success.

FOCUS ON THE FEET

When struggling on difficult move, it's a natural tendency to obsess on finding the next good handhold that will enable you to pull through. Ironically, the solution is usually a matter of better footwork and body position. Thus it's vital that you assume an intense foot focus and resist the temptation to search for a handhold solution to your difficulties.

Stellar footwork and never-ending foot focus are hallmarks of all top climbers. This is one area where you can, and should, model the actions of these elites. Observe how the best climbers in the gym use their feet in prevailing through heinous cruxes, and then strive to let your feet similarly run the show. You will also benefit by reviewing the fundamentals of effective technique (see chapters 5 and 6) and by performing a few of the foot-oriented drills (such the Downclimbing, Tennis Ball, High-Step, and Tracking drills).

Condition yourself to look down and *think feet* every time you begin to strain or tremble on a route. Make "focus on the feet" your climbing mantra and you will be surprised by the ease at which you surmount many so-called cruxes!

Rehearsing a Project

In rehearsing for your redpoint send, it would be wise to consider these common performance-limiting factors (and their cause): poor economy of movement (bad technique and physical tension), overgripping of handholds (anxiety and fear), missed holds and rests (climbing with blinders on), and shaken confidence (negative thoughts). Each of these factors accelerates energy drain, and failure is all but certain if you suffer from two or more of these handicaps.

While we have already covered all these influencing factors in one way or another, it's important that you review every aspect of efficient performance in practicing for a redpoint. Any overlooked detail or minor inefficiency might be enough to sink your ship. So, like cutting fat from a piece of steak, refine your sequence by cutting out any unnecessary movements or time spent hanging out in strenuous positions. Your goal is to move briskly from one rest position to the next, with the highest possible fuel economy. Make a game out of elevating the quality of your ascent with every practice lap, and soon the redpoint will be in the bag.

Redpointing a Project

The nature of projecting is to climb a route at your limit or to break new ground with a hardest-ever ascent. A successful redpoint, therefore, requires near-perfect execution as well as an anxiety-free and well-rested body. In the case of a route that you quickly solved and rehearsed, it may be possible to achieve the redpoint in the same session. But first take an extended break to recover from your practice efforts. Take off your climbing shoes, get a drink, and walk off any existing tension so as to feel completely fresh and relaxed for your redpoint attempt.

Depending on your degree of fatigue, you may want to rest anywhere from ten to thirty minutes before going for the send.

As you begin climbing, take the route one chunk at a time, whether it's bolt-to-bolt or rest-to-rest. The burden of looking up and considering the route as a whole can be too great and may plant the seeds of failure in the form of jitters and doubts. Mentally tick off each chunk as you complete it—this will build confidence and help propel you upward. Before you know it you will be clipping the anchors, and the route will be ticked!

An especially severe project may require that you return another day with a full gas tank in order to redpoint the route. Take two full rest days and then return to the gym with the intention of completing the project. Perform an extended warm-up and redpoint a few easier routes to get into a groove. Now take a ten- to twenty-minute rest and send the project.

Tips for Working a Route

1. Chunk down the route into workable parts. Hangdog (climb bolt-to-bolt with liberal hanging on the rope) up the entire route to identify the hardest chunk. Then work on solving this section first.

2. Analyze the route's feedback after each failed attempt. Are you missing a hold? Is there a better sequence or body position to be found? Do you need to climb faster or locate another rest?

3. Resist the tendency to lead with your hands and instead focus on your feet. The key to unlocking most crux sequences lies in discovering the optimal use of footholds and the requisite body positions.

4. Upon solving all the chunks, begin linking sections from the top down. Your goal is to rehearse and wire the top portion of the route, which is where you will be most fatigued when attempting your redpoint.

5. Take a long rest (ten to thirty minutes) before going for the send. If needed, take a couple of days off and return to redpoint the climb in a completely fresh state.

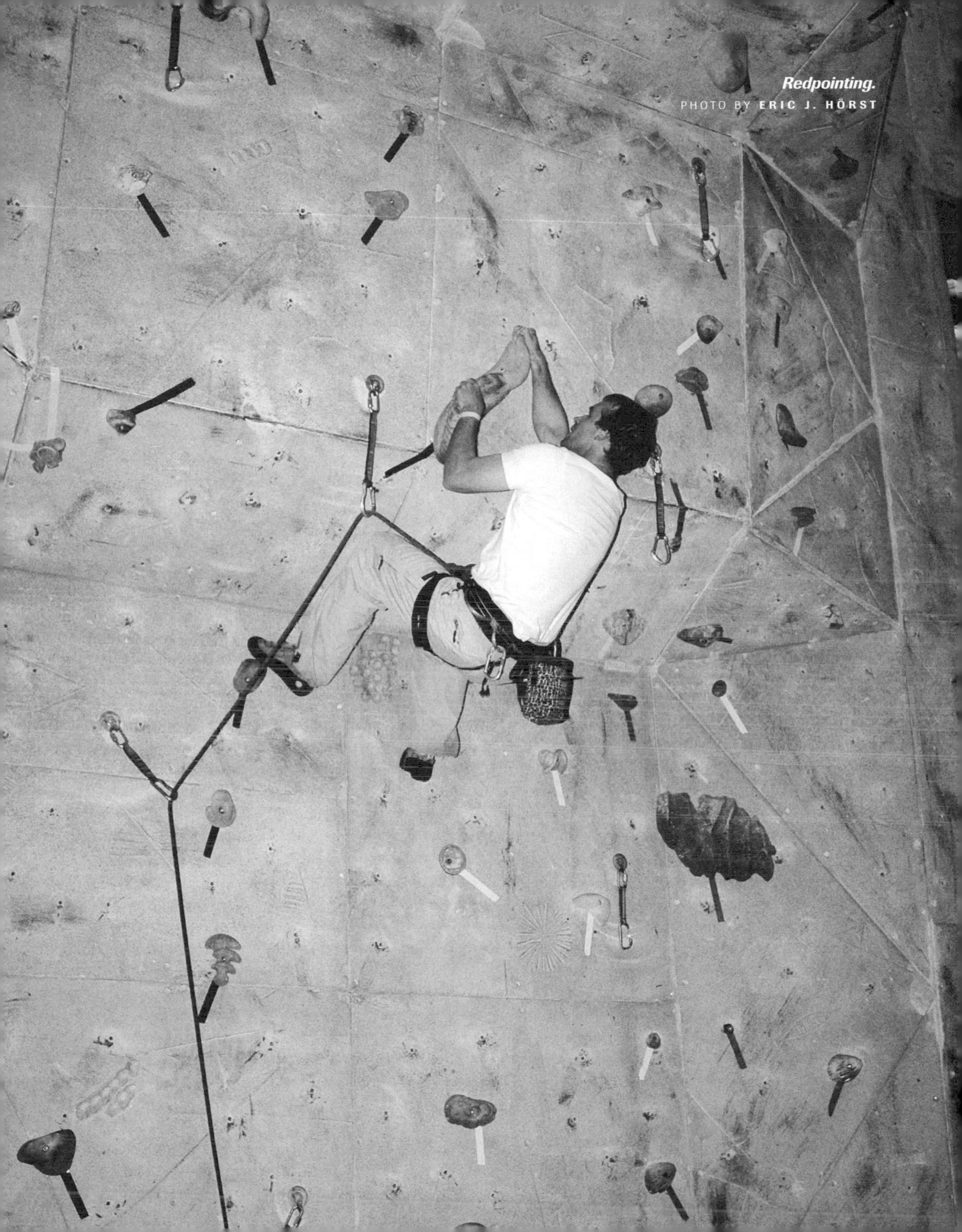

Redpointing.
PHOTO BY **ERIC J. HÖRST**

Mental Training and Fear Management

The brain is the most important muscle for climbing.

—Wolfgang Güllich, legendary German climber who established the groundbreaking Action Direct (5.14d) in 1991

A common adage among rock jocks is that "climbing is mostly mental." This saying is born from the fact that even the strongest, most stylish climber can be sunk by fearful, anxious, or doubtful thoughts.

Whereas I believe climbing performance is actually about one-third mental—with technique and fitness making up the other two-thirds—most climbers' skill levels in these three areas develop disproportionately. After a year or so of climbing, for example, your fitness and technical attributes will likely be more developed than your mental abilities. Consequently, your mental game may become the greatest constraint to your future growth and your ultimate degree of success in the sport.

The goal of this chapter is to help you turn this common weakness into a strength. For starters, you will learn the importance of self-awareness and how you can make regular self-assessments and course corrections. Next, you will learn how to control anxiety and fear, because you simply cannot climb well (or enjoy climbing) if you are weighed down by negative thoughts or the fear of falling. Lastly, you'll discover the keys to creating a peak performance state from which your best ascents will be born.

But let's begin with a look at getting your head into the game by developing a higher level of self-awareness.

Developing Self-Awareness

Name a top athlete in any sport—Peyton Manning, Tiger Woods, Serena Williams, Lance Armstrong, and the like—and you are naming a person with an uncommon sense of self-awareness. Similarly, the most talented amateur athletes and weekend warriors possess a level of self-awareness that enables them to maximize their ability, even though their sport is but an avocation. In climbing, self-awareness empowers you to manage stress and fatigue, redirect unproductive thinking, identify weaknesses, and refine your practice and training to be most effective. Let's dig deeper and take a look at a couple of techniques for increasing self-awareness.

Self-Assessing Your Performance

Self-assessment is a process of identifying both your strengths and weaknesses, yet it's the weaknesses on which you must shine the light if you want to climb better. While your real-life experiences with failure will seem to point to a lack of strength, such a conclusion is myopic and often dead wrong. Here's why.

When you get pumped and fall off a climb, there are almost always underlying causes that produced premature fatigue and failure. For example, poor footwork or a missed foothold, improper body positioning, overgripping of holds, fearful thoughts, climbing too slowly, lack of concentration, a botched sequence, or a missed rest will all lead to accelerated energy drain. Therefore, a meaningful self-assessment must go beyond the superficial issue of "lacking strength" and examine the mental and technical weaknesses that are robbing you blind. I estimate that average climbers unknowingly waste 50 percent (or more) of their energy resources due to lackluster technique and poor mental control. In this case, complaining about a lack of strength is like complaining about the price of gas while driving a gas-guzzling, out-of-tune car!

Here are two strategies for effective self-assessment. First, conduct a spot assessment after every fall or failure on a route. Ask yourself a series of probative questions such as *What pressures or fears held me back?* or *What technical or tactical errors did I commit?* or *What physical tension prevented fluid, controlled movement?* Asking questions like these will often reveal your limiting factor on a given route and thus allow you to make an effective course correction on the spot.

Identifying the theme of your weaknesses on a broader macro scale may require a more comprehensive assessment. Use the self-assessment checklist (Table 8.1) as a sort of magnifying glass to inspect and assess specific skills and tactics. Of course, it's the low-scoring questions that present major constraints on your performance.

Hire a Coach to Identify Technical and Tactical Flaws

Athletes in pretty much all other sports have coaches, so why shouldn't climbers? Interestingly, most climbers get no formal instruction beyond their first day or two as true novices learning to tie knots and belay. In using this trial-and-error approach to learning, you will inevitably hit some performance roadblocks.

Enlisting a coach to assess your abilities and help direct your training will put you on the fast track to better climbing. All you need is one consultation per month or quarter, during which time the coach can assess your climbing and then design an appropriate action plan for improvement. Hopefully, this program will include practice drills to improve technique, suggestions for improving your climbing tactics and mental control, and some fitness-training exercises that target critical physical weak-

nesses. If the coach simply prescribes a strength-training program, then it's time to find another coach.

Tuning into Your Thoughts

On any given day more than 20,000 thoughts surface in your conscious mind. If there is a natural tendency in the direction of thoughts, it's to focus on problems, fears, and frustrations. To some degree, this tendency to focus on the negative and threatening aspects in life is a genetic defense mechanism. However, the tendency to view things compulsively from the cup-is-half-empty perspective or the worst-case scenario is a conditioned habit that will hold you back.

Gaining higher self-awareness, then, must include tuning into your thoughts more often and supplanting negative thinking with positive imagery and productive self-talk. Consider that everything you are and everything you will become is a direct function of your thoughts. Thus, what could be more central to improving your climbing than fostering a curious, positive, goal-motivated way of thinking?

The impact of getting your climbing head on straight can't be understated both in terms of immediate results and long-term improvement. For example, just as finding a hidden hold on a desperate crux can make it feel way easier, the effects of eliminating fearful, doubtful self-talk can feel like a ten-pound weight is taken off your back. So if you want to climb better today, lose the mental baggage! The long-term aggregate effects of higher-quality thinking day-to-day could be the difference between you climbing 5.9 or 5.13 a few years from now.

Becoming aware of the unproductive self-talk and negative imagery is the first and hardest step to turning it around. Tune into your self-talk throughout the day, at home, at work, and at the gym. What are you hearing? Ultimately the goal is to modify your thinking in ways that will help you solve problems (instead of wallowing in them), challenge fears (instead of avoiding them), and compel intelligent action toward your goals (instead of backpedaling at the first sign of adversity). Learn to redirect your

Table 8.1 A Self-Assessment Checklist

Evaluate yourself in each area and check (✓) the box that best represents your current ability.

Technique	Good	Okay	Poor
Precise, quiet foot placements that carry body weight			
Grip handholds lightly and let arms play a secondary role			
Use of the Left–Right Rule for stable movement			
Economy of movement (rhythm, pace, poise)			
Use of rest positions			
Use of nonpositive handholds (side pulls, underclings, down-sloping holds)			
Optimal use of feet and climbing shoes (inside/outside edges, toe, sole, heel)			
Use of flagging to aid stability and prevent barndooring			
Mantling through long reaches; hand–foot matching			
Twist lock and backstep on steep terrain			
Dynamic moves (deadpoints and lunges)			
Clipping quickdraws			

Mental	Good	Okay	Poor
Trusting the belay system (and spotter)			
Reading sequences, clip positions, and rest locations			
Anticipating moves and developing a strategy			
Visualizing sequences and a successful ascent			
Deciphering cruxes			
Redpointing projects			
Controlling tension and anxiety			
Managing fear of failure and falling			
Getting focused and tuning out distractions			
Detachment from climbing outcome			

Physical	Good	Okay	Poor
Body composition (compared with ideal for climbing)			
Flexibility			
Pull-muscle strength (general pull-up ability)			
Core/abdominal strength			
Antagonist pull-muscle conditioning			
Lock-off strength			
Grip strength			
Anaerobic (climbing) endurance			
Speed of recovery (between climbs and workouts)			
Quality of diet			
Quantity of rest between workouts			

thoughts onto your goals, replace negative self-talk with can-do language, and focus your energy on current actions that will propel you forward.

Controlling Tension and Anxiety

As the saying goes, "Thoughts are things." If you possess fearful thoughts, these thoughts will result in anxiety and physical tension. Similarly, if you direct calming, positive thinking, you will naturally shift into a more relaxed, centered state. Given this intimate connection of the mind and body, you can consciously determine how you feel simply by redirecting your thoughts. This is a powerful concept that's vital for climbers to understand and leverage—such thought control is the essence of mental toughness.

In this section you will learn how to create an optimal, centered state for climbing via proactive thought control. Being centered encompasses the feelings of relaxation, balance, and confidence. You will always climb your best if you begin from this centered state. As you ascend a difficult or scary route, however, your mind and body can rapidly shift into a tense, inefficient state. Thus you must also learn how to regain control—or return to center—while on the climb.

Getting Centered

Whether you're climbing a five-move boulder problem or a 50-foot route, unchecked tension and anxiety will hold you back like gravity on steroids. Physical tension kills motor skills and technique, while mental tension (anxiety and fear) quells cre-

ativity, focus, and the opportunity to achieve flow. Interestingly, average climbers are so used to climbing with undue tension that they don't even realize its negative effects. Upon gaining awareness and learning to release the tension, however, they are amazed at their newfound freedom to move smoothly and more efficiently.

You, too, can learn to take control over tension and create a relaxed, balanced, centered state from which to climb your best. The six-step ANSWER Sequence is a highly effective process for identifying and eliminating tension. It's easy to learn and put to work, as evident by the thousands of climbers around the world who now use my ANSWER Sequence as their antidote to anxiety and physical tension.

Initial use of the ANSWER Sequence may require a quiet room and five minutes to perform. With a little practice, however, you will be able to incorporate it into your preclimb routine and create a centered state in just a minute or two. I invite you to make a copy of the ANSWER Sequence, and begin using it throughout the day, both in and outside of the climbing gym.

Regaining Control

Climbing near your limit can be stressful. Desperate moves, risk of falling, and the uncertainty of what's next can foster unproductive thoughts and physical tension that snowballs at a rapid rate. Left unchecked, such rising tension will cause you to pump out and quite likely fall. While every climber has been through this type of experience, it should be but a brief phase that you work through. Increasing confidence and experience will go a long way to mitigate this natural fight-or-flight response. Still, even expert climbers occasionally experience tension when attempting severe routes. They are masters at controlling tension on the fly, however, so that it never grows to a level that hampers performance.

Similarly, your goal should be to develop such awareness and control over rising tension. You can then use rest stances and clipping positions as an opportunity to release the tension and return to center. Here are two strategies for regaining control in the midst of a difficult route.

The A N S W E R Sequence

A **Step 1: Awareness** of anxiety, tension, or negative thoughts. Tuning into your "inner world" is the first step in creating a peak performance state. Use the following steps to counter the problem areas you diagnose.

N **Step 2: Normalize** breathing. Irregular breathing multiplies tension, so strive for smooth, even breathing when the pressure is on. Take several slow, deep belly breaths and feel the tension release from your core.

S **Step 3: Scan** for areas of muscular tension. To reduce tension, contract the affected muscles for a few seconds, then relax them and visualize the tension draining out like air from a balloon.

W **Step 4: Wave** of relaxation. Take a final slow, deep breath and feel the wave of relaxation wash from your head to your toes.

E **Step 5: Erase** thoughts of the past—engage the present moment with all your attention. Vividly visualize the ideal outcome and believe in it, but then redirect your thoughts with a laserlike focus onto the present moment.

R **Step 6: Reset** posture and flash a smile. Trust your abilities, let the outcome take care of itself, and have fun regardless of the results.

Lead climbing is stressful, and it's only through experience and conscious effort that you will develop the poise and mental toughness needed to excel.

FOCUS ON BREATH CONTROL

Deep, steady breathing is the number one antidote to tension. Not surprisingly, then, the common tendency to hold your breath on a difficult sequence is a prime cause of tension. While it's okay (and often beneficial) to hold your breath for a single challenging move that requires you to bear down hard, it is common to continue to hold your breath, or breathe unevenly, throughout a series of difficult moves. By being aware of this tendency, however, you can take conscious control of your breathing during stressful times on a route. Strive for slow, deep belly breaths during the moves leading up to a crux, and try to regain steady breathing as you move out of the most difficult moves. This strategy alone will go a long way toward controlling tension as you climb.

Before you start up a route, try to predetermine the location of all rest stances and clipping positions. These spots should offer you the opportunity to take a minute to steady your breathing. Upon reaching one of these spots, close your eyes for a moment and turn your thoughts inward to feel air filling your lungs with each slow breath. As you exhale, visualize the tension exiting your body and feel a renewed sense of being centered. This entire process might only take fifteen to thirty seconds, but it's invaluable for regaining an optimal state for attacking the next section of the climb. Make it a habit to steady your breathing at every rest; you might even consider using the ANSWER Sequence at good rest positions that allow you a minute or two to hang out.

KEEP YOUR THOUGHTS PRODUCTIVE AND GOAL-ORIENTED

Doubtful, fearful thinking is an on-sight or redpoint terminator. You simply can't climb well with the weight of these negative thoughts in tow. Once again, you need to seize every stopping point on a route as an opportunity to tune into your thinking. Is it productive or unproductive in nature? Quickly evaluate any fears to determine if they are legitimate or just phantom fears trying to scare you off the route. In gym climbing, most fears are fraudulent, and if this is indeed the case, you must write them

off as illusions and then redirect your attention onto your goal—sending the route!

The popular sports metaphor "keep your eye on the ball" is appropriate here. Resist the tendency to doubt your abilities or ponder the fall potential, and simply narrow your focus onto the next section of climb. As explained in chapter 7, it's best to attack a route one chunk at a time. Concentrate on the moves up to the next rest and forget about what's below you as well as what's yet to come above the next chunk. If your only goal is climbing the 6 feet (or whatever) to the next rest position, the burden is greatly reduced and a big cause of tension is erased.

View Failures as Part of the Success Process

An important part of emotional control is the ability to deal with failure in a productive way. The natural tendency for many folks is to react to failures with emotional outbursts and a torrent of negative, critical thinking. Of course, such reactive behavior will make future attempts on a climb even more difficult. Not only does this create physical tension, but it also creates an emotional anchor to the climb that will plague future efforts. Even if you return to the route with a clear mind on another day, your subconscious can recall the angst and potentially sabotage your efforts.

While no one likes to fail, it's important to embrace your failures as opportunities for growth and learning. Every time a route rejects you, it is also offering you a valuable lesson for becoming a better climber. If you simply write off the failure as "not being strong enough," you miss out on the lesson. Strive to dig deeper and identify the true cause of each failure—is it poor technique, poor strategy, bad sequencing, fear and doubt, or maybe just a lack of "go for it"?

The very best climbers, or peak performers in any field, tend to be uncommonly curious individuals. They are always on the outlook for new information, distinctions, or ideas that will help elevate their game, and they possess an intense curiosity as to why they sometimes fail. By training yourself to respond to failure in a similar way, you will gain some of the personal power of these elite performers. The bottom line: Don't curse your falls, embrace them! They are guideposts and stepping-stones to the higher grades.

Managing Fear

Climbing is a great proving ground to develop mental skills for the rest of your life. Given the safe environment of a gym, there's no reason to not challenge your doubts, your beliefs of what is possible, and, most of all, your fears.

Most common to climbing are the fears of failure and falling. In this section you will learn how to manage or even eliminate these fears, although you will do so with two very different strategies. Defeating fear of failure is an internal battle you'll need to win over your ego, whereas fear of falling can only be dissipated through experience at falling.

Defeating Fear of Falling

It's completely natural to fear falling, just as it is normal to feel fearful in your first-ever attempt to snowboard a black-diamond slope or jump off the high dive. Interestingly, it's not the activity that you actually fear, but instead the unknown of what it will be like. For this reason the fear of black-diamond slopes or the high dive abates with each additional exposure to the situation, because the unknown gradually becomes known. The same is true for the fear of falling—as you become aware of the real risks and log some air time, your fear will slowly dissolve.

Thankfully, an element of this fear remains and

will kick in at times when it's truly needed to save your neck. Based on your experience you'll recognize a situation that presents a potentially dangerous fall, and you'll be able to heed the warning of this legitimate fear.

Now let's take a look at two strategies for lessening your fear of falling: risk management and the act of taking practice falls.

ANALYZE AND MANAGE REAL RISKS

This first step in dealing with fear is to identify and mitigate legitimate fears while you dispel the illusionary ones. For example, fear of taking a ground fall before clipping the first bolt on a lead climb is a legitimate fear. Recognizing this, you can take action to reduce the risk (say, by stick clipping the first bolt or getting a spotter) and thus nix the fear completely. Same goes for a fear of taking a swinging lead fall toward a large protruding hold or wall feature. By analyzing the fall potential and approximating the angle and length of the fall, you can make an intelligent decision as to whether to climb on (and risk the fall) or downclimb to avoid the risk.

Of course, many fears are simply illusions created in the mind of an inexperienced climber. Fear of the belayer not catching your fall and fear of equipment failure are two common phantom fears that haunt many novices. In these cases you must challenge the fearful thoughts and win over them with reason—you *know* the gear is bombproof and you *know* you can trust your belayer (assuming he's a mature, experienced belayer). Silence the voice of such phantom fears by redirecting your thoughts to the moves at hand, and repeat a mantra such as "climb on," "relax," or "do it, do it!"

PRACTICE FALLING

The second strategy for beating the fear of falling requires that you embrace falling in the form of occasional practice falls. As described on page 93, taking a series of controlled lead falls is an effective way to stretch your boundaries on the sharp end. A once-and-done practice fall will do little to erase the fear, however; instead you need to take several falls each session over a period of several weeks. The fear of falling is strong, so it takes a committed effort over time to decondition this emotion. Assume a work-through-it mentality and expect the process to take a few months, if not longer, to yield the desired results. Trust that in taking this bitter medicine, you will eventually develop an indomitable go-for-it mentality that continually prevails over unreasonable fears of falling.

Crushing the Fear of Failure

Fear of failure wields tremendous power over climbers who possess an unbending need for success. Not surprisingly, the fear of failure tends to produce failure as you climb timidly in an attempt to not blow it. Consider how often a football team gives up the winning score when they shift into prevent defense.

In climbing, a try-not-to-fail "prevent defense" results in tentative movement and an apprehension over making tenuous or dynamic moves. Furthermore, it leads you into second-guessing sequences, doubting your ability, and focusing on the possibility of failure. This mental tension manifests itself as shallow breathing, overgripping of holds, jitters, and tense, inefficient movement. Before long, the very thing you are trying to avoid catches up with you.

Interestingly, this fear is completely self-imposed, and thus eliminating it is completely in your hands. Following are two strategies for killing this fear at its roots.

FOCUS ON THE PROCESS, NOT THE OUTCOME

Fear of failure results from an outcome-oriented mind-set that constantly ponders the odds and consequences of success versus failure. Therefore, you can defeat this fear by focusing single-mindedly on the process of climbing and never letting your mind wander to the possible outcomes. Concentrate on the things immediate to your performance, such as precise foot placements, relaxing your grip, moving quickly onto the next rest position, and such. You can accentuate this laserlike focus by sharpening your visual awareness of the holds and wall features before you. Notice the slight variations and imperfections that make each hold unique, and strive for

optimal placement of every hand and foot. If you capture your attention in this way, there will be little opportunity to think about success or failure. Climb in the present!

Any time your thoughts begin to shift away from process orientation, immediately respond by redirecting your thoughts to your breathing. If possible, pause and take a deep breath or two—feel the air rushing in and out of your chest, and your focus will immediately return to the present moment. Once accomplished, return your focus to climbing with a quick study of your current hand- and footholds. This will get you back into the process of climbing with an optimal mind-set.

Acute thought control and a commitment to always having fun are fundamental to climbing your best.
PHOTO COURTESY OF **NICROS, INC.**

PREDETERMINE THAT YOU WILL ACCEPT FAILURE SHOULD IT HAPPEN

A more global approach to permanently deleting the fear of failure is to simply adopt the attitude that it's okay to fail. By willingly accepting this fate (if it should even happen), you totally eliminate the fear and hence liberate yourself to climb to win! Embracing the potential of a negative outcome doesn't mean you aren't going to try your best or that you want to fail. Instead this position simply places you in a frame of mind from which you can try your best to win without reservation.

Of course, gracefully accepting failure is easier said than done for some people. You can only assume this mind-set by consciously detaching your self-image from your performance. This can be difficult in a climbing gym setting, since strangers tend to make first judgments on others based on what they see on the outside—appearance and performance. Your goal, then, must be to recognize that your true friends will like you regardless of your climbing ability, and the opinions of strangers are trivial. Whether or not you can completely embrace this mind-set is a measure of maturity and self-confidence, but striving to possess it is a great mental exercise for developing these traits. Given a long-term effort at assimilating this way of thinking, you will gain mental prowess and free yourself from the chains of needing to perform for others. Ultimately, it's in climbing for yourself—win, lose, or hanging from a quickdraw—that you will feel most happy and indeed climb your very best.

Creating a Peak Performance State

This final section provides a more holistic look at creating a peak performance state from which you can climb your best. The key is being able to dial in your mind, body, and emotions so they work together in perfect harmony and powerful synergy. In sports this optimal state is often referred to as "the zone."

First, you'll learn four key elements to getting into the zone. The most consistent climbers can create and maintain a highly distinct mental climate that transports them into the zone. You, too, will learn how to tap into this powerful state. Following

Tips for Managing Fear

1. Analyze your fears to determine if they are real or imagined. Take action to mitigate the risk(s) associated with your legitimate fears.

2. Overcome imagined fears with reason—know that these phantom fears are bogus. Redirect your thinking in productive ways and resolve to dismiss all other illusionary fears that might surface.

3. Practice falling (in a safe setting) to develop confidence and trust in the belay system. Your long-term goal is to be able to fall trying without fear or reservation (if indeed it's a safe climb).

4. Focus on the process of climbing, and detach from the possible outcomes. Let the climb unfold one move at a time.

5. Predetermine that you will accept failure should it happen. Recognize that you are not defined by your successes or failures—however, you are defined by the way you react to success and failure.

this we'll look at the importance of preclimb rituals for modulating your mind and body for peak performance. Learning to use these mental techniques will surely elevate your performance, regardless of your absolute level of ability.

Getting into the Zone

The zone is a state where everything comes together for the perfect ascent that seems almost effortless and automatic. Unfortunately, the zone is a state that eludes many athletes. The trick is learning to create this state on demand as opposed to just waiting for it to appear.

Think of the zone as a stable platform from which peak performance occurs. Like a table, this platform has four supporting elements or "legs": a relaxed body, confident emotions, a focused mind, and smooth unforced actions. If one or more of these legs are missing, the table will tip and the zone will be unattainable. This, of course, is the typical situation for many climbers who fail to quash tension, doubts, distractions, and apprehension. The end result is a performance roller coaster where the quality of climbing varies from route to route and day to day.

Following are strategies for solidifying the four supporting elements and getting into the zone more often!

RELAXING YOUR BODY

We've already discussed that you climb most efficiently when you are physically loose and experiencing no excess muscular tension. This is especially important in attempting to climb near your limit, when even the slightest muscular tension will erode fine motor control, drain energy reserves, and most likely lead to failure. Peak performance requires that your muscles feel warm, loose, and free of tension. The best way to achieve this state is to climb a few submaximal warm-up routes that get your blood flowing, yet don't pump you out. Routes two to four number grades below your redpoint level are ideal. After completing these routes take off your climbing shoes and perform several minutes of gentle stretching. This combination of warm-up climbs and stretching will prime your body to enter the zone.

Any remaining tension can be eliminated with the ANSWER Sequence described on page 105. After you've put your climbing shoes on and tied into the rope, spend a minute or two on the ANSWER Sequence and you'll be able to optimize your physical state before starting the route.

BUILDING CONFIDENT EMOTIONS

Self-confidence is a positive mental attitude and anticipation of a successful outcome. Climbing up to your abilities and, for that matter, pushing your limits cannot happen without sufficient self-confidence. On the other hand, an overconfident *I'll-try-anything disposition* will eventually lead to frustration and failure. Let's sort things out.

You develop self-confidence in proportion to your experience, training, and past successes. Therefore, building self-confidence begins with logging many hours on the rock as well as a steady string of successes on routes of increasing difficulty.

Similarly, engaging in a consistent, intelligent training program that improves upon known weaknesses will also build confidence.

Finally, there's positive self-talk and imagery to further fortify confidence. Statements such as "I'm well prepared," "I'll do great," and "This will be fun" will foster positive emotions. Likewise, visualization can be a powerful confidence builder. Close your eyes and spend a minute or two reliving a past great ascent. By *feeling* the emotions of that past success, you tap into this powerful resource to empower you in the present moment.

FOSTERING FOCUS

Entering the zone demands a steady, laserlike focus. Precise motor skills and synchronized movements require a tight focus; even a brief break in concentration can result in a botched sequence or fall. Narrowing your focus requires a combination of positive energy and a still mind. Any anxiety or distractions will shatter your focus and make getting into the zone impossible.

A detailed preclimb ritual (to be discussed in the next section) is one of the best strategies for fostering focus. Engaging in a series of preparatory activities—such as scoping the route, tying into the rope, and visualizing a successful ascent—conditions the mind to block out distractions and zero in on the task at hand. Similarly, going through the six-step ANSWER Sequence can help to further sharpen focus.

In order to understand how to maintain focus, you must understand that distractions are the enemy of focus. Therefore, anything you can do to eliminate distractions before beginning a climb will help foster focus. While climbing, the ultimate goal is to let the rest of the world disappear from your conscious. Narrowing your world to just you and the climb is the essence of focus.

TRYING SOFTER AND LETTING IT FLOW

Elite athletes often tell of how their best performances somehow seemed effortless or automatic. These experiences describe what is known as "the flow state." You can best access this state by detaching

Focused like a laser beam, Chris Sharma on-sights the finals route to win the 2005 ABS Sandfest.

PHOTO BY **ERIC J. HÖRST**

yourself from the past and future, and engaging the route without apprehension. It's also vital that you avoid pressing or trying too hard and instead let your natural climbing skills surface.

Anytime you begin to struggle with a sequence, ease up on the accelerator and assume a "try-softer" approach. If possible, downclimb a few moves to regain a stance so that you can gather yourself. Take a few deep belly breaths and try to return to a relaxed, confident state before you resume climbing. Sometimes you may not be able to downclimb, so you will need to make a few try-softer adjustments on the fly. Begin with a single deep breath, and then focus on improving your foot placements and softening your grip on the handholds. This entire process should take just ten to fifteen seconds, but it's vital for regaining control and fostering flow. Now continue climbing briskly, with confidence and style.

The Power of Preclimb Rituals

The things you think and do in the minutes leading up to a climb largely predetermine the quality of your performance. Rushed preparations and scattered thoughts usually give birth to a shaky performance, whereas detailed, careful preparation and targeted thinking tend to yield a solid, if not exceptional, performance. This exemplifies the power of preclimb rituals.

There are two parts to an effective preclimb ritual: proceeding through a preparatory checklist and the triggering of emotional anchors. The checklist covers all must-do physical tasks in the minutes leading up to the climb, while the leveraging of emotional anchors is a final mental step before launching up the route.

PRECLIMB CHECKLIST

Like a pilot's preflight checklist, a climber's preclimb ritual should consist of every single activity, big or small, that is necessary to ensure a safe, successful journey. For example, my typical preclimb ritual begins with scoping the route to determine the best path and, hopefully, figure out the key moves and rest positions. Next, I perform a couple of minutes of

mental rehearsal and visualization as I try to feel the moves and preprogram in the sequence. Upon gaining a sense of comfort and knowing about the route, I put on my shoes and tie into the rope. I complete my preclimb ritual by taking a few slow, deep breaths, straightening my posture, and cracking a smile in anticipation of a great climb. This entire ritual typically takes between three and ten minutes (depending on the difficulty and length of the climb), and it leaves me in an ideal state to make my best effort.

Develop your own unique rituals based on what makes you feel most prepared and psyched for a route. Think back to some of your best past performances to gain some clues as to what to include. What did you think and do in preparing for that climb? What did you eat or drink, how did you warm up, and how long did you rest between climbs? Awareness of all the factors—little and big—that lead up to your best performances is a key to being able to reproduce similar results in the future.

Experiment with different rituals and analyze what seems to work best. An effective preclimb rit-

Tips for Creating a Peak Performance State

1. Trust your abilities and don't anticipate the outcome.

2. Develop and use a preclimb routine before every ascent. Scope the route, analyze and mitigate potential risks, identify the keys to the route, and visualize the ascent.

3. Leverage past ascents to create positive energy and fortify confidence in the present moment. Reliving past successes in your mind's eye taps this valuable resource for use in the present.

4. Double-check your harness bucket, knot, and the belayer's device, and then trust the system implicitly.

5. Relax, crack a smile, and have fun climbing!

ual doesn't need to be extravagant or long. In fact, a short, concise ritual that quickly gets you prepared and focused to climb is best. Upon developing a ritual that works, stick to it!

EMOTIONAL ANCHORS

Emotional anchors are powerful triggers for peak performance. Have you ever experienced the relaxed pleasure that washes over your mind and body when you hear an old song that instantly connects you to some great past event? This experience exemplifies the power of anchors at transporting past emotions into the present. Your brain associates the song with the emotional state of a distinct period earlier in your life; upon hearing that tune, these emotions are relived in the present. Knowledge of this process empowers you to recall the positive emotions of a previous ascent to aid your performance in the present.

If you've been climbing awhile, you should have a few "perfect" ascents that you can leverage in this way. If not, then tap into some other great life event where you felt exceedingly confident, positive, and successful. Either way, your goal now is to relive this event by creating a brief mental movie that brings as many senses as possible into play. Most people find that bright, crisp visualization is the most effective way to trigger past emotions; however, listening to a particular song can be a powerful anchor, too. Experiment a little in order to discover what works best for you. Be creative and overlook no details in reliving the past event, and you'll learn to consistently release powerful emotions that yield great performances.

CHAPTER NINE

Getting into Climbing Shape

We cannot lower the mountain, therefore we must elevate ourselves.

—*Todd Skinner, prolific American climber and motivational speaker*

Climbing provides an excellent physical workout that will definitely pump you up. Thus the first step to getting into climbing shape is simply to climb on a regular basis. An hour or two at the climbing gym, three or four days per week, will increase your general level of fitness as well as producing rapid gains in climbing-specific strength. Cancel your health club membership and make indoor climbing your workout of choice!

While climbing offers the most specific training for climbing, there are several good reasons to also engage in supplemental training. First, a modest amount of aerobic training will benefit your climbing measurably by improving stamina and lowering percent body fat (more on this in a moment). Similarly, it would be advantageous for a novice who lacks the base strength needed to learn fundamental climbing moves (can you do ten pull-ups?) to perform some climbing-specific training of the pull muscles. Finally, some basic push-muscle training will help to prevent muscular imbalances (and reduce the injury risk) that can result from regularly pulling plastic at the gym.

As you progress into the realm of being an intermediate and advanced climber, you will also need to begin some highly targeted training beyond the aforementioned general conditioning. Success at the lofty grades of 5.11 and above often demands spe-cialized strength skills such as the ability to lock off on one arm, hang on a two-finger pocket, or throw a long lunge. Such physical attributes are best developed with a blend of climbing and intelligent training for climbing.

Given the many physical constraints to climbing performance outlined above, you may wonder: Why has it taken until chapter 9 to dig into the subject of fitness training? My answer comes in two parts that I hope you will take to heart and hold as fundamental principles during your formative days as a climber. First, during your initial months learning to climb, you will get enough of a muscular workout simply by climbing a few days per week; premature use of highly stressful exercises, such as the fingerboard, may lead to injury. Second, the steep learning curve of climbing technique means you will make the fastest gains in absolute ability by investing your available workout time into actual climbing versus taking away from climbing time to engage in strength training. The bottom line: For a beginner, climbing *is* the best training for climbing. Therefore, vow to make paramount the learning of climbing techniques, tactics, and strategy (the subjects of chapters 1 through 8) and you will be on the fast track to become a skilled, successful, and strong climber!

General Conditioning

Can you pinch an inch around your waist? Is it a major struggle to touch your toes while keeping your legs straight? Does it take a Herculean effort—or miracle!—to do ten consecutive pull-ups? If you answered yes to one or more of these questions, then you are in need of some general conditioning.

General conditioning focuses on developing the physical foundation needed to learn the fundamental climbing skills described throughout this book. The goal is to optimize body composition, increase flexibility, and build a base level of muscular strength. Let's take a look at effective training for each.

Optimizing Body Composition

If you've ever hiked with a heavy pack or carried someone on your back, you've experienced the negative effects of increased weight on physical performance. Conversely, a reduction in percent body fat or excessive nonfunctional muscle mass can have a positive effect on performance, especially in a sport such as climbing where a high strength-to-weight ratio is fundamental.

The optimal body fat percentage is 6 to 12 percent for men and 8 to 16 percent for women. If you're not sure how you measure up, consider having your body fat tested. Or you can use the economic pinch-an-inch method on your waistline (actually a good gauge). If you can pinch an inch (or more), you are not in the optimal range.

Similarly, excessive muscular weight is about as bad as excessive fat. In fact, since muscle weighs more than fat per unit volume, large muscles in the wrong place are worse than fat. Inappropriate training is the usual cause of unwanted muscle. For instance, the leg exercises performed by bodybuilders or bike racers are a waste of time for climbers since lack of leg strength is rarely a limiting factor on the rock. Biceps curls and heavy bench-press exercises will likewise have a negative impact on climbing performance. Sure, they will pump you up nicely for the beach, but they will also weigh you down on the rock. Fortunately, you can strip away unwanted fat and excessively bulky muscles with disciplined diet and aerobic exercise.

The dietary strategy is to reduce empty calories from junk foods and high-fat fast foods, while maintaining a steady consumption of protein and carbohydrate. The ideal macronutrient caloric breakdown for an athlete is 65 percent carbohydrate, 15 percent protein, and only 20 percent fat. Consequently, you can toss out the high-fat fad diets such as the Zone or Atkins—these are absolutely the wrong diet

strategies for a serious athlete!

An active male desirous of some weight loss might restrict his total dietary intake to around 2,000 calories per day (up to 50 percent more on extremely active days). This would break down to about 320 grams of carbohydrate, 80 grams of protein, and 45 grams of fat. Similarly, an active female wanting to drop a few pounds should limit total daily food consumption to about 1,500 calories (up to 30 percent more on extremely active days), striving for a macronutrient breakdown of around 240 grams of carbohydrate, 60 grams of protein, and 35 grams of fat. Upon achieving desired climbing weight, gradually increase caloric intake to determine the appropriate consumption to maintain a stable body weight.

Regarding aerobic exercise, running is by far the most effective method of incinerating fat and shrinking unwanted muscle. Don't worry about losing your climbing muscles, however; they will be preserved as long as you continue to climb regularly and consume at least 1 gram of protein per kilogram of body weight per day. Other popular aerobic activities such as steep mountain biking and the StairMaster will yield mixed results: They do eat up body fat, but they also tend to maintain (or build) undesirable leg muscle. Swimming or fast hiking are good alternatives, if you can't run.

Frequency of aerobic training should be proportional to the magnitude of your weight loss goal. For example, if you are significantly overweight, then daily twenty- to forty-minute runs are an important part of your training-for-climbing program. As you near ideal weight, two or three twenty-minute runs per week are sufficient. Upon reaching your optimal weight, very little aerobic training is necessary since indoor climbing requires only modest aerobic fitness. At this point, your training time is better invested on actual climbing and supplemental sport-specific exercises.

Improving Flexibility

While extraordinary flexibility is not needed in climbing, a modest degree of suppleness is necessary for fundamental techniques such as high-stepping, stemming, and heel hooking. Fortunately, just climbing a few days per week provides active stretching that will gradually increase lower-body flexibility. You can expedite the gains in flexibility with supplemental stretching exercises performed as part of your warm-up and cool-down activities. In fact, it's beneficial for all climbers, regardless of their natural level of flexibility, to engage in a few minutes of stretching to prepare the body for the stresses of climbing and help reduce injury risk.

It's important to understand that warm-up stretching should always be gentle and nonpainful, since forceful or ballistic stretching can injure muscles, tendons, and joints. Similarly, intense stretching of a cold muscle can be disastrous, so it's ideal to perform a few minutes of light exercise before stretching. For example, a few minutes of jogging, fifty jumping jacks, or a couple of fast-paced, up-and-down laps on a very easy route will increase your heart rate and warm the muscles for effective stretching.

Following are ten stretches to employ as part of your warm-up routine. Spend about one minute on each stretch, and you'll be ready to begin your climbing workout. It may be beneficial to perform some additional stretching on rest days if you feel that lack of flexibility is a constraint in your climbing.

FINGER AND FOREARM FLEXORS

This is the most basic stretch for climbers, since it works the forearm muscles that enable finger flexion and your grip on the rock. Before doing this stretch, perform twenty finger curls—quickly open and close your hands as if you were flicking water off your fingertips. Now, straighten the arm to be stretched and lay the fingertips (pad-side down) into the palm of the opposite hand. Pull back on the fingers/hand of the straight arm until you feel the stretch begin. Perform this stretch in two positions—with the thumb pointing inward and with it turned outward. Hold each stretch for ten to fifteen seconds.

Finger and Forearm Flexors

Fingers pointing up.

Fingers pointing down.

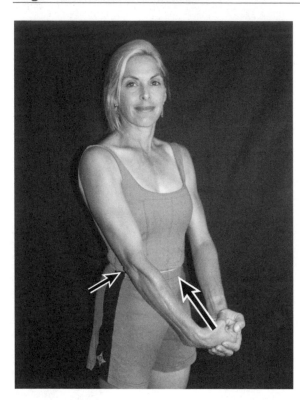

Fist pulled inward.

Forearm rotated to work stretch.

FINGER AND FOREARM EXTENSORS

This is a vital yet often overlooked stretch that can help prevent elbow tendinitis. Begin by straightening the arm to be stretched, then make a fist and place it in the palm of the other hand. Gently pull the fist inward so as to bend at the wrist and feel the stretch along the muscles of the back of your forearm. Hold the stretch for fifteen to twenty seconds, during which time you rotate your forearm to work the stretch with your fist turned upward, inward, and downward. Perform this stretch two times with each arm.

SHOULDER AND UPPER BACK

This is a great stretch for the shoulder and upper-back muscles used in climbing overhanging walls.

Raise your arms to a position parallel to the floor and grab behind the elbow of the arm to be stretched. Pull your elbow across your chest toward the opposite shoulder. While still pulling, slowly move the elbow slightly up and down to work the stretch.

UPPER ARM AND BACK

Yet another key stretch that works the large pulling muscles of your back as well as the upper arm. With arms overhead and bent at the elbows, grab one elbow and pull it behind your head until you feel a stretch in the back of the upper arm and shoulder. Finish by slowly leaning sideways in the direction of the stretch to extend it below the shoulder and into the lat muscles.

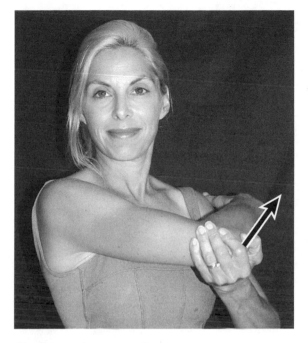

Shoulder and upper back.

Upper arm and back.

KNEE TO CHEST

This stretch helps loosen the often tense muscles of the lower back, thus enhancing your high-step ability. Lay flat on the floor and pull one knee toward your chest while keeping the other leg straight. Pull the leg until you feel stretching in the back of your leg, buttocks, and lower back. Hold this position for twenty to thirty seconds, then stretch the other leg.

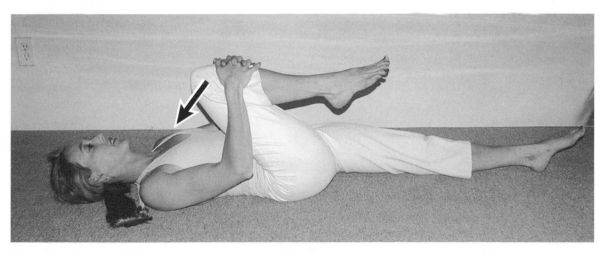

Knee to chest.

Getting into Climbing Shape

Back of leg.

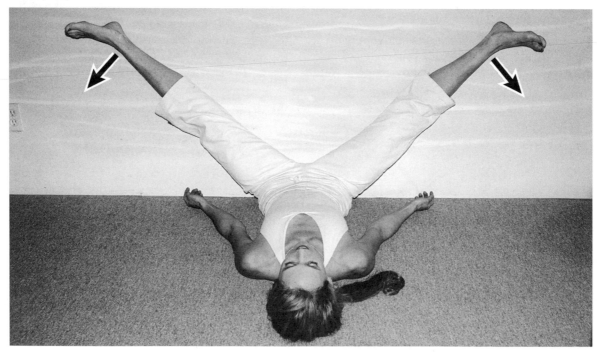

Wall split.

BACK OF LEG

The often tight muscles along the back of the leg are important to loosen up before climbing. Lie flat on your back with one leg straight and the other bent with the sole of the foot flat on the floor next to the opposite knee. Lift the straight leg upward, grab behind the thigh, and pull gently forward until you feel the stretch down the back of the leg. Hold this stretch for twenty to thirty seconds.

WALL SPLIT

This is an excellent passive stretch of the legs, hips, and groin that will enhance your ability to **stem**, or bridge between two widely spaced footholds. Lie on the floor with your buttocks about 6 inches from a wall and your legs extending straight up the wall with a 90-degree bend at the hips. Slowly separate your legs by sliding your heels out to the side.

Concentrate on relaxing throughout your body and allow gravity to extend the split. (It helps to wear socks so that your feet slide more easily down the wall.) Hold this split position for one to two minutes.

BUTTERFLY

This stretch works the hip turnout so crucial for climbing near-vertical walls. Lie flat on your back and place the soles of your feet together with your legs bent about three-quarters of the way. Relax and allow gravity to pull your knees toward the floor. Keep your spine straight and flat on the floor, and hold the stretch for one to two minutes.

ABDOMINAL STRETCH

This simple stretch works many of the core muscles of your torso that are so important in climbing. Lying flat on your stomach, press your shoulders away

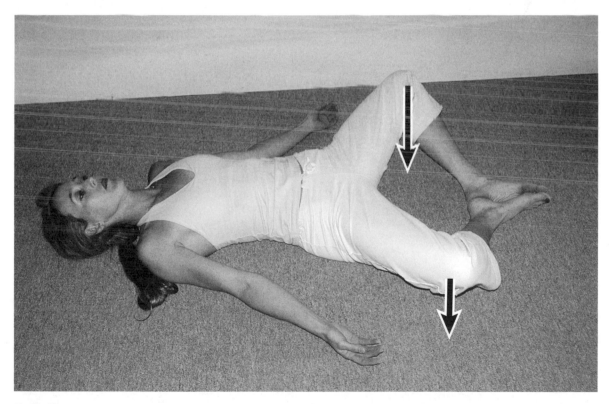

Butterfly.

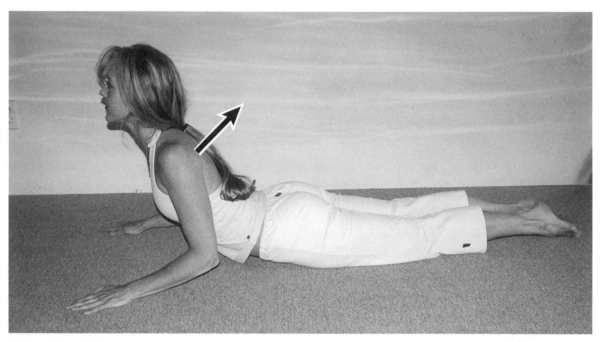

Abdominal stretch.

Calf stretch.

from the floor while keeping your legs and pelvis in contact with the floor (it helps to contract your buttocks to reduce stress on the lower back). Relax and allow the curve of your spine to extend up through your upper back and neck—go easy at it, especially if you have any history of back problems. Hold the stretch for fifteen to twenty seconds, relax, and repeat.

CALF STRETCH

In climbing, the calf muscles are the under-recognized workhorse that supports all the constant foot edging and front pointing. Stretching these muscles before and after each climbing session is important to enhance performance and recovery, respectively. Start on all fours and walk your hands and feet together until the angle formed at your hips is about 90 degrees. Relax one leg, moving it slightly forward, while keeping the rear leg straight. Hold the rear heel to the floor and move your hips forward/backward to regulate the tension of the stretch. Hold for twenty to thirty seconds and repeat. Alternatively, you can perform this stretch by leaning forward against a wall and similarly stretching the back of your lower legs.

Basic Pull-Muscle Strength Training

Learning to climb requires a modest level of base strength in order to move up the wall and learn climbing technique. Assess your level of base strength with the following fitness tests. Can you do: five to ten pull-ups, fifteen hanging (from a pull-up bar) knee lifts, and twenty abdominal crunches? A no answer to any of these questions indicates a need for some supplemental strength training. Such basic training is also beneficial if you cannot climb at least three days per week.

What kind of general strength-training program is best for a novice climber? You might engage in a standard health-club-style circuit-training program for a few months, although this is not the type of training-for-climbing program you'd want to engage in long-term. Understand that your workout needs to be more tailored to climbing, and of course the motions of a typical weight-lifting or bodybuilding workout have little in common with climbing. So while you may initially utilize a health club workout to get in shape, you should gradually transition into a more sport-specific training routine as your general fitness improves.

The pull muscles of the arms and back are typically the first muscles to pump out while climbing, so they are the focus of your strength training. As explained earlier, poor climbing technique and mental anxiety lead to excessive use of these muscle groups and premature failure. Therefore, you can rapidly increase your apparent strength in these areas by working to improve climbing technique. Still, some supplemental pull-muscle training is quite useful, especially if you can't make it to the climbing gym as often as you'd like.

In formulating an effective pull-muscle workout for climbing, it helps to consider what exercises are most specific to the motions of our sport. For example, pull-ups are far more similar to climbing movements than are biceps curls. Similarly, **fingerboard** exercises are extremely specific to the way you grip the rock in climbing, whereas the various handheld squeezers are not. Thus, fingerboard training will translate to better climbing performance, while squeezing one of the handheld toys will primarily make you better at, well, squeezing that toy!

Following are five excellent exercises for strengthening the pull muscles as well as the supporting core muscles of the torso. Perform these exercises three days per week, either at the end of a climbing session or as a replacement for climbing when it's not possible to get to the gym.

PULL-UPS

Perform your training on a pull-up bar, or the bucket hold of a fingerboard, or a set of free-hanging Pump Rocks. Train only in the palms-away position (the way you usually grip the rock) and with your hands initially at shoulder-width. Perform three to five sets to failure with a three-minute rest between sets. As your pull-up strength improves, begin to vary the distance between your hands to better simulate the wide range of hand positions you'll encounter in climbing.

A pull-up on the bucket holds of the Nicros NexGen hangboard.

AIDED PULL-UPS

If you are unable to do five consecutive pull-ups, employ one of these two powerful strategies. Place a chair below the pull-up bar and step up into a lock-off position with the bar just below your chin. Remove your feet from the chair and hold the lock-off for five seconds before slowly lowering yourself toward the straight-armed position. Immediately step back up on the chair to the top lock-off position and repeat the process exactly. Do five total repetitions, and then rest for five minutes. Perform two to three sets.

The second strategy is simply to have a spotter hold around your waist and lift a portion of your body weight so that you can do eight to ten less-than-body-weight pull-ups. Do three sets in this manner with a five-minute rest in between. Use these training strategies three days per week, and you'll be surprised how fast your pull-up strength improves.

LAT PULL-DOWNS

Do this in place of, not in addition to, pull-ups. This is the one weight-training exercise in which you can load on weight without limit. Select a weight that allows you just six to twelve high-intensity repetitions. Perform three to five sets to failure with a three-minute rest between sets. Vary the distance between your hands with every set.

Lat pull-down machine. Vary hand spacing, and pull the bar down to your chest.

PHOTOS BY **RANDY LEVENSALER** © 2005.
WWW.LEVENSALER.COM

HANGING KNEE LIFTS

This is a strenuous exercise that works the lower abdominals, hip flexors, and many of the core muscles of the torso. Hanging from a pull-up bar, the bucket holds of a fingerboard, or a set of Pump Rocks, lift your knees up to your chest, allowing your legs to bend naturally with the motion. Now lower your legs slowly until they return to a slightly bent position (not straight) and immediately begin the next upward repetition. Continue this knee-lift motion until failure. You goal should be two sets of twenty-five repetitions. It's important to maintain some tension in your shoulders and concentrate on the feeling of a stiff upper body while your abs are contracting and lifting the knees to the chest.

ABDOMINAL CRUNCHES

Perform this floor exercise with your feet up on a chair and knees bent at about 90 degrees. Cross your arms over your upper chest or place your hands

Hanging Knee Lift

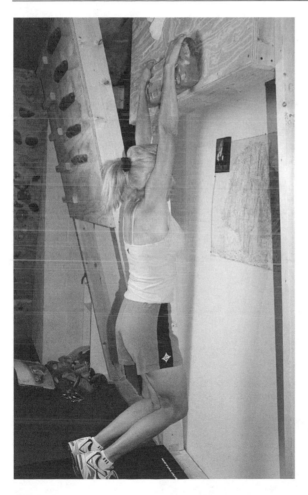

1. Begin with a slight bend at the hips and knees.

2. Lift the knees to chest level.

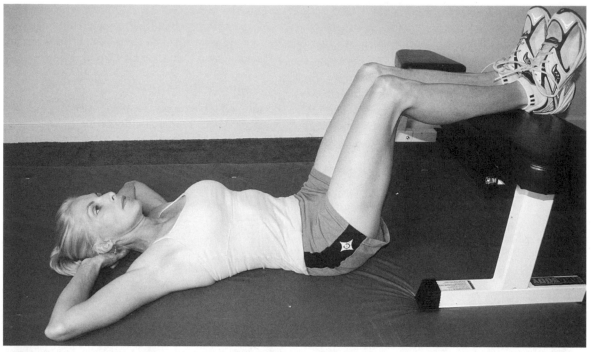

1. Cross your arms over your upper chest or place your hands behind your head (harder), but do not interlace your fingers behind your neck.

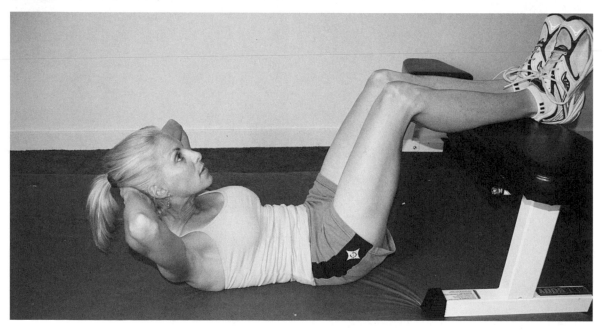

2. Lift your shoulders off the floor and exhale as you "crunch" upward.

behind your head (harder), but do not interlace your fingers behind your neck. Now lift your shoulders off the ground and exhale as you "crunch" upward. The range of motion for this exercise is small—the goal is to lift your shoulders and upper back off the floor, but *not* to ascend the whole way as in doing an old-school sit-up. Continue at a modest pace for twenty-five to fifty repetitions, then rest for approximately two minutes before doing a second set.

Antagonist-Muscle Training to Prevent Injury

While climbing provides a rigorous workout for the pull muscles, it demands much less of the antagonist push muscles of the chest, shoulders, and upper arms. In the long term this could lead to tendinitis or other injuries, as these stabilizing push muscles may fall out of balance with their opposing pull muscles. The two most common problem spots are the elbows and shoulders. Let's take a quick look at each.

First, consider how climbing ceaselessly works the finger-flexor muscles of the forearms, yet does little to strengthen the extensor muscles on the outside of your forearms. As a result, climbers tend to develop a significant muscular imbalance and a susceptibility to lateral epicondylitis—a painful tendinitis on the outside portion of the elbow (also known as tennis elbow). As many as one in four climbers will eventually suffer from this affliction, although you can greatly reduce your chances by performing a simple preventive exercise. Reverse wrist curls with a light dumbbell will strengthen the extensor muscles on the back of the forearm. Perform this exercise, along with stretching of the forearm muscles, before and after every climbing workout; chances are you'll dodge the elbow tendinitis bullet.

The shoulders are another common site of injury, especially among climbers with a preference for overhanging walls and steep, severe boulder problems. Climbs of this nature place great leverage and strain on the shoulder joint, and it's the push muscles of the chest and shoulder area that help maintain stability. Of course, climbing does a poor job at strengthening these vital muscles. The upshot, for some unfortunate climbers, is that shoulder instability can lead to tendinitis, subluxation (partial or complete dislocation), or rotor cuff injury. Again, the use of a few basic push-muscle exercises will help maintain balance and, hopefully, keep you injury-free. Push-ups, dips, and dumbbell shoulder presses are three exercises I advocate for this purpose. Two or three sets each, twice per week, is usually enough to keep the push muscles in condition to do their job. (Should you possess an existing shoulder injury, however, please consult a physical therapist for more appropriate rehabilitation exercises.)

LIGHT SHOULDER PRESS

Using two dumbbells or a health club machine, perform two to three sets of twenty to twenty-five repetitions, twice per week. Total resistance should be limited to between 20 and 40 percent of your body

Shoulder press.

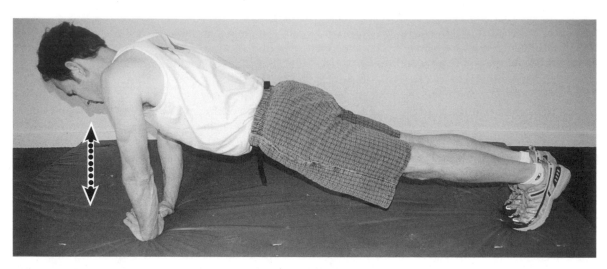

Push-up. Move your hands closer together to increase difficulty.

Dips on Free-Floating Pump Rocks

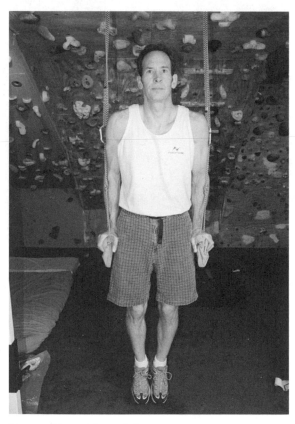

Top position with straight arms.

Bottom position with 90-degree bend at the elbows.

weight. If you plan to purchase dumbbells, I'd suggest women purchase two ten- or fifteen-pounders and men purchase two twenty- or thirty-pounders—there is no need to go much heavier.

PUSH-UPS OR LIGHT BENCH PRESS

Perform two to three sets of standard push-ups, twice per week. The goal is twenty to twenty-five push-ups per set. If you can do more than twenty-five repetitions, increase the difficulty by moving your hands closer together. If you have access to a bench-press machine, follow the same guidelines as in doing the shoulder press. Keep the total weight less than 50 percent of your total body weight—go much heavier and you risk adding unnecessary muscle mass that will only weigh you down while climbing.

DIPS

Dips are an excellent exercise for strengthening the many muscles of the upper arm, shoulders, chest, and back. Of course, the dip motion is similar to that of pressing out a mantle on the rock, so you have double the reason to perform this exercise twice per week. Most health clubs have a parallel bar setup ideal for performing dips. Similarly, you may be able to position two heavy chairs or even use an incut 90-corner of a kitchen counter to perform your dips. A good alternative for use in a home gym is a set of free-floating Pump Rocks, on which you can perform dips as well as various pull-up exercises.

If you haven't done dips before, you will discover that they are surprisingly difficult. Initially, shoot for doing two sets of six to ten repetitions, but strive for the eventual goal of fifteen to twenty reps. In the meantime employ a spotter to help lift around the waist (reduce body weight) so you can achieve at least six dips per set.

REVERSE WRIST CURLS

This exercise is mandatory for all climbers, in order to maintain forearm muscle balance and prevent injury. Using a five- to twenty-pound dumbbell (start light), perform these wrist curls palm-down and with your forearm resting on your knee, a bench, or table. Do approximately twenty half-

Reverse wrist curl.

repetitions; that is, begin with your hand in the neutral position (straight), then curl it upward until it's fully extended. Perform one set as part of your warm-up and two more sets at the end of your workout.

Climbing–Specific Training

The previous section on general conditioning presented a wide range of basic exercises ideal for developing a solid physical foundation for entry-level climbing. Such basic training is appropriate for all climbers from novice up to one year of experience. Beyond a certain ability level, however, more advanced training is required to build the very specific strength needed to break into the higher grades. To this end, the following section on climbing-specific training is all about developing the lock-off strength, power, anaerobic endurance, and contact (finger) strength that are essential for success at climbs rated 5.11 and above.

By definition, climbing-specific training must stress the muscles in ways that are extremely similar to their use in climbing. Furthermore, this advanced protocol must work the muscles at a sufficiently high intensity to trigger neuromuscular adaptations that may not be gained through regular climbing activities. This is a vital distinction—advanced strength training will not be effective unless it targets the climbing muscles at a higher intensity level than they are regularly exposed to while climbing routes. Upcoming are three different methods of achieving this outcome: bouldering as training, high-intensity pull-muscle training, and fingerboard or Pump Rocks training.

Before we move ahead, it's important to point out that the following exercises are not appropriate for a true beginner. While you may begin incorporating a few of these exercises after six months of regular climbing, it's best to hold off on serious climbing-specific training until you have at least a full year of climbing under your belt. Use the material in this chapter as a primer on the subject of advance training, but consult *Training for Climbing* (Falcon's How to Climb series) for comprehensive coverage of advanced training theory and instruction.

Bouldering as Training

Bouldering is arguably the best all-around training method for climbers since it can produce improvement in all three areas of the performance triad: physical, technical, and mental. Without the constraints of the rope and clipping bolts, bouldering allows you to narrow your focus onto the mission of climbing the hardest moves you are capable of doing. From a strength-training perspective, you can also select maximal boulder problems of differing lengths to target training of maximum strength and power (problems with less than ten hand movements), or anaerobic endurance (ten to forty hand movements), or endurance (greater than forty hand movements). In doing so, it is best to choose nontechnical routes that will test your physical capabilities, not your technique. Recognize that failure on a boulder problem because of technical limitations, not muscular failure, means that you have also failed to effectively train the muscles for strength gains.

Consider that in bouldering, it's the upper-body pull muscles and the forearms that take the brunt of the workout. With these muscles in mind, predetermine a purpose for a given session: to train for maximum strength and power, or to train for anaerobic endurance. Following are training guidelines for each type of workout.

TRAINING MAXIMUM STRENGTH AND POWER

Short, steep, high-intensity bouldering problems are the ticket for training maximum strength and power. The ideal problem should be hard enough to require a maximal physical effort, not necessarily a perfect technical effort—remember, the goal here is to train strength. In terms of length, select a route of between eight and twelve hand movements that will not allow you to rest and chalk up midroute. Each bouldering problem should be a definitive, continuous muscular effort that quickly zaps your finger strength and upper-body power. Your goal is to do six to twelve boulder problems or an equal total of laps on the same problem. Rest for at least three minutes between sets, so that you feel reasonably fresh and can make a strong effort on each set.

You can increase the efficacy of this program by selecting—or better yet, setting—a boulder problem that targets a specific move or grip position. For example, a steep problem featuring a series of long reaches between holds would train lock-off strength or lunging power. Or a series of six to twelve small crimp holds would be the ultimate for training crimp-grip strength. You could similarly apply this strategy to train pinch grips, pocket grip, Gaston strength, twist-lock strength, and more. Working such isolation problems is simply the best wall-training strategy for building maximum strength and power.

TRAINING ANAEROBIC ENDURANCE

Anaerobic endurance, also sometimes called AE, strength endurance, or power endurance, is the ability to perform long, continuous sequences of strenuous climbing. Your level of anaerobic endurance is tested on boulder problems or roped climbs possessing between ten and forty difficult hand movements

Short, steep, high-intensity boulder problems are ideal for training maximum strength and power.

without rest. It's this type of steady, near-maximal climbing that triggers the production of lactic acid, and the resultant pump and burning feeling in the forearm muscles.

Interval training is the gold standard for training AE. A staple of serious runners, or any athlete desiring more speed and stamina, interval training should also be a part of any serious climber's training program. Consider how a runner alternates a near-full-speed lap with a slow lap or rest interval; a climber's interval training must similarly cycle near-maximal climbing with brief rest periods. Here's how to do it.

First, forget about working specific boulder

problems—your focus here is to engage in effective interval training, not sending routes. Your interval-training goal is to complete five to ten "burns" with only a two-minute rest in between. Each interval, or burn, should be a continuously strenuous sequence that allows between twenty and forty moves before you *approach* muscular failure. The key here is to stop a few moves short of the forearm muscles reaching complete failure, so that you don't completely soak the muscles in lactic acid. Take exactly a two-minute rest, and then begin your next climbing interval. Consider using a stopwatch to time your rest breaks, or enlist a training partner to join in on the fun! No doubt you will soon discover the physical and mental pain inherent to interval training. In this case, however, the old saying is true: "No pain, no gain." Engage in interval training once or twice per week and you will develop remarkable anaerobic endurance.

High-Intensity Pull-Muscle Training

The standard pull-up has long been a staple exercise for climbers. Several sets of pull-ups performed a few days per week will provide most climbers with a base level of pull-muscle strength needed to learn all the basic climbing techniques. Beyond a certain intermediate level of difficulty, however, climbing requires more specific forms of strength such as the ability to lock off a handhold (to make a long reach) or make a quick, powerful upward movement. Consider the benchmark of being able to do fifteen solid pull-ups and solidly climb 5.10 as the point at which you should graduate to more targeted training of the pull muscles.

Before we dive into the details of three excellent pull-muscle exercises, it is important to reconsider what is exactly the ultimate constraint on your climbing performance. Sure, more pull-up power and lock-off strength is a good thing, but many climbers still fail due to lackluster technique, poor mental control, or simply because they climb too slow. If any of this sounds familiar, it would be wise to invest more training time on your true weaknesses rather than on acquiring more pull-muscle strength.

UNEVEN-GRIP PULL-UPS

This may be the best exercise for developing one-armed strength and lock-off ability. The technique here is to execute the pull-up motion with one hand on the bar and the other holding on to a towel looped over the bar (or with two or three fingers through a loop of webbing). Alternatively, you can use a set of free-floating Pump Rocks hanging in an offset position. Both hands pull, but the upper hand will do a disproportionate amount of the work depending on the vertical separation between hands. Initially, perform uneven-grip pull-ups with one hand about 1 foot below the other, but progress incrementally toward the goal of a 2-foot separation. Do a set to fail-

Uneven-Grip Pull-Ups

1. To start, grasp the Pump Rocks with a 1-foot vertical separation between your hands.

2. Pull up allowing the upper hand to do most of the work. Over time, increase the distance between hands to increase the difficulty.

Lock off the top.

Lock off the middle with an arm angle near 90 degrees.

Lock off low with an arm angle near 120 degrees.

ure, then rest for two minutes and switch sides. Repeat twice. Increase the vertical distance between hands if you can do eight or more reps.

FRENCHIES

Frenchies rule for building anaerobic endurance in the pull muscles—but they're also extremely strenuous and painful, due to the lactic acid release they trigger. The upside of this training technique is the marked improvement in pull-up and lock-off ability that you will undoubtedly notice after just a few weeks of training. Here are the details on these uniquely effective modified pull-ups.

Begin with a single pull-up (palms away, hands shoulder-width apart) and lock off in the top position for a five-second count. Now lower to the bottom and pull up to the top again; this time, however, immediately lower halfway down to an arm angle of 90 degrees. Hold a solid lock-off here for a five-count, then lower to the bottom. Immediately crank another pull-up, but this time lower to a lock-off with an arm angle of about 120 degrees. Again, hold this steady for a true five-second count before lowering to the bottom position. This sequence of three lock-offs constitutes a single cycle, but you should continue on with another cycle (or more) until you reach complete failure. Take a well-deserved five-minute rest between performing a second and third set.

WEIGHTED PULL-UPS

The quickest way to develop maximum strength is by means of my hypergravity training techniques, detailed in *Training for Climbing*. In a nutshell, this technique simulates hypergravity (greater than gravity's natural pull) by means of adding training weight to your body in the form of a ten-pound weight belt. Your neuromuscular system will gradually adapt its maximal pull-up and lock-off capabilities in proportion to your higher apparent body weight. Then, when you return to climbing at normal body weight, you will feel noticeably lighter and climb stronger given this überstrength.

As with the previous exercises, execute weighted pull-ups only on your normal training-for-climbing days, ideally towards the end of the session when your muscles are well warmed. Using a pull-up bar or bucket holds on a fingerboard, perform three to five sets of pull-ups with a ten-pound weight belt (available at most sporting goods stores) around your waist. Rest for at least three minutes between sets, and increase the weight to twenty pounds when you are able to do fifteen repetitions with the ten-pound belt.

Fingerboard Training

The fingerboard, also known as a hangboard, is a staple training tool for use in commercial and home gyms alike. Its popularity should be obvious, given that it addresses the common weakest link to the rock: the fingers. Unfortunately, this simple training tool can be misused (or overused), which can lead to

Grip training on Pump Rocks.

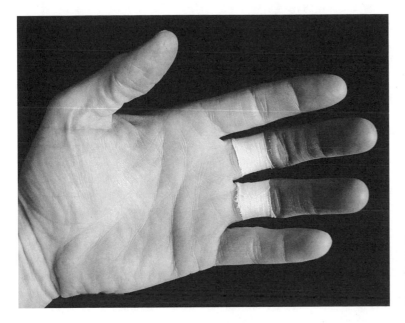

Three firm turns of tape around the base of the fingers may provide some additional support of the commonly injured tendon pulleys of the middle and ring fingers.

finger tendon and elbow injuries. You can best avoid this outcome by employing a fingerboard as just one part of a good training program, not the cornerstone. Furthermore, it's important to reiterate that fingerboard training is inappropriate for novice climbers or anyone with recent incidence of finger, elbow, or shoulder injury.

While the large holds of a fingerboard offer an ideal platform for many of the pull-up exercises presented in this chapter, the focus of this section is use of the board to train grip strength. The genius of a good fingerboard (see top photo on page 124) is the multitude of finger positions and grips that it enables you to train. This is especially useful if you are unable to regularly boulder or climb at a commercial gym. Why not install a fingerboard or set of Pump Rocks at home for some substitute training?

Regardless of where you work out, however, it's imperative that you perform a complete warm-up before commencing with finger training. Begin with a few minutes of light exercise such as jogging around the block or doing fifty jumping jacks. This might seem like a funny way to begin a finger workout, yet it's absolutely vital for elevating your heart rate and core temperature: Warm muscles are less

likely to be injured. Next, perform a few submaximal sets of pull-ups as well as the arm and upper-body stretches described on page 118. Complete the warm-up with some self-massage of the finger and forearm muscles to further loosen the muscles and enhance blood flow for a great workout. Finally, consider reinforcing the tendons at the base of your fingers with a few tight turns of tape (see photo). Following are two excellent fingerboard-training strategies.

TRAINING CONTACT STRENGTH WITH REPEATERS

Repeaters may be the single best fingerboard regimen, because they will build your **contact strength**—initial grip strength upon engaging a handhold. One set of repeaters involves a series of ten maximum-intensity hangs on the same pair of holds. Each hang should last just three to ten seconds, so you may need to wear a ten-pound weight belt (or use smaller holds) to make this a difficult task. Rest just five seconds between each of the ten hangs. The complete set of repeaters should take around two minutes and, of course, lead to a growing forearm pump.

Take a two-minute rest before launching into your next set of ten repeaters. Use a different pair of

Guidelines for Climbing-Specific Training

1. Make bouldering the foundation of your climbing-specific training. It's hard to beat steep-wall bouldering for developing lock-off strength and power.

2. Frequently dedicate entire sessions to training endurance. Climbing laps on submaximal routes and performing long, moderate traverses will build climbing stamina. Employ interval training on a bouldering wall to develop high-intensity anaerobic endurance.

3. Commit to regular training of your antagonist muscles. As little as fifteen minutes of push-muscle training, two days per week, will help maintain muscle balance and reduce injury risk.

4. Perform reverse wrist curls as part of *every* climbing session. The health of your elbows depends on it.

5. Err on the side of over-resting, instead of overtraining. Limit yourself to three or four days of climbing and training (in aggregate) per week.

holds for each set of ten repeaters, beginning with your most problematic grips, and then gradually progress to larger holds as you tire. It's also good to vary the grip positions trained to spread out the neuromuscular stimulus. For instance, you might begin with shallow two-finger pockets, then progress to small crimps, narrow pinches, small slopers, shallow three-finger pockets, medium crimps, deep two-finger pockets, medium slopers, medium crimps, and large slopers. Performing one set of repeaters (ten repetitions) for each of these ten grip positions would result in a total of one hundred near-maximal contractions—a pretty good finger workout!

TRAINING ANAEROBIC ENDURANCE WITH PYRAMIDS

Pyramid training simulates the way your forearm muscles might work in climbing a medium-length gym route. In this way, it tends to train forearm endurance over pure strength. As shown in chart 9.1, one run through the Fingerboard Training Pyramid involves seven hangs on the same pair of holds. The

Chart 9.1 Fingerboard Pyramid Training

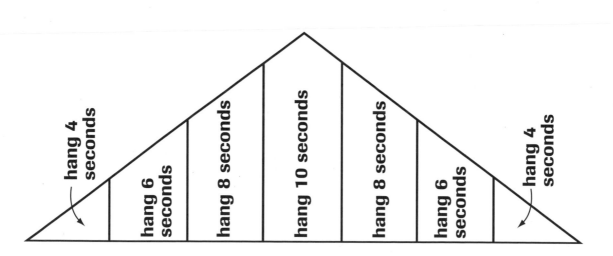

Using the same pair of holds, follow each step precisely with just a five-second rest between each step. That is, hang four seconds, rest five seconds, hang six seconds, rest five seconds, hang eight seconds, and so on.

LEARNING *to* CLIMB INDOORS

rest interval between each hang is only five seconds, so a complete cycle will take just under one and a half minutes. Take a one-minute rest before performing another pyramid cycle on a different set of holds. Your goal is seven to fifteen total sets.

As you progress through the sets, strive to hit all the primary grip positions, including full and half crimps, all the two-finger pocket teams, pinch grips, and open-hand slopers. It's good to vary the size of the holds used for a given set based on your level of fatigue, but be sure to stay on schedule in terms of the timing of your hangs and rest intervals.

Nutrition and Rest

A chapter on getting into climbing shape would be incomplete without a look at performance nutrition and rest habits. This often overlooked subject is especially important for serious, hard-training climbers. Proper nutrition and adequate rest are as important a part of the training-for-climbing equation as the workout itself, because training adaptations—getting stronger!—occur predominantly during rest days and while sleeping. Therefore, if you deny your body the time it needs to fully recover, your body will deny you the gains in strength you had hoped to achieve; you might even slip into the overtraining syndrome (more on this in a bit). Let's first take a look at rest and nutritional requirements for a serious climber.

Rest and Recovery

Complete recovery from a workout typically takes anywhere from twenty-four to seventy-two hours, depending on the intensity and volume of the training and climbing. For example, it might only take one day to recover from a session of easy toprope climbing that failed to produce a major muscular pump. Likewise, recovery from moderate aerobic activities such as running and biking usually takes but twenty-four hours. On the other hand, an evening of high-intensity boulder, pushing your limit on toprope or lead, or advanced training of the pull muscles can take two or three days (sometimes more) to recover from completely.

Consider that the body repairs itself and new

growth occurs primarily while you are asleep. Therefore, the amount of sleep the night of a hard workout is as important as your use of proper training exercises and consumption of sufficient nutrients. The bare minimum amount of sleep per night is seven to eight hours, with nine hours being optimal after an especially hard day of climbing. If you're like most people, that kind of free time is hard to come by, but you might be able to pull it off by giving up some nighttime activities (TV and such) in favor of going to bed earlier. Remind yourself that sleep is an essential part of your training. What are your priorities?

Nutrition

While your muscles can do little rebuilding until you go to sleep, they can begin restocking glycogen (sugar fuel in the muscle) immediately following a workout. You can shorten recovery time by kick-starting this repletion process with a sports drink and some liquid protein. Postworkout is the one time it's good to consume a sugar-based sports drink such as Gatorade. Chase the sports drink with a glass of high-quality protein like Designer Whey (available at all health food stores) and you'll be on the way to accelerating your recovery by as much as 50 percent. Research has shown, however, that you must consume the sports drink and protein within two hours of ending your workout (the sooner, the better) in order to accelerate recovery in this way.

Outside the postworkout period you benefit by eating well-balanced meals comprising low-fat proteins such chicken, fish, or skim milk, along with healthy portions of fruit, vegetables, and whole-grain carbohydrates. Forget everything you've heard about the value of high-fat, low-carbohydrate diets. Such fad diets may help overweight businessmen, desperate housewives, and Aunt Jemima lose some weight, but they are inappropriate and counterproductive for a serious athlete. Carbohydrate is, in fact, the primary source of energy for your training and climbing, so use of a low-carbohydrate diet will leave your muscles flaccid and weak on the rock.

A good nutritional strategy is to consume six smaller meals or snacks spaced evenly throughout the day as opposed to the typical three large meals per day. At least three of your meals should contain a significant portion of protein. For instance, breakfast could include a couple of eggs, skim milk, or whey protein; lunch might include some yogurt, skim milk, or a can of tuna; and for dinner it might be good to eat a piece of lean red meat, chicken, or fish. Each of these meals should also include some carbohydrate in striving to meet the 65/15/20 (carbohydrate/protein/fat) macronutrient profile detailed earlier in the chapter. The other three meals—actually snacks—are vital for maintaining steady blood glucose and continuing the recovery processes 24/7. A piece of fruit, a balanced-type energy bar, or glass of protein drink each makes an excellent choice.

Another important but often overlooked part of the performance nutrition equation is drinking lots of water. Proper cellular function—and peak mental and physical performance—requires full hydration. Make it a goal to drink a minimum of eight glasses of water (two quarts) per day and twice this amount when working or climbing in hot conditions. At the gym, make it a habit to sip water throughout your session at the rate of at least one pint per hour. (If you aren't going to the bathroom regularly, you aren't drinking enough water for optimal performance.)

So what foods should you avoid? Anything highly processed (which will unfavorably spike blood sugar), as well as foods containing a high amount of added sugar or any hydrogenated oils (check labels for "trans fats") whatsoever. Similarly, high-fat fast foods and anything fried should be left out of a serious climber's diet. Save these junk foods as a rare reward after a personal-best send or upon reaching a major training or climbing milestone. As a regular part of your diet, they will hold you back. Again, it's a matter of personal values and priorities—you set the rules!

Finally, in this age of pre-prepared foods, it's quite difficult to consume the vitamins and minerals that you need as an athlete striving for optimal recovery and peak performance. Taking a daily multivitamin each morning is a good first step, though you might further benefit by consuming an extra 500 to 1,000 milligrams of vitamin C and 200 to 400

IUs of vitamin E. Research has shown that both of these vitamins can enhance recovery and overall health in a hard-training athlete.

Avoiding Overtraining Syndrome

The antithesis of getting into climbing shape is the downward spiral of overtraining syndrome. Far too many enthusiastic and good-intentioned climbers have been drawn into the black hole of overtraining. In actuality, overtraining syndrome is often the result of a combination of under-resting and undereating. The bottom line: Climb too often, train too hard, rest too little, and eat a poor diet, and you will eventually slip into overtraining. You'll know that you have crossed into the dark side because you'll begin to feel weaker (not stronger), your climbing ability will plateau (or sink), and you might eventually get injured or sick. If any of this ever begins to sound familiar, view it as a red flag and immediately take a couple of weeks off from all training and climbing.

Of course, it's your goal to avoid this affliction altogether. Here are a few tips to help keep the grim reaper of overtraining at bay. First, keep your training and climbing session reasonable in length so as to not dig yourself too deep a hole from which to recover. Two to four hours of bouldering at the gym should be more than enough to get a good workout. Surely more than half of this time will be spent resting as you belay or spot other climbers, so your actual aggregate amount of climbing time should be more along the lines of sixty to ninety minutes.

On a more macro scale, it's important that you never climb (or train for climbing) more than four days per week. Unlike activities such as bicycle riding or playing golf, which you can engage in daily, subjecting yourself to the stresses of climbing day in and day out will eventually lead to an overuse injury. Three or four days per week at the gym provides plenty of muscular stimulus and motor learning to advance you toward your climbing goals—climbing more than this may actually prevent you from reaching them! Get on a regular training schedule and stick to it. One popular gym climbing schedule is Monday, Wednesday, and Saturday. Another popular schedule is Tuesday, Thursday, Saturday, and Sunday. There

Chart 9.2 Two Sample Workout Schedules

(three days of climbing)

Mon	Tue	Wed	Thur	Fri	Sat	Sun
CL	A/GC	CL	A/GC	Rest	CL	Rest

(four days of climbing)

Mon	Tue	Wed	Thur	Fri	Sat	Sun
A/GC	CL	A/GC	CL	Rest	CL	CL

CL— climbing day and/or climbing-specific training

GC— general conditioning (aerobics, stretching, and so on)

A— antagonist-muscle training

Rest— rest day (no training of any kind)

are many other possibilities. Either way, don't even think about going to the gym on your designated rest days. The only acceptable training on these days of rest from climbing would be aerobic activity, flexibility training, or training of the antagonist push muscles.

You also need to foster an uncommon sense of self-awareness and self-discipline. When you wake up in the morning with sore muscles (known as delayed-onset muscle soreness), it's a sign of microtraumas that will require at least another twenty-four hours for repair and complete recovery. You have two choices in this situation: Go climbing (or work out) for a second straight day, despite the soreness, with reduced performance and increased injury risk. Or take a day or two off and allow your neuromuscular system to recuperate to a level of capability higher than before the initial workout. The latter choice is clearly the more intelligent approach—one that will make you a better, stronger climber in the long run. Sure, you'll probably be okay climbing sore every once in a while, but if it becomes a regular practice, you risk the pitfalls of overtraining. Remind yourself constantly that the goal is to perform an optimal amount of training and climbing, not the maximal amount you can pack into your schedule.

Nutrition and Recovery Tips

1. Plan your workouts and rest days on a calendar, and then stick to the schedule. Any less than three days per week of rest (from climbing and sport-specific training) tempts injury and reduces workout effectiveness.

2. Eat three well-rounded meals per day with a portion of quality protein and carbohydrate in each feeding. Avoid most fast foods, anything that's fried or contains trans fats, as well as any calorie-dense junk foods (except as an occasional reward!).

3. Snack on fruit and balanced-style energy bars between meals and during workouts.

4. Drink at least eight glasses of water per day, and twice this amount in hot conditions. Sip water throughout your climbing session at a rate of one pint per hour.

5. Consider taking a daily vitamin, as well as small supplemental doses of antioxidants such as vitamins C and E.

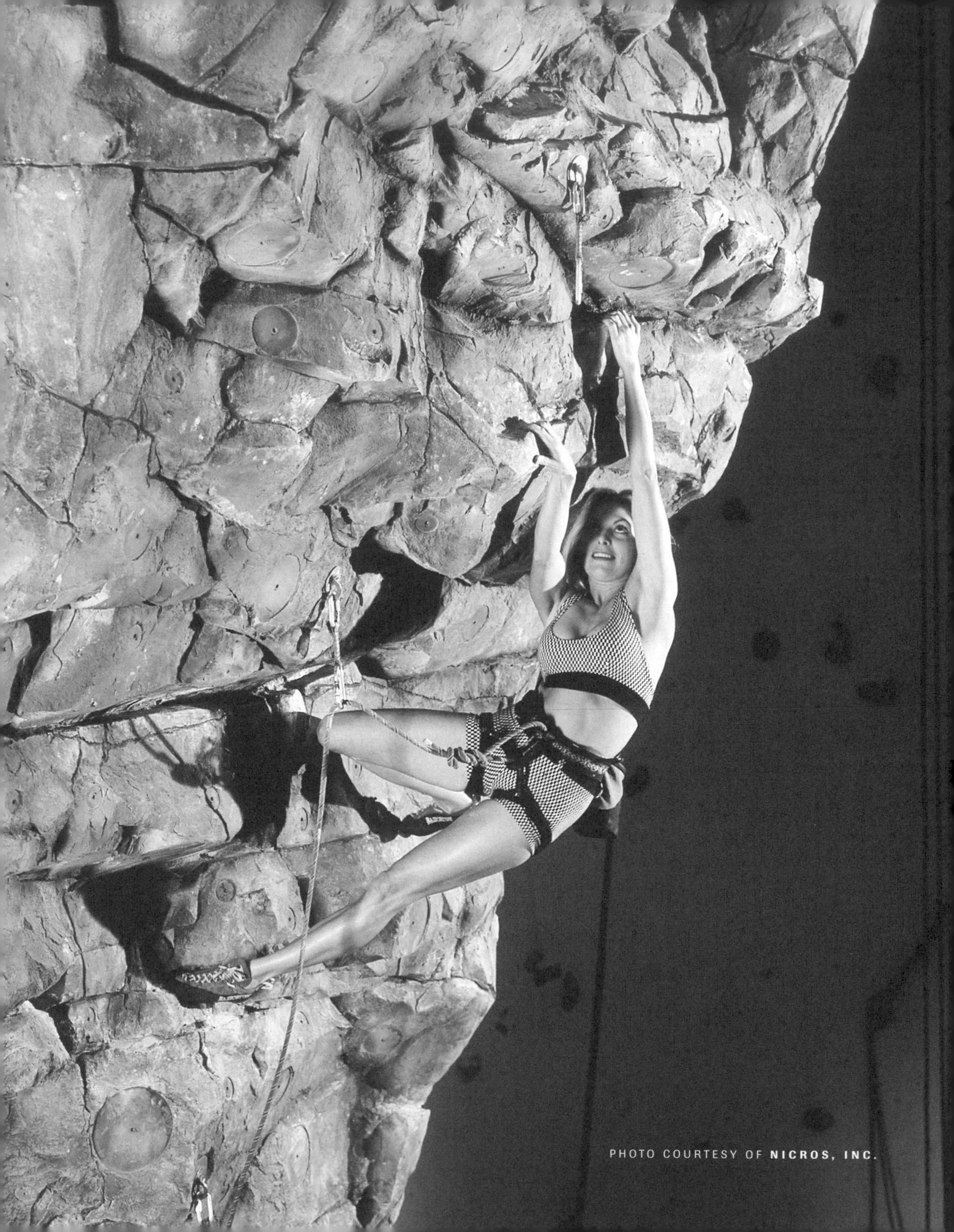
PHOTO COURTESY OF **NICROS, INC.**

10

The Secrets to Climbing Your Best

Climb the mountains and get their good tidings. Nature's peace will flow into you as sunshine flows into trees. The winds will blow their own freshness into you, and the storms their energy, while cares will drop off like autumn leaves.

John Muir, nineteenth-century American naturalist and mountaineer

Your initial days and months of climbing will yield rapid improvement and a corresponding sense of tremendous accomplishment. For this I say, "Kudos to you!"—for challenging your fears, pushing your physical boundaries, and resolving to extend your reach beyond your current grasp.

As a climber of nearly thirty years, I continue to find the experience rewarding and self-revealing. I trust you will, too, as long as you find ways to keep climbing fresh and avoid falling into a rut. If climbing ever becomes just a workout, then you will surely begin to lose interest and eventually look to some other activity for a new challenge. However, this need never be the case with climbing. There are hundreds of different indoor climbing gyms at which to test your mettle as well as myriad outdoor crags to

explore for a challenge should you decide to climb beyond the confines of human-made walls.

In closing this text on learning to climb, I'll reveal a few of the secrets to sustaining your excitement about climbing and maintaining a sense of steady growth. First, we'll examine the keys to staying motivated and upwardly mobile in ability. Next up is a look at the many benefits of building a home training wall. Lastly, we'll take a peek into the unique techniques, risks, and rewards of climbing outdoors. If you love indoor climbing, then you may someday venture outside and discover that real rock climbing is even more gratifying and addictive than pulling plastic indoors.

Create Long-Lasting Motivation

As in doing any sport or activity, if you engage in climbing long enough, you will experience occasional lapses in motivation. Sometimes this drop in desire is the result of a hard, stressful day at school or work. Such temporary motivational troughs affect us all from time to time, and they are something that you just need to resolve to push through. If you can prod yourself to the gym and climb a first route, chances are you will snap out of the funk into a more energetic, positive state. Interestingly, it may be this very state-changing power of climbing that makes it so addictive.

More long-lasting motivational doldrums are often related to a growing dissatisfaction with your climbing. For example, a plateau in performance, a rise in frustration and failures, or a feeling of persistent fatigue or mental stress can all lead to diminished motivation. In some cases these symptoms result from overtraining, as your mind and body begin to run aground. As discussed in chapter 9, excessive climbing and training beyond your body's ability to recover will lead to an unavoidable drop in performance—and possibly to injury. More commonly, however, the reduced motivation is simply the result of a stagnant climbing routine. If you do any activity in the same way, with the same people, at the same time, week after week, it will become monotonous and unexciting. Following are three prescriptions for pumping up your motivation and keeping your climbing sessions fresh, fun, and interesting.

Set Performance Goals

Goals are the ultimate motivator. As a new climber, you have a very clear, specific goal: "to learn to climb." Once you master all the basic techniques and develop a degree of success at climbing, however, you need to set new goals that will maintain a high level of motivation. Performance-related benchmarks are ideal, as they provide an open-ended structure to goal setting. Let's set some performance goals.

The most common type of performance goal is a desired climbing grade to achieve. This month it may be "to climb 5.10"; next month it may be "to boulder V4"; next year it may be "to redpoint 5.12." Similarly, you can set training goals that will pique motivation to achieve the physiological changes you desire. For instance, you might set a goal "to do ten pull-ups" or "to lose five pounds." Training goals are most effective if they are concrete and measurable, as opposed to a less specific goal such as "to improve flexibility." Over many weeks of training, you will see tangible progress toward your performance benchmark, and this will elevate your motivation even more.

The beauty of performance goals is that there is always room for more improvement—technically, physically, and mentally—and you can therefore continue to formulate new goals for the length of your climbing career. Here are five tips for setting effective goals.

1. Write down your goals—this makes them more real and far more achievable. Begin keeping a training notebook or climbing diary in which you can record your goals, workout plan, and climbing accomplishments.

2. Define your goals specifically and with as much detail as possible. While measurable goals are best, it doesn't hurt to set a few style or mental goals such as "to improve footwork" or "to climb with more economy." With such subjective goals, ask a partner or coach to observe your climbing and decide when you have, in fact, achieved the desired style goal.

3. Make your goals lofty and challenging, but keep them realistic. Setting unreachable goals—"to lose ten pounds this week" or "to climb 5.14 by year's end"—is counterproductive and a real motivation killer. Instead set incremental goals that will yield a motivation-generating "win" every few weeks.

4. Set a deadline for the accomplishment of each goal. A goal best inspires you into action when a deadline is affixed to the performance benchmark. Goals such as "achieving ten consecutive pull-ups by year's end" or "bouldering a V5 by my birthday" will light a fire for action—a fire that burns stronger as the deadline nears. Conversely, goals without deadlines are more fuzzy and tend to inspire halfhearted action.

5. Write down one thing that you will sacrifice in order to reach this goal. This final step is vital, and, interestingly, it's a step missing from most traditional goal-setting exercises. Considering what one thing you could give up to help attain your goal is a powerful exercise. This will open your eyes to the reality that achievement doesn't just come by doing more of something or trying harder; it also requires that you eliminate or detach from things that are holding you back.

Begin a Focused Training Program

In your first few months or even year or two of climbing, you will realize steady improvement by just climbing a few days per week and using a handful of basic training exercises. As you become a solid intermediate climber possessing sound mental and technical skills, however, your improvement curve may level off as physiological constraints come to light. This is a common and extremely frustrating situation that most climbers face at some point. Fortunately, most physical constraints can be shattered with an intelligent sport-specific training program.

As stressed in chapter 9, high-intensity sport-specific training is not something to jump hastily into—begun too early in the learning curve, it can have a negative effect on learning technique as you obsess on strength as the answer to all climbing woes. Therefore, I propose the following litmus test for beginning a targeted training-for-climbing program: *You should be able to climb 90 percent of 5.10s onsight and with good, efficient style.* Although there is nothing magical about the 5.10 grade, it's my experience that the majority of climbers become competent at this grade strictly through a program of climbing a few days per week supplemented with only basic fitness training.

Passing this test indicates that you are ready for some sport-specific training, as long as it's properly designed and executed. This distinction is critical, since sport-specific training will yield few positive results if it fails to target your physical weaknesses. Chapter 8 touched on the importance of self-awareness as well as the value of enlisting a coach to help assess your weaknesses and design an appropriate training program. Many gyms have a qualified coach on staff, so I encourage you to consider this option.

You may prefer a self-directed training program, and you can no doubt get excellent results given due diligence in researching and designing the program. Chapter 9 provided a primer on sport-specific training, but I encourage you to also consult *Training for Climbing* for comprehensive and cutting-edge instruction.

Regardless of your information source or the program details, it's important to create a written plan of action that will dictate a firm, long-term workout strategy. Irregular or haphazard training programs will produce mediocre results at best and may even lead you down the wrong path of action. You are better off just climbing as training as opposed to launching into the darkness of trial and error. The bottom line: Do your research, design an appropriate program, and then commit to executing the program long-term. This is the prescription for an uncommonly effective training program.

Tap into the Human Resource

While the social and often crowded nature of a climbing gym can pose many distractions and roadblocks to peak performance, it's important to recognize the tremendous resource that is present in the form of the aggregate experience of the membership. People are the ultimate catalyst for adding new life to your gym climbing sessions. In fact, the simple act of making new acquaintances will elevate your motivation to get to the gym more frequently.

View each person, no matter his ability, as a possible source of the secret you need to break into the next climbing grade. Use this as your incentive to reach out and open up to strangers, even if it's not exactly in your nature to do so. Make it a goal to rope up or boulder with one new person each week, and you'll discover a new kind of excitement and energy for climbing. Enjoy getting to know each person and attempt to gain a glimpse at what drives her. Similarly share your passions, and I guarantee a resultant synergy will develop and empower both you and your new comrade.

Keys to Maintaining Motivation

1. Set performance goals for both your climbing and training. Make the goals specific, incremental, and reasonable given your current ability.

2. Begin a regimented training program that is climbing specific and targeted on your weaknesses. Employ a climbing coach to provide objective, expert guidance.

3. Keep your climbing fresh by engaging new partners and alternating your sessions among two or three different gyms or home walls.

4. Begin climbing outdoors! Sign up for a group class or hire an AMGA-certified guide. (See page 147 for more details on taking your climbing outdoors.)

Build a Home Wall

For many climbers, time is the primary constraint on performance. Metropolitan traffic and the complexities of work and family life can make it difficult to get to the climbing gym on a regular basis. As I've stressed throughout this text, optimal results come from a firm schedule of climbing three or four days per week, yet for some folks this is just not possible. Given a limited climbing schedule, it's natural to get frustrated and lose motivation—but don't despond, *respond*, by building a home wall!

Although no match for a full-service commercial gym, a small home wall can provide a convenient, sport-specific workout that's highly effective.

What's more, a home training wall saves time and money (how many hours and gallons of gas do you burn driving to and from the gym?), and it allows you to do other things, such as study or play with the kids, while resting between burns on the wall.

So what's the investment needed for a modest home wall? A bare-bones, 8-by-10-foot, 45-degree overhanging wall could cost you as little as $300 or $400—the cost of wood and a few dozen handholds. Of course, you could easily spend $1,500 or more if you build a more lavish setup with a few different wall angles and a few hundred handholds. Straight ahead is a primer on building a home wall, followed by an overview of effective home-gym training.

A small home wall affords an effective and time-efficient workout for even the busiest climber.

Designing and Building the Wall

Designing a home gym has to begin with an analysis of possible locations for building the wall. While it's possible to construct a small freestanding wall in a dorm room or apartment living room (it's been done many times), the most popular site is a garage or basement. Garages provide the advantage of a higher ceiling, whereas the basement offers a site with more stable temperatures. If you have both options, weigh the pros and cons of each location recognizing the temperatures you'll face in winter and summer if you build the wall in the garage. I'm fortunate enough to have a basement with a high ceiling (well over 8 feet), so the decision to build my wall inside was an easy one.

As for design, recognize that it will be difficult to train vertical wall technique or endurance on a small home wall, so the primary goal is to train lock-off strength, power, and grip strength. And for this, nothing beats a "45"—an 8-foot-wide, 45-degree wall that begins 16 inches off the floor. This gives you an 8-foot-wide, 16-inch-high "kicker board" along the base of your wall onto which you'll mount some small footholds. Depending on ceiling height, the 45-degree wall will run 8 to 10 feet (the hypotenuse of the right triangle profile) to intersect the existing ceiling beams. The frame should be built with 2-by-8s on a 16-inch center. Make sure the frame is anchored in a bombproof way to existing wall and ceiling structure via lag bolts, galvanized truss plates, and concrete anchors. The climbing surface is ¾-inch plywood attached to the frame with drywall screws.

The hand- and footholds anchor to the plywood with special T-nuts available from any handhold company as well as most hardware or fastener stores. I suggest you purchase and install a minimum of three T-nuts per square foot of wall surface. The basic 8-by-10-foot wall described here would thus require 240 T-nuts as well as a couple of dozen more for the kickboard. While you may never fill all the T-nuts with holds at one time, the large number of T-nut holes affords you a wide variety of placements when you're moving holds around the wall to create new problems (important to keep things fresh).

Kids reveal the innate need for humans to climb. Here, two youngsters are learning to feel the footholds by climbing barefoot (a great practice strategy!).

You'll want to purchase the same types of modular holds that you are familiar with from your local commercial gym. Several companies make specialized training holds that are affordable and ideal for a home wall. Expect to pay anywhere from $1.00 for a tiny foothold up to $10.00 or even $25.00 for a large roof hold or mega-jug. Since your wall is steep, favor medium-sized shapes, which typically cost about $5.00 each (commonly sold as sets of ten for around $50.00). Select holds with what appear to be usable features and avoid any with sharp edges (skin shredders) or abrasive texture. Purchase a variety of holds that will train different grip positions such as crimps, two-finger pockets, pinches, slopers, and such. As a guideline, select hold sizes as follows: 10 percent tiny foot chips, 20 percent small crimp edges, 20 percent pockets, 20 percent medium-sized edges, 20 percent slopers and pinches, and 10 percent large buckets or roof holds. Now mount the holds and start climbing!

Many people start small and then add more wall surface as time, resources, and space allow. Consider adding a 4-foot-wide panel that overhangs 20 to 30 degrees past vertical, a supersteep section that overhangs about 60 degrees, and an 8- or 10-foot section of horizontal "roof" surface. Be creative and have fun with your design. Finally, if you have kids between the ages of about two and six, consider building a small section of vertical wall for them to play around on while you are training on the 45-degree wall. This will make for a joyous and rewarding time for Mom, Dad, and kids alike.

Home Training Guidelines

Home-wall training is all about the high-intensity, sport-specific training that is so beneficial for intermediate to advanced climbers. Such targeted training of the climbing muscles is highly stressful and demands adequate rest to realize the full fruits of your labors. As you then might expect, the one downside to home walls is the temptation to climb every day. Don't fall into this injury-producing, overtraining trap!

An effective home-gym workout comprises three parts: a twenty- to thirty-minute warm-up, thirty to sixty minutes of serious climbing, and ten to twenty minutes of supplemental and strength-training exercises.

As described in chapter 9, each workout should commence with a warm-up period. After completing your stretches begin climbing some easy problems using only the largest handholds. Avoid getting a rapid **flash pump**, and instead strive to slowly increase the intensity of your bouldering over the course of twenty to thirty minutes.

Now it's on to the core of your workout, thirty to sixty minutes of near-maximal bouldering. The goals of this portion are twofold: to develop efficient movement and to increase sport-specific strength.

If training maximum movements and upper-body power is the goal du jour, then working on difficult four- to ten-move boulder problems is the winning ticket. Exercise your creativity and develop boulder problems that test the movements and body positions you find difficult or most strenuous. Of course, working such movements will in the long run make you stronger and more competent at them. Make it a goal to establish specific boulder problems versus just climbing around on the wall. Rest a few minutes between each problem so that you can give each

---

Home-Wall Construction Tips

1. Search the Internet and talk to other climbers for home wall ideas. Enlist a friend with a background in construction if you are uncomfortable with framing and the use of power tools.

2. Sketch out the proposed design and determine all the beam lengths down to the inch based on the wall angles you choose (time to revisit your trigonometry from high school). Make a list of everything you need, then price out the supplies at a couple of building supply stores.

3. Don't skimp on wood. Buy 2-by-8s for framing and use only ¾-inch mid- or high-grade plywood for the climbing surface.

4. When framing, err on the side of overkill in terms of anchoring the support beams to existing ceiling and walls.

5. Drill the T-nut holes and hammer in the T-nuts before mounting the plywood sheets. Be sure to drill from the "good" side of the plywood, but then flip the panel and hammer in the T-nuts on the splintered backside of the holes. Install about one hundred T-nuts per 4-by-8-foot sheet of plywood. Attach the plywood to the framing with 2½-inch drywall screws placed every 6 inches.

attempt your best effort. Enlist a training partner to join in on the fun, and take turns setting problems.

Over the course of several sessions, you will come to know and perfect many different boulder problems of varying difficulty. This achievement opens the door to a powerful strategy for training anaerobic endurance—interval training. As the name implies, interval training involves alternating brief, intense bouts of climbing with brief rest intervals. Beginning with some of your hardest established boulder problems, send one at a time with just a two-minute rest in between each burn. The goal isn't necessarily to successfully ascend each problem, although it's ideal if each training interval does last between thirty and sixty seconds. Continue in this interval-training fashion for thirty to forty minutes. If you keep to the proper time structure, this will equate to about fifteen to twenty complete intervals—a heck of a workout that will yield big payoffs when redpoint or on-sight climbing.

The final stage of the workout takes place off the wall as you execute supplemental exercises such as pull-ups, dips, reverse wrist curls, sit-ups, and such. Most important are the antagonist push-muscle exercises that help maintain muscular balance in the elbows and shoulders. Conclude the session with some light stretching to encourage blood flow and speed recovery.

Begin Climbing Outdoors!

From a more holistic perspective, you will climb your best and tap into the full experience of being a climber only when you step onto rock in the great outdoors. While many of the technical skills and muscles used are the same as in climbing indoors, dancing up a cliff in all the natural elements (sun, wind, and sheer vertical exposure) produces a unique bond with this rock on which we were born.

Everything is amplified in climbing outdoors—

Soaking up the wonder of El Capitan and Yosemite Valley from midway up the East Buttress of Middle Cathedral.
PHOTO BY **ERIC J. HÖRST**

the need for efficient technique and use of strength resources, the demand of climbing partners to work together in synergy, and, of course, the level of absolute risk and reward. Clearly, climbing outdoors is not an activity to rush into without proper instruction in the many unique real-rock techniques and safety systems. Following is a primer on taking your climbing out to Mother Nature's domain.

The Secrets to Climbing Your Best

Get Proper Instruction

Competence, or even expertise, at indoor climbing carries little weight when venturing outdoors. Sure, you'll adapt to outdoor climbing more quickly than someone with no prior climbing experience, but all first-time outdoor climbers are novices when it comes to learning the specialized safety systems. Thus it is absolutely mandatory that your journey onto real rock begin with a few climbing lessons with a professional guide.

Many climbing gyms offer group classes on learning to climb outdoors. You can expect to pay $100 or more per day—money well spent, since you will learn the proper safety techniques from the get-go. Remember, it only takes one mistake to bring an ultimate end to the game. Don't be cheap (or foolish) and attempt to teach yourself!

Another option is to search the Internet or ask a local outdoor store for a local guide certified by the America Mountain Guide Association. Nothing beats one-on-one instruction for learning all the subtleties of real-rock technique. If you find climbing in the great outdoors rewarding, your next step would be to join a local climbing club or find an experienced and mature individual to partner up with for regular visits to the crags. Since lead climbing outdoors often requires placing of protection (if no anchors bolts are resident), it's vital that you initially confine your outdoor climbing to toproping and bouldering. Lead climbing outdoors is a very serious undertaking that most climbers don't engage in until after a few years of rock climbing.

Learn to Crack Climb

Though they're rare on indoor walls, vertical fissures, or cracks, are commonplace at many crags. Ascending such fissures demands a novel set of technical skills commonly classified as "crack climbing."

Central to crack-climbing technique is placement of your hands and feet into the crack in order to gain purchase and facilitate upward movement. Therefore, instead of gripping edges or pockets with your fingers as in gym climbing, crack technique involves inserting your fingers, hand, or arm (depending on the size of the fissure) into a crack and jamming them into place. Initially, such jamming techniques will feel insecure, painful, and a bit scary. With practice, however, you will discover that many jams offer a better fix to the rock than gripping a standard down-pull handhold at the gym.

Crack climbing also requires special foot-jamming techniques, although you will sometimes be able to edge or smear on small holds outside the crack as you are accustomed to doing indoors. Let's take a look at the fundamental crack-climbing techniques, but consult John Long's *How to Rock Climb* for a more comprehensive study of outdoor climbing.

HAND TECHNIQUES

Just how your hands engage a crack depends on the size of the fissure. The narrowest cracks—only about ⅜ inch wide—will accept little more than the tips of your fingers. The jamming technique to use here involves inserting the tips of your index and middle fingers as deep as possible into the crack—often your ring and pinkie fingers will be left floating outside the crack, or barely gripping the crack edge. Most often you'll place this jam with your index finger on the bottom and your elbow out to the side. This way, when you pull on that arm the elbow will rotate downward and produce a twisting of the fingers that further anchors them into the crack. Slightly larger cracks ranging from about ½ to 1 inch in width require a similar technique—you simply insert as much of your fingers into the rock as possible. One thing you will notice in large finger cracks (around an inch wide) is that the fingers tend to slide down this oversized crack. In these situations, it's vital to look for constrictions or bottlenecks along the crack and attempt to place your jams in or just above these narrow spots.

Cracks ranging from 1 to 3 inches wide are the domain of hand jams. As the name implies, you need to insert as much of your hand as possible and then jam it into place. There are several different ways to perform hand jams, and with practice you'll learn to quickly assess the best technique for a given situation.

First, it's important to point out that you can execute a hand jam in the thumb-up or thumb-down

Toprope crack climbing at Swan Slab area, Yosemite, California.
PHOTO BY **ERIC J. HÖRST**

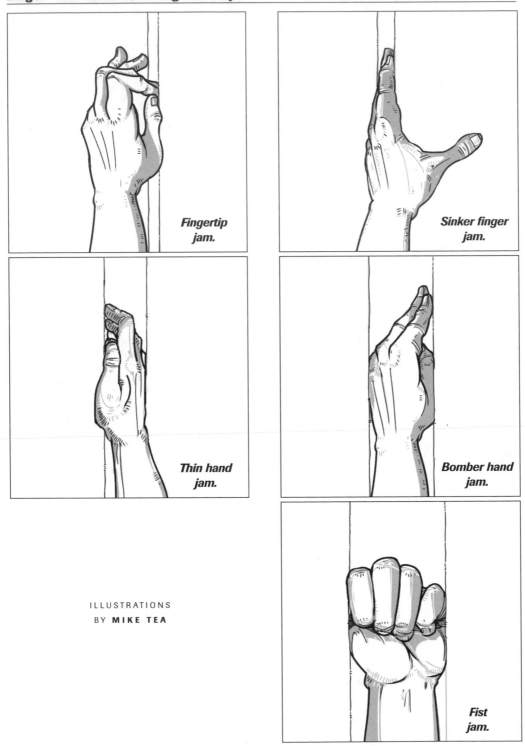

Fingertip jam.

Sinker finger jam.

Thin hand jam.

Bomber hand jam.

Fist jam.

ILLUSTRATIONS
BY **MIKE TEA**

position. Vertical cracks are often better climbed in the thumb-down position, whereas cracks that slant slightly are more easily climbed with the lower hand jamming thumb-up and the high hand jamming thumb-down. Next, you'll want to scan the hand crack for a constriction or bottleneck that will provide the most bombproof jam imaginable. Cracks with little variance are more challenging, as they require a bit more effort to create a solid jam. The key is to cup your hand inside the crack to generate outward pressure and friction on the inside of the crack. Furthermore, jamming thumb-down exerts a twisting force on the jammed hand as you pull down, and this tends to increase the security of the jam.

Fist jamming is the optimal technique for cracks about 4 inches wide. The technique here is simply to insert your hand with the palm facing into the crack and then make a fist. In closing your hand tightly, the width of your fist increases, making it stick like an oversized cork stuck in the top of a wine bottle. Cracks larger than 4 inches are less frequently encountered, and the techniques required to ascent these wide fissures are beyond the scope of this entry-level book.

FOOT TECHNIQUES

There are two primary foot techniques used in crack climbing: feet inside the crack and feet on the rock face. On many climbs it will be obvious which technique you'll need, because a hand or fist crack will readily accept your feet while most finger cracks will not. Let's break things down.

In climbing thin finger cracks, you have little choice but to search for edges on the rock surface on which you can edge or smear. The exceptions are offset cracks (where one edge of the crack is set out from the opposite edge of the crack) and larger finger cracks, which occasionally afford a foot smear on the exposed edge of the crack. As a rule, however, small cracks require that you think like a gym climber in terms of footwork. Look for stems, high steps, outside edges, and even backsteps in attempting to use your feet optimally.

Cracks wider than about 1 inch in width provide exceedingly solid foot placements by means of foot

Cracks too small for foot jamming require you smear on the edge of the crack or step on some other feature on the rock face.
PHOTO BY **KEITH MCCALLISTER**

jamming. The simple technique involves turning your foot sideways—so that the sole of the shoe is facing inward and your knee is bent outward—and inserting as much of your foot as possible into the crack. Depending on the size of a crack, you may be limited to jamming just the toe portion of the shoe (narrow hand cracks) or its entire front half (fist cracks). Once you're secured in the crack, your knee will naturally rotate back to center as you stand up

Larger cracks allow for more solid foot placements by jamming part or all of your foot into the crack.
PHOTO BY **KEITH MCCALLISTER**

The lieback technique is most useful when climbing a crack in a corner.
PHOTO BY **KEITH MCCALLISTER**

on the foot. In climbing a continuous hand or fist crack, you will simply need to leapfrog one foot above the other in a series of foot jams about 1 foot apart.

LIEBACK TECHNIQUE

Finally, there's liebacking, a unique method of climbing cracks that are located in the vertex of a dihedral or corner. The lieback technique places your body in a sort of rowing position with your arms pulling and your legs pushing in a powerful opposition. Feet smear on one wall of the corner while your fingers cling to the edge of the crack and

arms remain as straight as possible. Move upward by simply walking your feet up the wall and sliding (or leapfrogging) your hands up the crack.

Most people find liebacking to be more intuitive and easy to learn than other crack climbing techniques—but they also discover that it's extremely strenuous.

With practice you'll learn to position your hands and feet in an optimal way that provides the greatest leverage at the lowest possible energy expenditure. Of course, as in all kind of strenuous climbing, moving quickly is fundamental to maximizing your performance.

CRACK-CLIMBING STRATEGY

Effective crack-climbing strategy is virtually identical to the optimal indoor climbing strategy you know so well—climb briskly and efficiently, utilize the legs as much as possible in generating locomotion, and pause for long periods only at definitive rest stances.

Just as in your clumsy first days at attempting indoor climbing, expect your initial forays at crack climbing to feel awkward and frustratingly difficult. But as in gym climbing, you will rapidly learn the many unique motor skills. Jamming cracks will quickly become less strenuous and a heck of a lot of fun.

Use the security of a toprope to experiment with different techniques and subtle variations on the basic jamming skills described above. Don't be satisfied with just thrashing up a crack to the top, but instead strive to learn the best way to do each move with the goal of climbing each crack in good style and with minimal use of strength. To this end, it's a great practice strategy to climb a few laps on each crack in the attempt to achieve a smooth, proficient use of crack-climbing technique.

Guidelines for Beginning to Climb Outdoors

1. Obtain professional instruction! Self-instruction may work in learning most other sports, but applied to outdoor rock climbing it can get you killed. Hire a veteran instructor, ideally one certified by the AMGA.

2. Engage only in bouldering and toproping for your first year (or more) climbing outdoors. Outdoor lead climbing is not something to rush into.

3. Learn to crack climb. The experience and skills gained from your crack-climbing ventures will feed back and enhance your skill at all other types of climbing.

4. Travel to crags near and far to experience all the wonder and joy of outdoor climbing.

Climb at Many Areas

There is a world of rock climbing wonder awaiting you—go explore it and enjoy it!

In terms of growing your ability, exposing yourself to a wide range of rock types is another one of the secrets to climbing your best. Consider that each new area requires distinctly unique skills and techniques that you cannot learn elsewhere. Only through a diverse sampling of climbing areas can you achieve true mastery.

As an indoor climber transitioning to the great outdoors, it's ideal to pursue a 50–50 split in days spent climbing indoors and outdoors. The most practical and popular approach is to climb indoors on two weekday evenings then spend Saturday and Sunday pulling down on the real stuff outdoors. In this way, you obtain quality sport-specific muscular training during the week, but gain in the important technical and mental areas by cragging or bouldering outside on weekends. It's a great schedule from a training perspective, and it's an unbeatable game plan from a motivational and experiential standpoint.

Finally, I want to tell you the biggest secret to climbing your best: Decide to love climbing unconditionally. Embrace the notion that any day climbing—indoors or out, and success or failure—is a great day. With this disposition you will climb more confidently and at peace with whatever the results may be. Your mind and body will work in magical unison and most often lead to a superb and transcending outcome.

The author, climbing the steep,
pocketed limestone at Wild Iris,
Wyoming.
PHOTO BY ERIC MCCALLISTER

Afterword

In my three decades as a climber, perhaps the biggest breakthrough occurred when I realized that almost all the mental skills and strategies I learned through climbing could be applied to other areas in my life.

Detailed below are some of the powerful lessons of the vertical world, as revealed on the pages of *Learning to Climb*. Learn more success strategies "from the steep" at www.MentalWings.com.

On achieving success:
To succeed, you must embrace and learn from failure.

On stretching personal boundaries:
Pushing through discomfort and harnessing anxiety into productive energy is the strategy for uncommon experience and personal success.

On the importance of elevating quality of thinking:
Everything you are and will become is a direct function of your thoughts. Self-improvement, then, must begin with a fine-tuning of your internal dialogue or self-talk throughout the day. The goal is to modify your ways of thinking so as to help you solve problems (instead of wallowing in them), challenge fears (instead of avoiding them), and compel intelligent action toward your goals (instead of backpedaling at the first sign of adversity).

On the performance mind-set:
The best mental approach for peak performance is to focus on the process and let the outcome unfold on its own. Enjoy the process regardless of the results, and you'll always be a winner.

On self-induced pressure:
The more pressure you place on yourself, the more difficult it becomes to think and act proficiently. Paradoxically, you will perform better by not needing to!

On fear of the unknown:
In pushing personal boundaries and confronting the unknown, it's common to ponder the benefits of a retreat. Acknowledge such mental battles—between your desire to do new things and your primal instinct to avoid discomfort and failure—as being a normal part of the process. Resolve to persevere and you'll redefine your abilities and perception of what is possible.

On leveraging past experience:
Another powerful strategy for persevering in times of challenge and self-doubt is to think back to a similar encounter and subsequent success. Close your eyes and review that successful past event. How did you rise to the challenge, what strategies did you use, and, most important, how did you feel upon achieving success? This process of vividly visualizing all the details and feelings of a past success will recycle these resources for use in the present.

On using feedback and criticism:
View the feedback of failed attempts not as a sign you can't do something, but instead as a dynamic source of clues leading toward your inevitable success. Embrace each failed attempt as a signpost directing you toward a better course of action and the pathway to success.

On problem solving:

Breaking through sticking points and solving problems demands that you must get outside your current mind-set. Exercise flexibility of perspective by detaching from the situation and visualizing the problem from a perspective outside yourself. Imagine a wide range of possible solutions and give them a try without prejudice. Be creative and have fun, and the solution will reveal itself to you.

On developing mental toughness:

Your thoughts are precursors to both failure and success. Fearful thoughts will generate performance-killing anxiety and tension, whereas calming, positive thinking will foster a relaxed, optimal performance state. Knowing this intimate mind–emotion–body connection, you can control how you feel and perform by consciously directing your thoughts in productive ways. Such thought control is the essence of mental toughness.

On developing self-awareness and elevating performance:

Acute self-awareness empowers you to manage stress and fatigue, redirect unproductive thinking, identify weaknesses, and refine your actions and strategy to be most effective. Perform regular "spot assessments" by asking yourself a series of probative questions, such as *What pressures or fears are holding me back?* and *What mental or physical errors am I committing?* Pay close attention to the answers, since they hold the keys to effective course correction and enhancing performance.

On dealing with setbacks and failure:

Top performers in any field possess uncommon resilience to criticism, setbacks, and failure. They are always on the lookout for new information, distinctions, or ideas that will help elevate their game, and they possess an intense curiosity as to why they sometimes fail. Learning to respond to adversity in this way is tantamount to gaining some of the personal power possessed by these elite performers. So don't curse setbacks—view them as guideposts and stepping-stones to eventual success.

On managing fear:

The two steps to managing fear: First, identify and mitigate legitimate fears via risk management; second, dispel illusionary fears born of an inexperienced mind. Such phantom fears are the scourge of novices in any activity or venture. In these cases, you must challenge fearful thoughts head-on and conquer them with reason and courage.

On eliminating the fear of failure:

Fear of failure wields tremendous power over those who possess it—ironically, the fear of failure often leads to failure! Consider how a football team often gives up the winning score when they shift into prevent defense. Such a prevent defense in your personal action will result in apprehension, doubt, and, worst of all, thoughts of failure. Fortunately, you can defeat this fear by focusing single-mindedly on the process of effective action and purging any thoughts of possible outcomes. Concentrate on the things immediate to your performance—technique, strategy, and relaxation—and the ideal outcome will likely unfold.

A more global approach to permanently deleting the fear of failure is simply to adopt the attitude, *It's okay to fail.* By willingly accepting this fate (if it should even happen), you totally eliminate the fear and, hence, liberate yourself to play to win!

On building confidence:

Pushing your limits (in anything) demands a healthy self-confidence. You can best elevate self-confidence with positive self-talk and visualization. Statements such as *I'm well prepared, I'll do great*, and *This will be fun* will foster positive emotions. Likewise, visualization can be a powerful confidence builder. Close your eyes and spend a minute or two reliving a past great ascent. By *feeling* the emotions of that past success, you tap a powerful resource for use in the present moment.

Eric's powerful five-step, goal-achievement strategy:

1. Write down your goals. This makes them more real and therefore more achievable.

2. Define your goals specifically and with as much detail as possible.

3. Make your goals lofty and challenging, but keep them realistic. Set incremental goals—a goal gradient will yield a motivation-generating win every few weeks.

4. Set a deadline for the accomplishment of each goal. A goal best inspires you into action when a deadline is affixed to the performance benchmark.

5. Write down one thing that you will sacrifice in order to reach this goal. This will open your eyes to the reality that achievement doesn't just come by doing more of something or trying harder; it also requires that you eliminate and detach from things that are holding you back.

On tapping into the human resource:

People are the ultimate catalyst for adding new ideas and life to fledgling projects. View each person, despite background or ability, as a possible source of the secret you need to break through a given obstacle. Reciprocate by sharing your passion and energy. The resultant synergy will empower all parties involved to a new realm of possibility.

On what defines character:

You are not defined by your successes or failures. You are defined by the ways in which you react to success and failure.

On the secret to happiness:

Love the process of living, unconditionally. Embrace every day as a gift, no matter what it brings. With this grateful disposition, you will experience a richer, more joyful and transcending journey.

Wonderfully featured climbing at Rocks State Park, Maryland.
PHOTO BY **ERIC J. HÖRST**

Glossary

The following is a compilation of some of the technical terms and climbing jargon used throughout this book.

adaptive response—Physiological changes in structure or function particularly related to response to a training overload.

aerobic—Any physical activity deriving energy from the breakdown of glycogen in the presence of oxygen, thus producing little or no lactic acid, enabling an athlete to continue exercise much longer.

American Decimal System (ADS)—The primary rating scale for technical rock climbs.

anaerobic—Energy production in the muscles involving the breakdown of glycogen in the absence of oxygen; a by-product called lactic acid is formed, resulting in rapid fatigue and cessation of physical activity.

anaerobic endurance—The ability to continue moderate- to high-intensity activity over a period of time; commonly called power endurance or power stamina by climbers, though these terms are scientifically incorrect.

antagonist—A muscle providing an opposing force to the primary (agonist) muscles in action.

arête—The sharp vertical edge of an outside corner, as in the exterior corner of a building.

auto belay—A mechanical device that provides a secure belay, via a toprope cable, thus eliminating the need for a belay partner.

backstepping—Outside edging on a foothold that's behind you while climbing a move with your side to the wall.

barndoor—Sideways swinging or uncontrolled turning of the body resulting from poor balance or body positioning.

belay—A rope-management technique that allows a pair of climbers to protect each other during an ascent.

beta—Any prior information about a route, including sequence, rests, gear, clips, and so on.

bouldering—Ropeless climbing on short, often overhanging, sections of wall or along the base of larger walls.

bucket hold—A large, secure handhold.

campusing—Climbing an overhanging section of rock or artificial wall with no feet, usually in a dynamic left hand, right hand, left hand (et cetera) sequence.

campus training—A sport-specific form of plyometric exercise developed by Wolfgang Güllich at the Campus Center (a weight-lifting facility at the University in Nürnberg, Germany).

carabiner (biner)—A spring-loaded aluminum alloy snap link used to connect ropes to other pieces of gear such as harnesses and anchor bolts.

center of gravity—The theoretical point on which the total effect of gravity acts on the body.

chimney—A crack wide enough to admit a climber; typically ascended by opposing forces of the arms, legs, and back pressing against opposite walls of the crack.

chronic—Continuing over time.

concentric contraction—Any movement involving a shortening of muscles fibers while developing tension, as in the biceps muscle during a pull-up.

contact strength—Initial grip strength upon touching a handhold.

crash pad—A portable gymnastics-like pad, specifically designed to provide cushioning below climbs or boulder problems.

crimp grip—The most natural (and stressful) way to grip a rock hold, characterized by hyperextension of the first joint in the fingers and nearly full flexion of the second joint.

crimp hold—A small, sharp hold requiring a desperate cling by the fingertips.

crux—The hardest move, or sequence of moves, on a route.

deadpoint—The "peak" position in a dynamic movement where, for a moment, all motion stops.

dihedral or open book—A wall feature formed by the intersection of two wall planes, as in the inside corner of a room or building.

dogging—Climbing a route, usually bolt-to-bolt, with the aid of the rope to hang and rest while practicing the sequence. Also known as hangdogging.

dropknee—An exaggerated backstep, commonly used on overhanging rock, where the inside knee is dropped toward the ground, resulting in a stable chimneylike position.

dynamic move—An explosive leap for a hold otherwise out of reach.

dyno—Short for "dynamic."

eccentric contraction—Muscle action in which the muscle resists as it is forced to lengthen, as in the

biceps during the lowering phase of a pull-up.

endurance—Ability to perform physical work for an extended period of time. Cardiovascular endurance is directly related to VO$_2$ max, whereas muscular endurance is influenced by circulation and oxygen available.

epicondylitis—Inflammation of the tendon origins of the forearm flexors (medial) or extensors (lateral) near the elbow.

extension—A movement that takes the two ends of a jointed body part away from each other, as in straightening the arm.

fall—Disengaging the rock wall, intentionally or unintentionally, as in "falling onto the rope" or "falling off of a boulder problem."

fingerboard or hangboard—A training apparatus, commonly found in climbing gyms or installed above a doorway at a climber's residence, that facilitates climbing-specific finger and arm training (pull-ups, finger hangs, and such).

flagging—A climbing technique in which one foot is crossed behind the other in order to avoid barndooring and to improve balance.

flash—To climb a route on the first try without ever having touched it, but with the aid of beta.

flash pump—A rapid, often vicious, muscular pump resulting from strenuous training or climbing without first performing a proper (gradual) warm-up.

flexion—A movement that brings the ends of a body part closer together, as in bending the arm.

forerunner—A professional route setter, who establishes the climbs at a climbing gym or competition.

Gaston—A technique for grabbing an inward-facing vertical edge near your face, typified by an elbow-out, bent arm position and a thumbs down hand orientation.

gripped—Extremely scared.

Research has shown the G-Tox technique to be effective in speeding forearm recovery at marginal rest positions.

ILLUSTRATION BY **MIKE TEA**

G-Tox—A technique that uses gravity to help speed recovery from a forearm pump. It involves alternating (about every five seconds) the position of the resting arm between the normal hanging-at-your-side position and a raised hand position above your shoulder.

heel hook—Use of the heel on a hold, usually near chest level, to aid in pulling and balance.

highball—An uncommonly high and dangerous boulder problem, typically more than 15 feet in height.

honed—In extremely good shape, with low body fat.

hypergravity training—A highly effective method of training maximum strength, which involves climbing or training with weight added to the body (simulates hypergravity).

hypertrophy—Enlargement in size, as in muscular hypertrophy.

interval training—A method of anaerobic endurance training that involves brief periods of intense training interspaced with periods of rest or low-intensity training.

isometric—Muscular contraction resulting in no shortening of the muscle (no movement).

jamming—The technique used to climb vertical cracks, in which the hands and feet are wedged, or jammed, into the fissure.

kinesthetic—The sense derived from muscular contractions and limb movements.

killer—Extraordinarily good, as in a killer route.

lactic acid—An acid by-product of the anaerobic metabolism of glucose during intense muscular exercise.

lead climbing—The challenging climbing style in which the rope hangs downward from climber's harness, as opposed to being secured atop the climb via a toprope.

ledge—A flat, horizontal stance on an otherwise steep wall.

lieback—A technique, usually used in crack climbing, in which the hands pull and the feet push in opposition.

lunge—An out-of-control dynamic move; an explosive jump for a far-off hold.

mantle—A movement technique in which a handhold is pressed downward, in a motion similar to pushing yourself out of a swimming pool.

maximum strength—The peak force of a muscular contraction, irrespective of the time element.

modeling—A learning technique where an individual watches, then attempts, a skill as performed properly by another person.

motor learning—The set of internal processes associated with practice or experience leading to a relatively permanent gain in performance capability.

motor skill—A skill where the primary determinant of success is the movement component itself.

muscular endurance—The length of time a given level of power can be maintained.

offwidth—A crack too large for hand jams, yet too small to admit a climber's body.

on-sight—When a route is climbed on the first try and with absolutely no prior information of any kind.

open-hand grip—The less stressful finger grip involving only slight flexion of the finger joints.

overhang—A section of wall that juts out horizontally, parallel to the floor.

overhanging—A wall surface that angles outward beyond vertical, so that the top of the wall overhangs its base.

overtraining—Constant severe training that does not provide adequate time for recovery; symptoms include increased frequency of injury, decreased performance, irritability, and apathy.

overuse—Excessive repeated exertion or shock that results in injuries such as inflammation of the muscles and tendons.

problem or boulder problem—A short climb, typically 7 to 15 feet high, which is ascended without a safety rope.

projecting—The process of working on and rehearsing a difficult route with the goal of eventually climbing the route bottom-to-top in one push.

psyched—Raring to go or very happy.

pumped—When the muscles become engorged with blood due to extended physical exertion.

quickdraw—A short webbing sling with a carabiner on each end, used to clip the climbing rope into anchor bolts.

redpoint—Lead climbing a route bottom-to-top in one push.

roof—A large overhang that juts out horizontally more than a body length.

schema—A set of rules, usually developed and applied unconsciously by the motor system in the brain and spinal cord, relating how to move

and adjust muscle forces, body positions, and so on, given the parameters at hand, such as steepness of the rock, friction qualities, holds being used, and type of terrain.

screamer—Slang term used to describe a scary lead fall.

send—Short for "ascend."

sharp end—The lead climber's end of the rope.

skill—A capability to bring about an end result with maximum certainty, minimum energy, and minimum time.

slab—A wall surface with an average angle that is less than vertical.

sport climbing—Usually refers to any indoor or outdoor climbing on bolt-protected routes.

spotter—A person designated to slow the fall of a boulderer, with the main goal of keeping the boulderer's head from hitting the ground.

stabilizer muscle—A muscle that is stimulated to help anchor or stabilize the position of a bone.

stem—The technique of bridging between two widely spaced footholds.

stick clip—Preclipping the lead rope to the first anchor bolt on a climb with a specially made "stick clip" pole.

strength—The amount of muscle force that can be exerted; speed and distance are not factors of strength.

supercompensate—The body's recovery process of adaptation and overcompensation to the stress of exercise.

tendinitis—A disorder involving the inflammation of a tendon and synovial membrane at a joint.

tendon—A white fibrous cord of dense connective tissue that attaches muscle to bone.

trad—Short for "traditional"; outdoor climbing that requires placement of natural protection.

toprope—The most secure roped climbing setup in

which the rope passes through an anchor atop the route.

traverse—Climbing sideways across a wall without any gain in height.

tweak—To injure, as in a tweaked finger tendon.

undercling—An inverted, downward-facing handhold.

vert—Short for "vertical," as in a vert climbing wall.

visualization—Controlled and directed imagery that can be used for awareness building, monitoring and self-regulation, healing, and, most important, mental programming for good performances.

V-Scale—An open-ended scale for grading the difficulty of boulder problems.

wired—Known well, as in a wired route.

working—Practicing the moves on a difficult route via top rope or hangdogging.

Suggested Reading

Ament, Pat. *How to Be a Master Climber*. Boulder, CO: Two Lights, 1997.

Burbach, Matt. *Gym Climbing*. Seattle: Mountaineers Press, 2005.

Goddard, Dale, and Ugo Neumann. *Performance Rock Climbing*. Mechanicsburg, PA: Stackpole Books, 1994.

Hörst, Eric J. *How to Climb 5.12*. Guilford, CT: Globe Pequot Press/Falcon Guides, 2003.

———. *Training for Climbing*. Guilford, CT: Globe Pequot Press/Falcon Guides, 2003.

Hurni, Michelle. *Coaching Climbing*. Guilford, CT: Globe Pequot Press/Falcon Guides, 2003.

Ilgner, Arno. *Warrior's Way*. La Vergne, TN: Desiderata Institute, 2003.

Lewis, S. Peter. *Top Roping*. Guilford, CT: Globe Pequot Press/Falcon Guides, 1998.

Long, John. *How to Rock Climb*. Guilford, CT: Globe Pequot Press/Falcon Guides, 2004.

Sagar, Heather Reynolds. *Climbing Your Best*. Mechanicsburg, PA: Stackpole Books, 2001.

Sherman, John. *Better Bouldering*. Guilford, CT: Globe Pequot Press/Falcon Guides, 1997.

Resources

Web Resources

Accessfund.org

The Access Fund is a national, nonprofit organization dedicated to keeping climbing areas open and to conserving the climbing environment. If you plan to venture into outdoor climbing, please support the Access Fund by becoming a member and contributing some time to local grassroots stewardship.

ACMG.ca

Association of Canadian Mountain Guides (ACMG).

AMGA.com

American Mountain Guide Association (AMGA).

BDEL.com

Web site for Black Diamond Equipment, Ltd., one of the world's leading manufacturers of gear for indoor, outdoor, and alpine climbing.

La Sportiva.com

Manufacturer of top-shelf climbing shoes for climbers of all ability levels.

Learning2Climb.com

The companion Web site for this book, and a rich resource for information on gear, instruction, training, and much more.

Nicros.com

The nation's leading manufacturer of commercial climbing walls and modular handholds.

Podclimber.com

A great site with hours of informative podcasts from around the world.

RockClimbing.com

Launched in 1995, this fantastic site contains information on more than 7,000 climbing areas (in a hundred countries and all fifty states), but it's the large photo database and discussion forums that make RC.com a favorite site of many climbers. For beginners, this site represents an endless treasure trove of information.

SterlingRope.com

Manufacturer of premium ropes for indoor and outdoor climbing, rappelling, and rescue.

Training4Climbing.com

The planet's number one resource for information on training for climbing and climbing performance research. This free Web site provides new training tips and articles each month.

USAClimbing.org

USA Climbing is the national governing body for multiple disciplines of competition climbing: Difficulty, Bouldering, and Speed. The group's mission is to promote and encourage climbers of all ages in competitive climbing, and to sanction, organize, and promote competitive climbing events in an atmosphere of camaraderie and respect, utilizing the support of climbers, parents, coaches, climbing facilities, and industry. It's run and supported by volunteers.

Magazines

Climbing

Published nine times per year ($14.97/year). Subscribe at Climbing.com.

Gripped

Canada's only climbing magazine, published six times per year ($22.95). Subscribe at Gripped.com.

Rock & Ice

Published eight times per year ($25.95/year). Subscriber at RockandIce.com.

Urban Climber

Published six times per year ($24.95). Subscribe at UrbanClimberMag.com.

Index

A

abdominal crunches, 125–27
abdominal stretch, 121, 123
Access Fund, 167
ACMG (Association of Canadian Mountain
    Guides), 167
adaptive response, 159
Add-On (game), 82
ADS (American Decimal System), 16, 159
advanced drills, 76–78
AE (anaerobic endurance), 131–32, 136–37, 159
aerobic activity, 159
Air Traffic Controller (ATC), 22, 30–31
Ament, Pat, 7
American Decimal System (ADS), 16, 159
American Mountain Guide Association
    (AMGA), 8–9, 167
anaerobic endurance (AE), 131–32, 136–37, 159
anchors, emotional, 113
ANSWER Sequence, 104, 105, 106, 110
antagonist muscle, 60, 159
antagonist-muscle training, 127–30
anxiety, 104–7
arête, 14, 159
arm flexibility, 118
arm positions, 48–50
arms, using opposing forces, 68–69
ascent, style of, 17
Association of Canadian Mountain Guides
    (ACMG), 167

ATC (Air Traffic Controller), 22, 30–31
auto belay climbing, 12–13, 159. *See also* belay

B

back flexibility, 118
backstepping, 72, 74, 159
barndoor, 59, 159
belay, 10, 29–33, 159. *See also* auto belay
    climbing
belay commands, 31–32
belay devices, 22
belay gloves, 24
belay plates, 22, 30–31
belay tests, 10
beta, 17, 159
biners, 22–23, 159
Black Diamond Equipment, Ltd., 167
body composition, optimizing, 116
books, recommended, 165
bouldering, 10–11
    defined, 159
    drills, 81–82
    games, 82–83
    safety, 33–34
    as training, 130–32
boulder problems, 10, 94, 162
breath control, 61, 106
bucket hold, 159
butterfly stretch, 121

C

calf stretch, 123

campusing, 159

campus training, 159

carabiners, 22–23, 159

centered, getting, 104

center of gravity, 4, 56, 159

chalk, 23–24

character, 157

checklists

    equipment, 25

    preclimb, 112–13

    self-assessment, 103

chimney, 159–60

chunking down a route, 96

climbing

    auto belay, 12–13, 159

    challenges and rewards of, 7

    crack, 148–53

    indoor *versus* outdoor, 8–9

    on-sight, 17, 162

    outdoor, 147–53

    sport, 162

    trad, 162

    types, 10–13

climbing drill, fast-paced, 78

Climbing (magazine), 168

climbing-specific training, 130–37

    bouldering as training, 130–32

    fingerboard training, 134–37

    guidelines, 136

    high-intensity pull-muscle training, 132–34

climbing walls, 13–17

    classifying ascent style, 17

    difficulty rating scales, 16–17

    naming of climbs, 14, 16

    route setting, 14, 16

    wall features, 14

clipping quickdraws, 86–91. *See also* quickdraws

    clipping technique, 89–90

    optimal clipping position, 86–89

    preclipping first bolt, 91

    rope placement through carabiner, 90–91

clothing, 25

coaches, 37–38, 102

commands, belay, 31–32

concentric contraction, 160

conditioning, general, 115–37

    antagonist-muscle training, 127–30

    basic pull-muscle strength training, 123–27

    climbing-specific training, 130–37

    guidelines, 130

    improving flexibility, 116–23

    optimizing body composition, 116

confidence building, 110, 156

contact strength, 135–36, 160

contraction

    concentric, 160

    eccentric, 160

control, regaining, 104, 106

crack climbing, 148–53

    foot techniques, 151–52

    hand techniques, 148–51

    lieback technique, 152

    strategy, 153

crash pads, 11, 34, 160

crimp grip, 47, 160

crimp hold, 160

criticism, 155

crunches, abdominal, 125–27

crux, 14, 97–98, 160

D

Davis, Steph, 27

deadpoint drill, 82

deadpoints, 79–80, 160

deadpoint traversing, one-arm, 82

Destivelle, Catherine, 37

difficulty rating scales, 16–17

dihedral, 14, 160

dips, 128, 129

dogging, 96, 160

down climbing drill, 78

down pull, 48

drills
 advanced, 76–78
 basic, 63–65
 deadpoint, 82
 down climbing, 78
 fast-paced climbing, 78
 finger-press, 77
 foot-flagging, 77
 frog-foot, 65
 high-step, 65
 inside/outside foot edge, 77
 isolation, 64–65
 matching, 64
 one-arm deadpoint traversing, 82
 shuffle, 64
 steep-rock bouldering, 81–82
 straight-armed, 65
 tennis ball, 65
 toprope, 65
 tracking, 77–78
 traverse training, 64–65
 twist-lock bouldering, 81–82
 undercling, 77
dropknee, 160
dynamic moves, 4, 78–81, 160
dynamic ropes, 24
dynos, 80–81, 160

E

eccentric contraction, 160
economy, moving with, 59–61
edging, 51, 53
emotional anchors, 113
endurance
 anaerobic, 131–32, 136–37, 159
 defined, 160
 muscular, 161
 power, 131–32, 136–37, 159
epicondylitis, 160
equipment and safety gear, 19–25
 belay devices, 22

belay gloves, 24
 carabiners, 22–23
 chalk, 23–24
 clothing, 25
 equipment checklist, 25
 harnesses, 21–22
 helmets, 25
 quickdraws, 22–23
 renting, 9–10
 rope and rope bag, 25
 shoes, 19–21
equipment checklist, 25
experience, leveraging, 155
experimentation, 41–42
extended grip, 47, 162
extension, 160
extensors, finger and forearm, 118

F

failure
 fear of, 108–9, 156
 as part of success process, 106–7
falling, fear of, 107–8
falls, 12, 93–94, 160
fast-paced climbing drill, 78
fear
 of failure, 108–9, 156
 of falling, 107–8
 of the unknown, 155
feedback, 97, 155
fees, 9, 10
feet. See also foot flagging
 crux sequence, 97–98
 inside/outside foot edge drill, 77
 placements that carry your
  weight, 54–56
 quiet, 59
 using opposing forces, 68–70
finesse, 4
fingerboards, 123, 134–35, 160
fingerboard training, 134–37

finger extensors, 118

finger flexors, 117

finger grips, 45–48

finger-press drill, 77

first visit to climbing gym, 9–10

fitness conditioning, 130

flagging, 71, 160. *See also* foot-flagging
    drill

flashing, 17, 160

flash pump, 146, 160

flexibility, 116–23

   abdominal stretch, 121, 123

   back of leg, 121

   butterfly, 121

   calf stretch, 123

   finger and forearm extensors, 118

   finger and forearm flexors, 117

   knee to chest, 119

   shoulder and upper back, 118

   upper arm and back, 118

   wall split, 121

flexion, 47, 160

flexors, finger and forearm, 117

foot flagging, 71, 160

foot-flagging drill, 77

foot-hand matching, 72

foot positions, 51–53

foot techniques, crack climbing, 151–52

footwork, advanced, 74–76. *See also* feet

force vectors, 4

forearm extensors, 118

forearm flexors, 117

forerunners, 14, 160

Frenchies, 133

friction grip, 48

frog-foot drill, 65

front-pointing foot placement, 51

full-body harnesses, 21–22

full-crimp grip, 47

G

games, bouldering, 82–83

Gaston, 48, 50, 69, 160

Gill, John, 85

glossary, 159–63

gloves, belay, 24

goals, performance, 142, 157

gravity

   center of, 4, 55–56, 159

   line of, 4

Grigri, 22, 30

gripped, 160

Gripped (magazine), 168

G-Tox, 62–63, 161

Güllich, Wolfgang, 101, 159

gym types, 9

H

half-crimp grip, 47

hand-foot matches, 72

hands, using opposing forces, 69–70

hand techniques, crack climbing, 148–51

hangboards, 123, 134–35, 160. *See also* fingerboard
    training

hangdogging, 96, 160

hanging knee lifts, 125

happiness, secret to, 157

harnesses, 21–22, 27

heel hooking, 74–75, 161

helmets, 25

highball problems, 11, 161

high-intensity pull-muscle training, 132–34

high-step drill, 65

Hill, Lynn, 19

home training guidelines, 146–47

home walls, 144–47

honed, 161

human resource, tapping into, 143, 157

hypergravity training, 161

hypertrophy, 161

I

indoor climbing
history, 7–8
versus outdoor climbing, 8–9
injury prevention, training for, 127–30
inside/outside foot edge drill, 77
instruction, 10, 148
interval training, 131–32, 161
isolation drill, 64–65
isometric, 161

J

jamming, 45, 148–51, 161

K

killer, 161
kinesthetic, 161
knee lifts, hanging, 125
knee locks, 76
knee to chest stretch, 119

L

lactic acid, 161
landing zone, 34
La Sportiva, 20, 167
lat pull-downs, 124
lead climbing, 13, 85–99
learning to lead, 85–94
reading boulder problems and routes, 94–95
working a route, 95–98
learning, rapid, 37–43
Learning2Climb.com, 167
ledges, 14, 161
Left-Right Rule, 58–59
leg flexibility, 121
lessons, 10, 148
liability, waiver of, 9

lieback technique, 152, 161
light shoulder press, 127, 129
line of gravity, 4
Long, John, 45
lowering off a route, 32
lunges, 80–81, 161

M

magazines, 168
mantle, 48, 50, 72, 161
matching drill, 64
maximum strength, 131, 161
mental training and fear management, 101–13
controlling tension and anxiety, 104–7
creating peak performance state, 109–13
developing mental skills, 38, 156
developing self-awareness, 101–4
managing fear, 107–9
mental preparation for lead climbing, 95
Metolius, 24
modeling, 40–41, 161
momentum, 59–60
motivation, 141–43
motor learning, 161
motor skill, 161
moves, anticipating, 94
moving with perfect economy, 59–61
Muir, John, 141
muscular endurance, 161

N

Nicros, 167
nutrition, 137–38, 139

O

offwidths, 14, 162
one-arm deadpoint traversing, 82
on-sight climbing, 17, 162

open book, 14, 160
open-hand grip, 47, 162
opposing forces, using, 68–70
outdoor climbing, 147–53
    crack climbing, 148–53
    guidelines, 153
    versus indoor climbing, 8–9
    instruction for, 148
    scheduling, 153
overhang, 14, 162
overhanging, 14, 162
overtraining, 43, 138–39, 162
overuse, 47, 162

P

pace, 61
palm/friction grip, 48
peak performance state, creating, 109–13
perfect economy, moving with, 59–61
performance evaluation, 156
performance goals, 142, 157
personal boundaries, stretching, 155
Petzl Grigri, 22, 30
photo symbols, 4
pinch grip, 48
pocket grip, 47–48
Podclimber.com, 167
power endurance, 131–32, 136–37, 159
power stamina, 131–32, 136–37, 159
preclimb checklist, 112–13
preclimb rituals, 112–13
press-down position, 48, 50, 161
pressure, self-induced, 155
problems, 10, 94, 162
problem-solving, 156
projecting, 95–98, 162
psyched, 162
pull-muscle training
    high-intensity, 132–34
    strength, 123–27
pull-ups, 123

uneven-grip, 132–33
    weighted, 134
pumped, 162
push-ups, 129
pyramid training, 136–37

Q

quickdraws, 22–23, 162. *See also* clipping
    quickdraws

R

reading routes, 94
redpointing, 17, 98, 162
rehearsing a project, 98
relaxing your body, 60–61, 110
renting equipment, 9–10
repeaters, 135–36
resources
    books, 165
    magazines, 168
    Web sites, 167–68
rest and recovery, 137, 139
rest positions, 61–63
rest step, 53
reverse side pull, 48, 50, 69, 160
reverse wrist curls, 129
rhythm, 59
risks, analyzing and managing, 107
rituals, preclimb, 112–13
RockClimbing.com, 168
Rock & Ice, 168
roofs, 14, 162
rope bags, 25
ropes
    equipment, 25
    placing through carabiner, 90–91
    tying into, 27–29
routes
    chunking down, 96
    lowering off, 32

reading, 94
setting, 14, 16
working, 95–98, 163

S

safety gear. *See* equipment and safety gear
safety systems, 27–35
    belay, 29–33
    bouldering and spotting, 33–34
    putting on harness, 27
    tying into the rope, 27–29
scales, difficulty rating, 16–17
schedules, 43, 139, 153
schemas, 41, 162
screamer, 13, 162
self-actuating belay devices, 22, 30
self-assessment, 101–2, 103
self-awareness, developing, 101–4, 156
sending, 162
Send Me (game), 82–83
Sharma, Chris, 67
sharp end, 13, 162
shoes, 19–21
shoulder flexibility, 118
shoulder press, light, 127, 129
shuffle drill, 64
side pull, reverse, 48, 50, 69, 160
side pulls, 50, 68–69, 69–70
skill, 162
Skinner, Todd, 115
slabs, 14, 162
smearing, 53
sport climbing, 162
spotters, 11, 33–34, 162
stabilizer muscle, 162
static ropes, 24
steep-rock bouldering drills, 81–82
steep terrain, 72–74
stemming, 121, 162
Sterling Rope, 168
stick clips, 91, 162

Stick Game, 82
straight-armed drill, 65
strength, 162
    contact, 135–36, 160
    maximum, 131, 161
strength training, pull-muscle, 123–27
stretches. *See* flexibility
success, achieving, 155
supercompensation, 43, 162
symbols, photo, 4
system weaknesses, 91–93

T

tendinitis, 162
tendon, 162
tennis ball drill, 65
tension, controlling, 104–7
thoughts
    elevating quality of, 155
    productive and goal-oriented, 106
    thinking out of the box, 97
    tuning into, 102, 104
toe hooking, 75–76
toe-in foot placement, 51
toprope, 11–12, 32, 162–63
toprope drills, 65
tracking drill, 77–78
trad climbing, 162
training
    anaerobic endurance, 131–32, 136–37
    antagonist-muscle, 127–30
    beginning, 142–43
    bouldering as, 130–32
    campus, 159
    climbing-specific, 130–37
    contact strength, 135–36
    fingerboard, 134–37
    home training guidelines, 146–47
    hypergravity, 161
    interval, 131–32, 161
    maximum strength and power, 131

pull-muscle, 123–27, 132–34
pyramid, 136–37
Training4Climbing.com, 168
traverse, 163
traverse training drills, 64–65
traversing, one-arm deadpoint, 82
Tuber belay plates, 22, 30–31
tweaking, 163
twist lock and backstep, 72–74
twist-lock bouldering drill, 81–82

U

undercling, 48, 50, 69, 163
undercling drill, 77
uneven-grip pull-ups, 132–33
unknown, fear of, 155
Urban Climber, 168
USA Climbing, 168

V

vert, 14, 163

visualization, 94–95, 163
V-Scale, 16–17, 163

W

waiver of liability, 9
wall features, 14. *See also* climbing walls
walls, home, 144–47
wall split, 121
warming up, 38
weaknesses, system, 91–93
Web resources, 167–68
weighted pull-ups, 134
wired, 78, 163
women's harnesses, 21
working a route, 95–98, 162, 163
workout schedules, sample, 139
wrist curls, reverse, 129

Z

zone, getting into, 109–12

About the Author

An accomplished climber of nearly thirty years, Eric J. Hörst (pronounced "Hurst") has ascended cliffs all across the United States and Europe. Driven by his passion for adventure and challenge, he has established more than 450 first ascents, primarily on his home cliffs in the eastern U.S.

A student and teacher of climbing performance, Eric has personally helped train hundreds of climbers, and his training books and concepts have spread to climbers in more than fifty countries. He is widely recognized for his innovative practice methods and training techniques, and since 1994 he has served as a training products design consultant and online Training Center editor for Nicros, Inc., a leading manufacturer of climbing walls and handholds.

PHOTO BY **ERIC MCCALLISTER**

Eric is author of the best-selling *Training for Climbing* and *How to Climb 5.12*. He regularly contributes to outdoor and fitness magazines such as *Climbing, Rock & Ice, Urban Climber, Outside, National Geographic Adventure, Men's Health, Muscle & Fitness,* and *Men's Journal,* and he has appeared on numerous TV broadcasts. Eric maintains a climbing performance blog for MountainZone.com and broadcasts twice-monthly Training Tip podcasts on Podclimber.com. Visit Eric's website, TrainingForClimbing.com, for training articles and information on all his books, or to schedule a training seminar, an editorial interview, or a speaking engagement.

Eric currently lives in Lancaster, Pennsylvania, with his wife, Lisa Ann, and his sons, Cameron and Jonathan.

Other Books by Eric J. Hörst

Training for Climbing (Falcon, 2003) is a comprehensive, science-based tome that presents a unique synthesis of leading-edge strength training, tried-and-true practice strategies, and powerful mental-training techniques that will empower you to climb better, regardless of your current ability. TFC is the ultimate resource on all aspects of climbing performance, and it's the training text of choice used by climbers around the world!

How to Climb 5.12 (Falcon, 2003) is a performance guidebook to attaining the most rapid gains in climbing ability possible. It provides streamlined instruction on vital topics such as accelerating learning of skills, training the mind and body, and becoming an effective on-sight and redpoint climber.

Mental Wings is not just about climbing performance, but about elevating all human performance. This CD program presents a highly unique and effective program for enhancing performance in any activity or endeavor. The eighty-minute audio program details thirty-five powerful strategies that you can immediately put to work. Visit MentalWings.com for more information.